T H E

HYBRID-CORN MAKERS:

PROPHETS OF PLENTY

By

A. Richard Crabb

New Brunswick

RUTGERS UNIVERSITY PRESS

1947

DEDICATED TO

Paul Angle

PREFACE

This is how you happen to be reading this book.

One evening in October more than ten years ago when I was Farm Editor for the *Moline Dispatch* in Illinois, I stopped in Morrison, Ill. to pay the Shumans one of those "no thank you, I can't stay visits." F. H. Shuman was then and still is one of the most capable farm advisers or county agents in the corn belt. Although it was well past the regular supper time, Frank was just coming home for he had been down to the south part of Whiteside county observing the harvest results of some special experimental plots where hybrid corn was being checked against the old standard open-pollinated corn.

"What's there to this new hybrid corn anyway?" I questioned.

Frank Shuman, who always has been decisive in his every move and thought, whipped back, "Greatest food plant development in 500 years, greatest plant discovery since Columbus found corn itself." My interest in hybrid corn has been high from that moment to this.

Shortly afterward I did my first writing on hybrid corn, a series of articles for the farm pages of the *Dispatch*. I continued to write about it as the new hybrid corn began sweeping aside the old open-pollinated varieties in northern Illinois and Iowa in a manner closely akin to Sherman's march through Georgia.

About this time my Uncle Merle Crabb, who operates a farm in western Illinois that has belonged to our family well over a hundred years, switched to hybrid corn, which gave me an over-the-supper-table interest and source of information on it. Much later I joined the agricultural department of a Chicago advertising organization which served further to keep my interest in hybrid corn unbroken.

Several years ago, Paul Angle, who was then generalissimo of the Illinois State Historical Society, mentioned in one of our visits that it was high time someone took the trouble to look into this matter of hybrid corn deeply enough to find out for sure who was responsible for it. Most of the men who made it possible, he pointed out, must still be living, and someone ought to go directly to them and get the information. Knowing of my special interest in agricultural writing, he suggested that I prepare a paper to be given before an annual meeting of the Illinois State Historical Society.

I began by making a few interviews and contacting other persons by letter. After hearing my paper before the society the next year, Paul Angle's appraisal was, "Why, you have material for a book." I was leaving the same day on a business trip, so that evening I called Mrs. Crabb and reported to her what Angle had said. She immediately endorsed the idea, something I am sure that she on occasions repented later because of the tremendous amount of help I required of her—help without which there would not now be this book which you hold in hand.

As soon as I began to work on the book, I decided to see every living person who had taken a major role in hybrid corn development and get an account of his work from his own lips rather than depend upon letters and secondary sources of information. Since every outstanding member of the practical corn-breeding group is still living and only one of the men prominently associated with the earliest hybridizing is dead, this was a real opportunity as well as a major undertaking.

In the weeks, months, and years that have followed, despite

hardships imposed by the war, I have travelled from New England to the Nebraska plains and from Minnesota to Tennessee and Louisiana to talk with all the principal hybrid-corn makers. These visits and a constant correspondence, some of it extending over more than four years, have enabled me to become acquainted with these breeders as perhaps no one else ever will know them. I liked them to the last man, and I deeply appreciated the opportunity to make the acquaintance of these scientists who gave America and the world hybrid corn.

Soon Paul Angle made another most valuable suggestion, urging that at the earliest possible time I prepare a first draft of the book so that each of these informants might be sent the portion of the manuscript dealing with his work. By mid-1946 I began sending manuscripts to the hybrid-corn makers, and the results were of much greater significance than I had expected. Seeing how determined I was to treat their work in a specific, relatively complete and accurate manner, these men re-examined their records and their memories and produced enough additional information so that entire chapters had to be reorganized and rewritten. This process continued until some portions of the book were rewritten as many as four times.

As this additional information began to accumulate, many of the most widely held beliefs about the development of hybrid corn were swept away. Here is an example. The first successful strain of hybrid corn was the Connecticut Agricultural Experiment Station's Burr-Leaming hybrid made up of two inbreds from Illinois Burr White corn and two inbreds from Illinois Leaming corn. Even in the highest botanical circles, it had for years been thought that this Burr White and Leaming corn had been brought to Connecticut from Illinois by Edward Murray East and that he had initiated and developed the inbreds for this Burr-Leaming double-cross hybrid. Even at the Connecticut Station the

Burr White and Leaming lines entering into the first hybrid were affectionately referred to as the "old East inbreds."

Little by little, we pieced together how it did happen and actually East didn't bring the Burr White or Leaming corn with him from Illinois to Connecticut, he didn't begin the inbreeding of any of the four inbred lines, and, in fact, East never worked with or handled the Burr White inbreds at all. Only by making the personal acquaintance of half a dozen men living as much as a thousand miles from one another was it possible to uncover the truth in this situation.

As a result of the additional information of this kind unearthed, the book now presents material seventy-five per cent of which has never before been told for the general public, and at least a third of which has never before been set down in print anywhere. Fortunately, it has been possible to find a number of previously unpublished photographs, some of them more than forty years old, to appear in the book as the best kind of documentary evidence for some of this new information.

I would like to point out that the men who read the manuscript before publication were asked only to check upon the accuracy of the facts. At no time were they invited to share the responsibility for the deductions made from the facts which they so willingly and without exception supplied and checked.

My special thanks are due to Professor H. D. Hughes of Iowa State College for having written the introduction answering the question so often asked, "What is Hybrid Corn?" I asked Professor Hughes to write this introduction for two reasons. One is that the question should more properly be answered by a recognized authority on botany. The other reason is that Professor Hughes, while not directly involved in the breeding of hybrid corn, is undoubtedly personally acquainted with and beloved by more of the hybrid-corn makers than any other university or experiment station agronomist.

I am confident that given an opportunity to choose, Professor Hughes would have been the hybrid-corn breeders' choice for this task. Professor Hughes must also be absolved from any responsibility for the conclusions or interpretations in the book since the manuscript was already in the hands of the publisher before he saw it.

So many individuals have made important contributions to this book that I dare not attempt to name them here. I should, however, indeed be ungrateful were I not to express appreciation of the help given me in the preparation of the book by Sarah Lemon and Ellen Korngiebel, who helped with the library research and processed all-told enough manuscript to fill ten moderate sized novels before the final version went to the Rutgers University Press. I wish to thank my long-time friend, Ken Smith, for having read and made the last minute manuscript alterations that are so valuable.

A. RICHARD CRABB

April, 1947.
Naperville, Illinois

CONTENTS

xiv   *Contents*

INTRODUCTION:

WHAT IS HYBRID CORN?

Long before history began to be recorded, man strove constantly to get plants that would produce greater amounts of food with less labor. Sometimes he obtained this improvement by increasing the food-producing ability of an existing plant, at other times by selecting a more capable new plant. Hybrid corn is the greatest example in recent time of increasing the value of a food-bearing plant by improving one already in common use. The development of hybrid corn is truly one of the most important advances made in all the thousands of years since man first began cultivating special food-bearing plants.

What is hybrid corn, and how does it differ from the corn grown before it was developed?

Hybrid corn is the result of a new system of breeding, an achievement made possible chiefly by two things. First is our increased knowledge about the physical make-up of the corn plant. In the last two hundred years, our plant scientists have learned a great many things about corn never known to the Indians who discovered corn and worked with it for several thousand years. Second are the series of discoveries we have made within the last few decades about the nature of heredity and the degree to which it can influence the function of plants.

In a broad sense, there is little that is new in the objective of the hybrid-corn breeder. Both plant and animal breeders have searched for hundreds of years to discover those particular individuals within a species with unusual capacities to produce outstanding offspring. Once discovered, these rare individuals have been prized as parent stock. Thus the beef cattle breeder has developed excellent bulls and cows, and the breeder of pure-bred horses has developed famous studs and mares. Once these animals were discovered and proved, they were kept in production as long as possible so that their superior germ plasm, and their fine hereditary characteristics could be transmitted to the maximum number of progeny.

The hybrid-corn breeder has done the same thing in general. The chief feature which has been revolutionary about his work is that he has devised means of controlling the genetic or hereditary factors in the corn plant much more strictly than even the most careful plant or livestock breeder had been able to do previously with orthodox breeding practices. In other words, no "blue blood" in the animal world developed by conventional breeding methods was ever so completely purified, so carefully bred, or so thoroughly proved as one of our outstanding strains of hybrid corn.

In developing hybrid corn we have searched through our old open-pollinated corn and selected outstanding individual plants to serve as parent stock. This parent stock has been purified by self-fertilization, which we usually call *selfing* or *inbreeding*. After a satisfactory degree of purification is achieved, we refer to this parent stock as an inbred. These inbreds are used exclusively as breeding stock in producing the good hybrids planted by our farmers. By using only the first-generation seed, that is, the first controlled cross between inbred parent stock, a maximum use has been made of hybrid vigor. The phenomenon of hybrid vigor is not a new discovery by corn breeders. The breeders of animals and plants already appreciated the value of crossing unrelated strains to secure more vigorous offspring. But the modern hybrid-corn breeder has understood and harnessed the magic of hybrid vigor to a degree and on a scale never before achieved.

To appreciate what the hybrid-corn breeder does, it is

necessary to understand how corn reproduces itself—something that the American Indian, who worked with corn for thousands of years, was never able to explain. Corn produces both the male and female elements on the same plant. The male cells are produced in the tassel at the top of the plant and the female cells on the ear shoots which develop at the nodes of the stalk, usually about midway between the base of the plant and the tassel.

The trouble to which nature goes in producing a kernel of corn is a dramatic story in itself. First, a microscopic pollen grain lands on the tender, sticky silk emerging from the young ear shoot. Under favorable circumstances, a tiny pollen tube emerges within a few minutes from this little pollen grain and grows down through the corn silk until it reaches the female cell on the soft cob.

As the pollen tube elongates, the male sperm cells advance with it, the older portion of the tube collapsing even before the growth of the tube has been completed. The growth of this pollen tube is one of nature's most stupendous acts. To appreciate what a construction job is involved, one need only consider that if the pollen grain were as large as a baseball, the average pollen tube would be several hundred feet long. As soon as the pollen tube reaches the base of the silk where it is attached to the cob, the male cells, which have moved through the length of the silk as the pollen tube has advanced, unite with the female cells at its base, and the development of a kernel of corn is begun immediately.

Thus every silk represents the possibility of one plump kernel of corn. Since there are about 800 to 1,000 silks emerging from the ear shoot of an ordinary field corn plant, there are approximately 800 to 1,000 kernels of corn on the average ear when it is harvested in the fall. If for any reason pollen does not come into contact with the ear silks, no kernels will be formed, and nothing but a big, fluffy cob will be found in the husk at harvest time.

The fact that the corn plant produces seed in such abundance is an important factor in breeding, since it makes possible the rapid multiplication of the seed supply of any desirable type. This has an important bearing on hybrid-corn breeding in that the corn breeder can undertake a large expenditure for research if he knows that he can expect to spread the cost over a large number of seed units once the value of a particular hybrid strain is proved.

With the processes of reproduction in plants more fully understood, men began to observe closely the effect of heredity upon the succeeding generations of corn plants. Several important discoveries, all hinging upon an increased understanding and control of heredity, were eventually made about corn and cross-pollinated plants in general. These discoveries are:

1. The open-pollinated corn plants are chance-born hybrids between numerous subtypes.
2. These subtypes can be separated from one another by controlling the pollen so that the plant fertilizes itself, making it possible for the corn breeder to separate the highly desirable subtypes from those which are inferior.
3. Once separated, the characteristics of the rare superior subtypes can be preserved as inbreds and used for parent stock indefinitely.
4. By crossing inbreds effectively the qualities of a number of inbreds can be combined into one strain of corn.
5. Such a first generation of an outstanding hybrid strain can be depended upon to possess such a degree of hybrid vigor that its yield will be tremendously increased over the chance-made hybrids of an open-pollinated stock.

While it is not difficult to trace the broad outlines of what the hybrid-corn breeder does, it is almost impossible to convey an appreciation of the vast amount of work necessary to find and develop good inbreds and to discover the most effective crosses between them. No means has ever been found to evaluate accurately either an inbred or a hybrid cross by any method other than growing them and checking closely their field performance and final yield. The hybrid-corn breeder, therefore, has to work with tremendous numbers of plants in order to find the infrequent combinations of real promise. Breeders seem to agree that they must expect to discard more than 99 per cent of the material with which they work in order to develop outstanding new hybrids.

In order that you may have a more concrete idea of what hybrid corn is, let us trace in chronological order the major steps taken by the plant breeder who develops a hybrid from open-pollinated corn. The very first thing he has to do is to select from open-pollinated corn the material which appears to him to offer the most promise for inbreeding. This search for the truly outstanding material to be used in breeding corn is a major phase of the work.

Inbreeding plots are usually laid out so that one row of plants can be grown from each ear. Since the corn breeder must maintain absolute control over pollination, he fastens paper bags securely over the tassel and the ear shoots before pollen is shed or silks appear. After the tassel bag has a good supply of pollen in it and the silks have grown out from the ear shoot, the pollen is transferred to the silk. To do this the breeder transfers the tassel bag to the ear shoot, manipulating it in such a manner as to insure that only the pollen from the tassel of the same plant has a chance to fertilize the ear. In this way selfing, or inbreeding, is forced upon the plant.

The wide variety of types of open-pollinated corn is the outward evidence of the great number of strains or subtypes present. When corn which has been selfed only once is planted, it usually produces a rather wide variety of plants, noticeably smaller and less vigorous than the original open-pollinated corn—smaller because of the loss of hybrid stimulation. The obviously inferior strains can be eliminated immediately, this being one of the advantages provided by inbreeding.

The more desirable strains are selfed again. In the second inbred generation the plants will be still smaller, and there is not likely to be as much variation. The corn breeder continues to save only the most desirable material for further inbreeding and discards the rest. As the inbreeding progresses, with repeated selfing each year through several generations, there comes a point when there is no further reduction in vigor and the inbred lines that have survived the elimination process are relatively uniform.

Unfortunately the physical appearance of inbreds is not necessarily an indication of their worth. Some inbreds most disappointing in appearance have been found to have unusual value when combined in crosses with other inbreds. The converse is often true. Only by careful testing can the corn breeder tell which of his inbreds have real value. Those that prove to have great usefulness are few in number.

How can these inbreds which are the very basis of hybrid corn be maintained in their original form year after year? The hybrid-corn breeder accomplishes this by never permitting pollen from other strains of corn to reach the silks of these inbreds, thus insuring self-fertilization. No form of plant life is absolutely static, but any changes which may occur in these proved inbreds are so slight that they can be depended upon year after year to produce a progeny of known capacities.

Corn breeders use different techniques in testing their inbred lines. Some begin testing earlier than others. The objective is to discover which particular combinations of inbreds will produce superior crosses. A cross between two inbreds is called a "single cross." Since the seed of a single cross has to be produced on inbred plants, which generally produce small, misshapen ears, single cross seed is too costly to be practicable for crops intended for marketing or feeding livestock. The high cash income of sweet corn and popcorn, however, justify the use of single-cross seed.

In producing a large volume of single-cross seed, the breeder cannot profitably make controlled crosses by hand-pollination. He chooses a plot well isolated from other corn so that there will be no pollen in the field except that shed right there. He usually plants two rows of one inbred designed to bear the seed, alternated with one row of the inbred selected to be the male parent. Before the tassels of the plants expected to bear hybrid seed begin to shed pollen, the breeder removes them so that the only source of pollen in the field is the plants in the rows planted to the male parent. In this way a cross is forced upon the plants in the rows used to produce seed. The inbred plant left to produce pollen fertilizes itself, and consequently another generation of inbred seed is produced by the plants in the row of male parents.

For field-corn hybrids, the breeder generally uses two carefully selected and previously proved single-cross hybrids as foundation seed and combines them into what is known as a double-cross hybrid. One of these single crosses is used as a parent to bear seed and the other to produce pollen. Seed of the double-cross hybrid is produced on the large, uniform ears of a single cross, and consequently there is a tremendously greater seed supply than is possible on inbred plants. In producing seed of the double-cross hybrid, the breeder uses the same technique employed in the production of single-cross seed. Using well isolated fields so that there will be only a minimum of foreign pollen, the breeder usually plants three rows of seed-bearing single cross to one row of single cross for pollen. Before the tassels on the seed parent begin shedding pollen, they are removed by crews of detasselers. The only source of pollen in the field, therefore, is the plants in the row of male parents. As a result a cross occurs in the seeds harvested from the detasseled rows. The ears from the pollen-producing rows are disposed of as ordinary commercial corn.

Sometimes a corn breeder finds that he has three inbreds that when combined give better results than he can get when he adds a fourth, and in such an instance he may develop a three-way hybrid or a three-way cross—one that brings together only three inbreds. This is done by combining two of the inbreds into a single-cross hybrid which is used as the seed-producing parent with the inbred used as the male or pollen-producing parent.

Under certain conditions, like the testing period to determine which inbreds are superior, a corn breeder may wish to combine an inbred or single cross with an open-pollinated variety. When this is done the resulting combination is called a top-cross hybrid.

One of the greatest advantages of the technique of breeding hybrid corn is the opportunity afforded to develop strains especially well fitted to particular conditions of weather, soil, disease, and insects. By bringing together the right combinations of inbreds, hybrids are "custom built" for particular needs. Hybrids have been developed that have the capacity to produce much greater yields during short seasons than were possible with open-pollinated corn. As a result corn is now an important crop in northern areas where a decade ago very little corn was produced. Hybrid strains with resistance to specific insects have been developed. The availability of these insect-resistant hybrids has made corn a more important crop than it otherwise would be in areas where insect damage to open-pollinated corn was great. Certain hybrids have been shown to be markedly more resistant to heat and drouth than the open-pollinated varieties they have replaced.

From this we can see how important it is to find the particular hybrids best adapted to the conditions likely to prevail at a given location. Many hybrids, especially those used in the northern corn-growing areas, are so closely adapted to particular conditions that they are superior to other hybrids only in an area no more than fifty or one hundred miles north or south. Since our belts of similar weather extend east and west, hybrids usually have a maximum of usefulness over greater east-west distances than over north-south distances.

The first widely successful hybrids were adapted to the central part of the corn belt. Gradually hybrids were adapted to areas farther north and farther south. Not many superior hybrids have yet been developed for areas in the Deep South, as in Louisiana, Alabama, or Florida, but rapid progress is being made.

We have tried to picture for you this new development which we know as "hybrid corn"—how it differs from the open-pollinated varieties that everyone was growing only a few years ago; something of the advances which the new breeding technique has made possible; and an insight into the vast amount of work the corn breeder must undertake to bring to the surface the few really superior inbreds, as well as the difficult problem of finding exactly those inbreds that fit together to make corn a more efficient producer of food.

My hope is that these brief introductory remarks will make even more interesting your reading of this book about the makers of hybrid corn. Since this is not a technical account, there is a minimum of "how" and "why," but a limited understanding of such terms as *inbreeding, inbreds, single-cross* and *double-cross hybrids,* as well as some knowledge of the general procedures of the modern corn breeder, will add to your pleasure in reading this book.

It has been my great good fortune to know practically all of the men who have made hybrid corn what it is, many of them somewhat intimately, beginning with Hopkins, Shamel, East, and Craig at the Illinois Station from 1900 to the present time. Because of my associations with them through the years and the opportunity to observe closely the great superiority of the new hybrids, I thought that I foresaw its future somewhat more clearly and more certainly than others not so fortunately situated.

But how limited was my vision! At a conference of representatives from several central corn belt states held in Chicago in 1934 to consider limits on corn acreage in keeping with the possible uses of the crop, it was pointed out that the use of hybrid corn would increase yields 20 per cent or more, and that acreages must be reduced accordingly. When the group broke up for lunch, a good friend from an adjoining state took my arm.

"Hughes," he said, "doesn't it make you a bit tired to have some of these academically minded folks talk about increased acre yields from hybrid corn and its effect on the total crop? You know as well as I do that neither of us will live long enough to see enough hybrid corn planted to have any effect at all on our total crop."

"You surprise me," I replied. "Is that the way you think about it in your state? Iowa farmers are already pretty well sold on hybrid corn as a result of our state tests. I am anticipating that the acreage planted to hybrid corn in Iowa will increase just about as fast as the seed can be made available. *Half of our acreage* may be planted to it."

Thus did I display my own lack of vision, for it is well known that in Iowa the acreage planted to hybrid corn increased from less than 1 per cent in 1933 to over 98 per cent in 1942. Similar increases have occurred in most other states in the corn belt.

Hybrid-Corn Makers is an account of the contributions made by many persons in developing a great discovery and bringing it rapidly to full fruition. It is a story of great personal achievement. To me it is not only an intensely interesting story, but also an accurate historical statement made possible only by a vast amount of painstaking effort. It is a statement which will be more and more appreciated with the passing of the years. Corn growers the world around, today and in the years ahead, are greatly indebted to Richard Crabb for doing the task that so obviously needed doing—writing the story while the important actors in the drama could aid not only in making it as accurate as possible but also in supplying a host of interesting and significant details which in a few short years would have been irretrievably lost.

—H. D. HUGHES

THE HYBRID-CORN MAKERS

PROPHETS OF PLENTY

CHAPTER I

Eternal Servant

MAN IS A GUEST on this earth of the green plants. Of all our planet's creatures and objects, the green plants alone are on dealing terms with the world's only great source of energy and power—the sun. In spite of all our efforts to crack their monopoly these green plants still hold an exclusive franchise in the vital business of gathering and storing the sun's energy as food and fiber without which neither man nor any of his animals could survive for more than a few hours. This was true ten thousand years ago, and it is just as true now in what we speak of as the atomic age, a somewhat misleading reference since life on our earth has from the beginning been sustained by the sun's energy generated by the process we now popularly refer to as "atom splitting."

Every green plant is, in effect, a power pipeline extending directly to the sun. Most plants pipe in this precious sun's energy as a miserable little trickle; others make it available more abundantly. A very few bring us the sun's power in a veritable gush, and discovering one of these rare green plants is like tapping a geyser of life and energy that never can run dry.

This is the story of the discovery of one of these rare superplants, hybrid corn, and of the men who fashioned it. Since the hybrid-corn makers worked with a plant already of world wide importance and of ancient origin, the story will be more interesting if we take a sweeping glance at corn in its unique role as a builder of civilization.

The American Indian developed nearly two dozen plants of present-day economic importance, including both white and sweet potatoes, pumpkins, beans, chocolate, squashes, tomatoes, peppers, peanuts, pineapples, tobacco, cocoa, cotton—and corn, greatest of all his food-providing plants. Corn was known to the Caribbean tribes who introduced it to Christopher Columbus as "mahiz," from which our word maize was derived. Scouts sent by Columbus to explore what is now the Island of Cuba became the first white men of record to see corn. On November 5, 1492, the first corn fields they encountered stretched across the Caribbean countryside continuously for eighteen miles.

How did the Indians develop corn? No one knows. Although the wild ancestors of many of our other major food and fiber-yielding crops have been found, no wild or clearly primitive corn has ever been discovered—although scientists throughout the world have spent more time attempting to fathom the mystery surrounding the origin of corn than has been spent on the historical background of any other plant.

Regarding the origin of corn, most plant scientists now look with increasing favor upon the theory widely discussed in the nineteenth century and recently revived—with extensive new evidence to support it by two noted botanists of the present day, Paul Mangelsdorf of Harvard and R. G. Reeves of the Texas Agricultural Experiment Station. This view holds that the cradle of corn is to be found in the extreme southwestern part of the great Amazon River basin in South America. Some of this region has not yet been explored, and there is a remote possibility that wild corn may yet be found in one of the inaccessible valleys of eastern Bolivia. The first Indians to plant and cultivate corn were probably those living in what is now Peru, Bolivia, and northern Chile.

In this area, it is believed, the new plant first supplied food

Edward Murray East making a chemical analysis of corn
samples from the Hopkins Corn Breeding project

Previously unpublished photograph taken on the University
of Illinois farm in 1905. *Left*: W. T. Craig beside a "Leaming hand-pollinated three years inbred." *Right*: H. H. Love
beside a "Leaming hand-pollinated four years inbred."
Center: Leaming open-pollinated

The first Burr-Leaming cross (1917), from which the first successful hybrid was grown (1918) at the foot of the Sleeping Giant so abundantly that it provided the energy and leisure to plant and build the first of several ancient American civilizations. This corn-supported empire of the Incas developed a culture and a standard of living that rivaled those of ancient Egypt, Babylon, and Greece.

As corn moved north, it touched off a number of later and also highly developed Indian civilizations in Latin and North America. The empires of both the Mayans in what is now Guatemala in Central America and the Aztecs in Old Mexico were in some respects even more advanced than that of the Incas. The march of maize continued northward into what is now the southwestern United States, and other Indian cultures blossomed in the Arizona–New Mexico area. Then corn crossed the desert barriers into the central and northeastern areas of North America so that at the time Europeans reached the New World they found varieties of corn being grown generally east of the Rocky Mountains and as far north as southern Canada.

The coming of the spice-seeking Columbus broke the seal of New World isolation and permitted corn to continue its march throughout the other continents.

The Indians, highly dependent on maize, were wholly responsible for its survival. Had North and South American Indians neglected to plant, hoe, and harvest corn and at the same time discarded their reserve supplies of seed during any one of the thousands of years they preserved it, the maize as we know it would have disappeared from the earth, for there is not a single recorded instance of corn having ever survived in the wild. Not only did the Indians preserve corn for themselves and for us; they developed and improved it to such a point that even today most corn being grown strongly resembles the maize that was passed on to other races by these red men. All five of the common types of corn in use today —popcorn, sweet corn, flour, flint and dent corn—were developed by the Indians.

Equally surprising has been the rapidity and degree to which this maize crop has been accepted by other races following its discovery by the Columbus expedition. Entering most other countries after the great food plants of the Old World were already solidly entrenched, this Indian corn quickly won a position of world-wide importance.

The men from Columbus' ships came ashore in the New World early in the fall of 1492. They thought they had reached the shores of India; consequently they gave maize the name "Indian corn" because it was raised by "Indians" and somewhat resembled their own cereal crops called "corn" since ancient times. Columbus returned to Spain early in 1493, carrying with him the first maize ever seen in Europe. That year corn grew in the royal gardens of Spain and within two generations was growing as a food crop in every country of sixteenth-century Europe. In less than a century, Indian corn had moved completely around the world. Today the maize of the American Indians has become a crop of virtually all nations. So great has been corn's relative indifference to changes in environment that every week of the year maize is being planted, cultivated, and harvested at some point around the earth. Corn is filling a role of such wide usefulness that it has won for itself a place apart from all other cultivated plants of the world.

Although the rapid spread and acceptance of corn throughout the world has added an intensely interesting and significant chapter to the romance of maize, corn has found its greatest usefulness and service right in North America. Corn has figured just as prominently in life on both American continents since the coming of white men as it did before, a fact that is likely to be overlooked by many of us today. The story of America under the white men has many incidents which dramatically highlight the importance and contribution of corn.

So important was the Indian's corn to early colonists in

America that the historian, Parker, concluded that ". . . the maize plant was the bridge over which English civilization crept, tremblingly and uncertainly, at first, then boldly and surely to a foothold and a permanent occupation of America."

The English, who were the first Europeans to realize fully that the greatest wealth of the New World was in its soil, established their first colony at Jamestown, Virginia, in 1607. The wheat and small grains that they intended to grow in America failed so miserably that, except for their discovery of Indian corn, everyone would have starved. Fortunately Captain John Smith had mingled with the Indians enough to appreciate the value of corn and the ease with which it could be grown. Seeing the critical condition of the Jamestown Colony he allotted an acre of ground to every man and ordered him to grow corn on it, or be deprived of the protection of the fort.

The Pilgrims landed from their overloaded *Mayflower* in mid-November of 1620 on the New England shore. Aware that they had neither the time nor the energy to clear a new home site from the forest, they selected an Indian corn field as the place to build the white man's first permanent settlement in New England. Food supplies brought from England were running low by the time the Pilgrims reached our shores. The scourge of hunger was soon among them. Fortunately Miles Standish and a few companions, while returning from a fruitless hunting expedition, came upon some mounds obviously built recently in which they found buried baskets of Indian corn.

In addition, the Pilgrims were able to buy eight hogsheads of maize and beans from the Indians to tide them over until their first harvests in the summer and fall of 1621. Squanto, trusted Indian friend, taught the men of the Plymouth Colony how to plant and care for corn, instructing them in such things as the preparation of the ground for planting, the use of fish in each hill for the fertilizer so greatly needed in the moderately fertile Cape Cod soil, the number of seeds to plant in a hill, and the best time and means of cultivation.

Few of us today realize the extent to which the colonists used and depended upon Indian corn. Thomas Ash, a clerk on the English ship *Richmond*, visited Carolina and other New World places in 1682 and was surprised to observe the universal use made of maize. Writing of the colonists, Ash reports, "Their Provision which grows in the Field is chiefly Indian Corn, which produces a vast Increase, yearly, yielding Two plentiful Harvests, of which they make wholesome Bread, and good Bisket, which gives a strong, sound, and nourishing Diet; with milk I have eaten it dress'd in various ways . . . The Indians in Carolina parch the ripe Corn, then pound it to a Powder, putting it in a Leathern Bag: When they use it, they take a little quantity of the Powder in the Palms of their Hands, Mixing it with Water, and sup it off: with this they travel several days. In short, It's a Grain of General Use to Man and Beast . . . The American Physicians observe that it breeds good blood . . . At Carolina they have lately invented a way of *making* with it good sound Beer; but it's strong and heady."

With the close of the colonial period, public appreciation of corn began to decline, ironically, just as the production and use of corn began to increase by leaps and bounds. Maize yielded such bountiful harvests that we could afford to feed corn to animals that in turn produce the meat and milk foods which have now for a hundred years been the backbone of the American diet. Only vast supplies of corn, other cereal grains, and forage have made possible this rich diet for America, as approximately seven pounds of grain and forage must be fed to produce one pound of the highly nutritious meat or milk.

With the opening of the Erie Canal, connecting the big cities of the seaboard with the Lake Erie region, Buffalo,

New York, surrounded with new corn country, became the nation's livestock processing center. The Indians were rapidly pushed from their lands in the valleys of the Ohio, upper Mississippi, and Missouri Rivers during the early years of the 1800's. Typical of the struggle of the whites to wrest away from the red men their corn grounds was the Black Hawk War of 1832.

The Sac and Fox Indians occupied what is now northwestern Illinois, southern Wisconsin, and a large part of Iowa. The center of the Sac and Fox nation was the villages situated along the Rock and Mississippi Rivers, near the sites below the present cities of Rock Island, Illinois, and Davenport, Iowa. There Indians had more than eight hundred acres under cultivation, most of which was in corn.

The whites began pressing in on the Sac and Fox Indians about 1800. In 1804 a highly questionable treaty requiring the Indians to move west of the Mississippi was drawn up in St. Louis between the Americans and two Indians who Chief Black Hawk, great leader of the Sac and Fox, said were not authorized to negotiate. Pressure upon the Indians increased constantly. During the next quarter of a century the Indians yielded territory grudgingly but bloodlessly. Illinois became a state in 1818, and matters came to a climax in 1831 after the Sac and Fox women had planted their corn along Rock River—their last crop on the corn fields of their ancestors.

Early that summer General Gaines of the United States Army issued an ultimatum to Black Hawk, giving him just two days to accept the terms of the St. Louis treaty and move his people across the Mississippi River. Although protesting vigorously, the Indians did retreat to the west bank of the Mississippi. Deprived of an opportunity to harvest their crop, the Indians were hungry during the ensuing winter, and in the spring Black Hawk and his braves recrossed the river. The Black Hawk War—in which Abraham

Lincoln and Jefferson Davis served as fellow officers—followed, and the Indians were soon decisively beaten. Victory gave the whites complete possession of the great corn lands east of the Mississippi River.

Farmers moved into these fertile areas as soon as treaties, rifles, or both had been effectively used to remove the threat of Indian troubles. The meat packing industry followed westward as the new corn lands were opened. Whereas in 1825 Buffalo, New York, had been our great meat processing area, by 1850 the packing industry was centered in the Ohio River city of Cincinnati, known in its early days as "Porkapolis," so numerous were its swine-slaughtering plants.

This was the era of the "land whale," when fat hogs, fed two years or more on a concentrated corn diet, supplied the oil that largely replaced the whale oil used earlier so extensively in the seaboard area of the United States. Sixteen million pounds of hog oil—each pound representing a scoopful of corn—were processed at Cincinnati in 1849 alone. Fifteen hundred men were engaged at that time making the barrels and kegs in which was shipped this oil that was used for illumination, lubrication, medicine and numerous other purposes.

One may well wonder if the Confederacy's president, Jefferson Davis, did not reflect sadly on the fact that he had helped clear the Indians from the Illinois and Wisconsin prairies. By the time his Confederates were fighting the Civil War, those prairies had been broken, and corn was being funneled into Chicago, in the form of livestock and grain, in such volume that Chicago was bidding for Cincinnati's position as capital of the American livestock industry. Chicago's P. D. Armour got his start toward fame and fortune by supplying meat from corn-fed livestock to the Union Army. In 1861 Chicago traders handled twenty-five million bushels of corn, and livestock representing many times that much corn. Feeding the Union and its armies gave Chicago such a stimulus that by 1870 it was recognized as the food center of the entire world—capital of a vast economic empire built largely on corn.

Corn growing became big business in the Civil War period and immediately after. In 1880 our farmers were raising more than thirty-four bushels of corn for every man, woman, and child in the United States.

Farmers began to feel a tremendous interest in improving their corn. The maize of the Indians, good as it was, must now be made better. During the closing decades of the last century, there emerged men in almost every corn belt community who took a special interest in developing better varieties of corn. With some of them, such as J. S. Leaming of Ohio, James Reid and Gene Funk of Illinois, and R. Hogue of Nebraska, the improvement of corn became a life-long interest, making them sages of the great corn country.

From 1890 on through the early years of the present century, competition among farmers to produce the best corn became an institution in the corn belt. Corn shows reached a climax in the National Corn Exposition and Chicago's International Hay and Grain shows.

So widespread was the interest in the corn show that when the National Corn Exposition voted to hold its 1908 session in Omaha, the governor of Nebraska appointed a special "state commission" to assure the state of a creditable show. Greetings to the exposition were received from far and near including one from President Diaz of Mexico. Prizes ranged all the way from ribbons to expensive pieces of farm equipment.

Corn shows did much to concentrate the interest of agriculture upon the importance of corn. An increasing number of persons determined to improve our corn production. Research facilities of our state agricultural colleges were brought to bear upon the problem of increasing corn production through improvement of corn varieties and development of better corn farming methods.

In 1912 American farmers produced their first three-billion-bushel crop of corn, which was more than half of all the corn produced throughout the world. To do this farmers planted approximately one-fourth of all the land under cultivation in the United States to corn, a proportion that has been roughly maintained ever since. These greatest crops of corn, ninety per cent of which are fed to livestock, exceed in both volume and value the combined American crops of wheat, oats, barley, rye, rice, and buckwheat.

Against this background of achievement, we might expect, since there were no new corn lands to be opened up and exploited, that corn culture in America had reached its peak. But for all our earlier achievements with maize, the improvement of corn had just begun. Early in this century a group of men, so few they could be counted on the fingers of two hands, began working out a totally new approach to the development and improvement of corn. They conceived entirely new techniques for making better corn; they tapped new and hidden resources in the maize turned over to us by the Indians. They developed what we know today as hybrid corn. Suddenly this new kind of corn plant swept aside the old corn prized so highly by Leaming, Reid, Funk, and Hogue. In a single decade most of the farmers in the corn belt ceased to raise this old open-pollinated corn.

In all the history of this great crop, no more opportune time could have been set for unveiling the miracle of hybrid corn. Just as its advantages were becoming fully available to farmers in the great corn belt, our corn-buttressed American economy met its most severe test. It became necessary to pit our total strength against a coalition of ruthless, lawless aggressor nations in a life-and-death struggle. Immediately, American corn was projected into unprecedented importance around the world. Our farmers were asked for and delivered four successive three-billion-bushel corn crops in the four war years from 1941 to 1944. Hybrid corn gave America the equal of an extra corn crop of pre-war size during those four war years. The United States raised one three-billion-bushel corn crop during the first World War, but our farmers had to plant 110,000,000 acres of land to get it. In 1942 by using hybrid corn we were able to harvest a three-billion-bushel corn crop from only 89,000,000 acres. The land and labor saved by the new kind of corn were channeled into other war crops and into our war factories, where they helped tip the scales in our favor in a war to the finish.

In the chapters that follow is told the story of hybrid corn, with special emphasis on the men who made it possible, and the events, decisions, and achievements that enabled the current generation of Americans to enjoy its blessings.

CHAPTER II

Dawn on the Prairie

COLUMBUS IS CREDITED with the discovery of America, and Thomas Edison is recognized as the father of the incandescent light, but no man can with justice be described as the discoverer or originator of hybrid corn. Possibly the lone wolf era in scientific advance is coming to a close, for hybrid corn, like radar, synthetic rubber, the atomic bomb, and most of the new miracles of modern research was developed by not one person or even two or three, but by a group of men.

To be sure, the band of hybrid-corn makers, those whose contributions can be considered indispensable, is small even to this day. Hardly more than two dozen plant-breeding scientists are to be found in this little group of men who shoved back the darkness that hovers eternally over our scientific frontiers and exposed the natural laws from which hybrid corn has been fashioned. Their accomplishments take on even greater importance when one considers that the principles they discovered and proved are now being used to present to mankind an entire array of superplants and animal servants. The hybrid-corn makers were the first to convert into great usefulness the pool of knowledge tediously pieced together through the preceding two and one-half centuries by such great minds as Camerarius, Cotton Mather, Charles Darwin, and Gregor Mendel.

The star of hybrid corn first shone over the peaceful

campus of the University of Illinois. Early in March, 1896, a small group of men met in the Illinois Agriculture experiment station office for a conference called to consider a job that had never before been done or even seriously considered. Two of those persons present were Eugene Davenport and Cyril G. Hopkins, both young scientists just beginning brilliant careers in agricultural research at the University of Illinois. Davenport, a livestock expert, stated the problem.

Our livestock industry, said young Mr. Davenport, is of vital importance to the great majority of Illinois farmers. This livestock industry is built upon a foundation of corn, a grain which, although admittedly better for feeding livestock than any other, still has great shortcomings. Corn is so deficient in some food elements such as protein, Davenport pointed out, that Illinois farmers were spending vast sums to import special feeds to make up for the shortcomings of corn. While many other changes had been brought about in corn since white men got this great plant from the Indians four hundred years before, nothing had been done to improve the important balance of food elements inside the corn kernel. Probably corn was fine for the Indians, but we use corn for vastly different purposes. It was time, said Mr. Davenport, that something be done to improve corn as a livestock feed for which purpose practically all of Illinois' corn was being used.

Probably Davenport's most interested listener was Cyril G. Hopkins, energetic South Dakotan directing the study of soils and crops for the Illinois Experiment Station. Hopkins was by training a chemist, and the idea of altering the internal chemistry of the corn kernel challenged him. Hopkins himself perhaps had done sufficient chemical analytic work with corn to know that strains differed much in their content of certain nutrients such as protein. Enthusiasm for

the experiment to develop a new kind of corn with better
feeding qualities rose higher and higher as the meeting progressed.

Before the conference broke up late that afternoon, a
bold decision had been made to throw the prestige and resources of the University's Agricultural Experiment Station
behind an effort to develop new kinds of corn which would be
better suited to present needs. Davenport, in his capacity as
director of the experiment station, appointed Hopkins to
take full charge of the project. It was agreed that more
plant breeders and chemists would be added to Hopkins'
agronomy staff at such time as they might be needed. This
was to be no classical study of corn, but rather it was to be
a practical corn-breeding job with an assigned objective
and a yardstick for measuring results.

The Hopkins' corn-breeding project was the first undertaking of its kind in the almost ageless story of corn. White
men had learned many things about corn which the Indians
never knew, and this was the first attempt of a research
organization to use this new knowledge to bring about major
changes in corn itself. As early as 1694 the Dutch botanist,
Camerarius, discovered pollen and the fertilization process
in corn, something that untold generations of Indians had
wondered about but had been unable to fathom. Cotton
Mather of Salem witchcraft fame observed and recorded in
1716 how wind carried Indian corn pollen and the immediate
effects of cross pollination. England's Charles Darwin in the
middle of the last century discovered that increased vigor
could be secured in corn by crossing unrelated strains. In
1879 James Beal, Michigan State's great pioneer botanist
who studied at Harvard with Asa Gray, friend of Darwin,
became the first person of record to cross varieties of corn
for the sole and expressed purpose of increasing yields. A
dozen years later Morrow and Gardner of the University of
Illinois checked Beal's conclusions in experiments of their

own. This was done only two years before the Hopkins corn-breeding project was begun.

The weeks from March until planting time in May of 1896 were busy ones for the young scientists who had set out to remodel the corn of the Indians along lines of their own choosing. Hopkins knew that this corn-breeding project was so different from anything ever done before that a completely new set of techniques would be needed. So he devised and put into operation the "Illinois ear-to-row" method of corn improvement. Within a half dozen years the ear-to-row plan had been adopted in a number of other state experiment stations, and the ear-to-row technique is still used to some degree or other by practically all hybrid-corn breeders.

Hopkins' new plan provided for taking enough kernels from each test ear to plant a row of twenty-five or more hills. Each row would be harvested and studied separately so that an almost endless amount of vital data and comparisons could be secured. Not only could the performance of each row be compared with every other row in the breeding plot, but it would be possible to check later generations back against the original ear, since only a few of its kernels would be required to plant the first test row.

The new ear-to-row plan also made it possible to trace the mother or ear parents of every plant in the breeding plot, and by detasseling certain plants the male or pollinator parents could also be classified at least in general terms. Thus Hopkins became the first corn breeder to employ the pedigree technique on a broad scale. While his type of pedigree would not satisfy today's hybrid corn breeder, it did represent a tremendous step from the mass selection methods of the Indians in the direction of what is now the science of hybrid-corn breeding.

Before corn-planting time in 1896, Hopkins personally supervised the selection of 163 ears of Burr White corn, a white variety popular with central Illinois farmers. White

corn was purposely chosen so that there would be no diffi-
culty in determining whether there occurred unwanted cross
pollination from the yellow corn commonly raised in fields
near the university farm.

Claude C. Chapman, just beginning his forty-odd-year career as superintendent of the University's experimental
farms, set aside a plot of prairie ground on which Hopkins
himself directed the planting of the first large-scale corn
breeding plot. Weather was favorable during most of the
season, and the experiment got off to a fine start.

That fall Hopkins and Chapman carefully harvested the
corn. Every ear from a given row was placed in a sack and
sealed so there could be no opportunity to mix other corn
in it later. At the end Hopkins had 163 sacks of corn each
containing about a fourth of a bushel. The whole future of
the project, and the future of much more than was then
realized, depended upon the corn in those sacks.

Would there be enough variation in the vital elements of
protein and fat to justify further experiment? Would the
amounts of protein and fat show a definite and close relationship to the protein and fat in the mother ears, establishing
clearly that these qualities can be passed along from one
generation of corn to the next? Today, answers to these
questions seem almost too elementary to deserve consideration, but this only indicates how much has been added to our
knowledge in the last half century. Hopkins was standing at
the edge of the darkness which confronts every scientist who
attempts to probe the unknown.

Immediately after harvest, Hopkins went to work to find
out the answers to these vital questions. Kernels from a
representative number of ears out of each of the 163 sacks
had to be analyzed. Calling on his mastery of chemistry,
Hopkins undertook that first year to handle much of the
burden himself, and it is understandable that the night

lights often burned in his office and laboratory until near
morning.

Indications of the first tests were promising. A few of the
samples contained much greater than average amounts of
protein and oil; some had much less. By checking the samples
back against the unplanted kernels of the mother ears,
Hopkins established clearly that there was a close relationship between them and that the qualities and characteristics
were being passed from one generation to the next. Now the
way was open to separate his 163 corn families into special
classifications such as the high protein group, the low protein group, the high oil group or the low oil group, and
then go back to the breeding plot to intensify their respective
qualities.

As was anticipated, the work connected with the corn-
breeding project increased sharply after the first season. Accordingly, in 1897, during the second year, Louis H. Smith,
who had just been graduated from the University, was added
to Hopkins' staff. Trained in both agriculture and chemistry,
young Louie Smith was an ideal choice for the new position.
Not only could he direct the work in the breeding plot, but
he could assume responsibility for an important part of the
tedious work in the laboratory. Between them, Hopkins and
Smith were able to keep pace with the project's expansion
during the next three years.

In 1899 Hopkins presented his first public report on the
Illinois corn breeding program. It gave a frank statement of
the objectives, and announced that in four growing seasons
there had been developed special strains of corn never before
known. Some of them produced a third to a half more protein or fat than ordinary field corn. The announcement
aroused intense interest among experiment station agronomists in the Mississippi Valley and among research-minded
farmers throughout Illinois and far beyond. As the news

spread, Hopkins became one of the most popular speakers at farm institutes and other gatherings of persons interested in agriculture.

By 1900 it was clear that more help was needed, especially in the laboratory, to keep up with the work of chemical analysis. This development was not entirely unexpected, and we may be sure that Hopkins had for some while been observing the promising young men in the school of chemistry. His choice at commencement time in 1900 was Edward Murray East, a somewhat shy individual who had earned a fine reputation as a student in chemistry but whose training included almost nothing concerning agriculture.

The moment at which this young chemist decided to go to work on the Hopkins' corn-breeding project proved to be one of those historic turning points not only for him personally, but for the cause of plant breeding, America over. Today there is hardly a plant breeding scientist in the country who is not either a student of East or of one of East's students or associates. East's association with the University of Illinois corn-breeding program, among other things, was to prepare him to be a dominant force among the small band of men who were to make possible hybrid corn in our time.

CHAPTER III

Edward Murray East

EDDIE EAST, as he was known to his campus associates at the University, had been born October 4, 1879, at DuQuoin, Illinois, a small town about midway between Springfield and Cairo. The young chemist's father was William Harvey East, who studied mechanical engineering at the University of Illinois in 1875.

As a child, Edward East showed unusual ability. Hardly more than a baby, he used his letter blocks to spell words, and at five he was reading sentences from the Bible. As a boy he worked at the grocery store, and eventually saved enough money to buy a rifle with which he demonstrated excellent physical as well as mental co-ordination by becoming an expert marksman, a sport he continued to enjoy well into later life. His work in the village grade and high schools was good and indicated a wide range of interests and activities. He was already a rapid and constant reader of books, a habit that remained with him all the rest of his life.

Probably as a result of parental influence, young Edward Murray East made up his mind early that he wanted to go to college. He finished high school when he was fifteen and went to work immediately in a machine shop to earn college money. Two years later he went to Cleveland, Ohio, and began his college career at the Case School of Applied Science.

Years later as a teacher at Harvard University, Dr.

East used to tell his own students of the mathematics professor at Case who gave him a zero on a crucial examination
with the explanation that a bridge or mechanical structure
could easily be rendered completely worthless by a single
error in mathematics. Lest his students get the impression
that he worshipped accuracy to the point of being a fanatic,
Dr. East would add that one of his chemistry teachers once
told him, "There is little to be gained by weighing a ton of
hay on an analytical balance." The influence of both incidents
is easily seen in East's later work. He always insisted upon
high standards of accuracy when accuracy was essential,
yet at the same time he had little patience for persons who
insisted upon being accurate merely for the sake of accuracy.

Soon after entering Case College, young East decided he
was not sufficiently interested in applied mechanics to continue the course at the Cleveland school. General science,
he felt, offered opportunities more to his liking, so the next
fall found him at the University of Illinois, where he decided
to major in chemistry. His progress during the first year
at Illinois was so impressive that he was awarded during
his junior and senior terms the position of "student assistant
in chemistry." It was a practice at that time to engage
promising students as department assistants while they completed their regular courses. He was graduated in June,
1900, and immediately took up his duties as chemist on the
Hopkins' corn-breeding project.

As might be expected, the young chemist found himself
well engaged at first just keeping up with details of his new
position. His laboratory work was so well done from the
start that Hopkins took a pardonable pride in his choice
of chemists. Very early East began to show interest in corn
breeding which exceeded his call of duty as a laboratory
technician.

In completing the records of each chemical analysis, it was
necessary for him to record the pedigree of each corn sample

brought to him for study. These pedigrees—first ever written for corn—were especially interesting to young East. It was his first exposure to the power of heredity to determine the characteristics and usefulness of plants. These observations first focused East's attention on the then relatively unexplored science of heredity to which he was later to make such great contributions.

East soon became so interested in the corn breeding project that he decided to take some courses that would throw additional light upon the things he was encountering on his new job. Among the professors with whom he took courses in agriculture was Dr. Charles Hottes, a young botanist just back at Urbana after a period of study in Europe.

Hottes' study in Europe had been especially opportune. He had met and absorbed the most recent botanical concepts directly and indirectly from such men as Correns the German, Terschermak the Austrian, and DeVries the Dutchman, giants in the rapid advances being made on plant studies in Europe at this time. Dr. Hottes was in Europe the year that these three scientists almost simultaneously discovered the important Mendel papers, written forty-odd years before, from which were to stem the Mendelian principles regarded today as the real explanation of the evolutionary processes which had been well described to the world for the first time by Darwin.

All this new information about the natural laws governing the behavior of plants Dr. Hottes brought back to the campus of the University of Illinois, where for nearly forty years he established and maintained an enviable reputation of being one of this country's great teachers of botany. To East the chance to study with Dr. Hottes was a matter of the greatest importance. Probably more than either of the men realized, Hottes influenced young East at this crucial time when he was considering the decision to shift his major interest from chemistry to the plant sciences. Not only did the teacher and student soon develop a mutual respect for one another, but their personal relations were especially pleasant, providing an additionally favorable atmosphere for effective work.

Recalling his work with East during this period, Dr. Hottes says, "I liked East very much. He was a good student. He didn't have to be driven, although he was a rather retiring pleasant sort of a fellow who as a youth gave rather little indication of the fine qualities of aggressiveness which he developed later. He always constructed his sentences with great care, speaking in a rather thin high voice. He was many times studious to the point of being preoccupied."

We may be sure that Hopkins encouraged East to take this increased interest in the corn-breeding project, and he probably was among the very first to realize that his young associate had been forever lost to the world of chemistry in which there was little doubt he had a promising future. East's decision as to his career had crystallized by late summer of 1903, when he and Miss Mary Lawrence Boggs of Wilmington, Delaware, a school friend, were married.

The next year East earned his Master's degree from the University. His thesis was based on chemical and bacteriological studies on the self-purification of running streams. While his training as a chemist was of great and lasting value to him, East's career as a chemist was now all but over. A few months later he was named first assistant in plant breeding of the Illinois Agricultural Experiment Station.

Even before this promotion, Hopkins had approved the idea of East having a special experimental plot of his own on the University's farm, nor is there any doubt that Hopkins made every reasonable effort to keep East interested and challenged by the corn-breeding program.

Shortly after East became first assistant in plant breeding, H. H. Love, who in a career at Cornell was later to become another of the country's great names in plant breeding,

joined the Hopkins staff. Love, like Smith and East before
him, came to the project largely to help with the laboratory
work which every year seemed to demand more and more
technicians' time.

Mr. Love had just graduated from a chemistry course at
Illinois Wesleyan, then as now one of the fine colleges in
Illinois. He was one of Wesleyan's good athletes, and in the
spring of 1903 he accompanied the Wesleyan baseball team
to play the University of Illinois. While in Urbana he visited
the agriculture building and talked with Professor Hopkins
about the possibility of his working on the corn-breeding
project the following year while doing graduate work. He
met Eddie East that same day and again that evening on a
streetcar when East, with the soon-to-be Mrs. East, was
going to a party.

Love won a place in Hopkins' corn-breeding project because he was already familiar with the work which was being
done. Hopkins and Dean Davenport had impressed the
rising young seedsman, Gene Funk of Bloomington, with the
possibilities of their new approach to corn improvement, and
Mr. Funk had put his staff to work on Funk Farms to develop special high protein and high oil strains of corn. So
impressed was Gene Funk with the possibilities that with an
attractive three-year contract he lured away from the University of Illinois Professor P. G. Holden, undoubtedly the
country's greatest corn evangelist of that day, to help with
the development and to popularize the new corn that would
be developed.

Mr. Funk realized that he would need laboratory facilities
to make the important chemical analyses, so he proposed to
R. O. Graham, professor of chemistry at Illinois Wesleyan,
that he permit the Funk interests to give the college a new
laboratory fully equipped in return for the opportunity to
have the chemical analysis work done on their corn samples
in the fall and winter. Graham and the Wesleyan authorities

accepted the offer, and Funk suggested to Professor Graham that he not attempt to do the routine work on the corn analyses but that he hire, at Funk expense, some good student to handle this phase of the work. Graham put young Love to work on the Funk corn samples in 1902, and he handled much of the work again in 1903 and the early months of 1904 before he left to begin his work with Hopkins and East.

East and Love divided a small office on the third floor of the Old Agricultural Building, only a few doors removed from Hopkins' office. Their room was so small that when they both leaned back in their desk chairs, their heads would bump. East and the newcomer were soon good friends. Love was married shortly after he came to the Hopkins project, and he and Mrs. Love established their new home within a block of the Easts so that the two men had the opportunity to visit frequently off the campus.

East and Love ran their little office as a sort of retreat from the atmosphere of formal discipline maintained rigorously by Professor Hopkins throughout his agronomic domain, evidence of his uncompromising nature. Hopkins visited East and Love in their little office on one occasion soon after Love came to Urbana. Love was leaning and sitting on his desk, and Hopkins left almost immediately. East told Love that he was fortunate to have been spared the reprimand Hopkins had once given East (and others at various times) for sitting on desks in his presence.

In June, 1904, only a few weeks after East and Love were established in their third floor office, Louis Smith left for an extended period of study in Europe. Hopkins put East in direct charge of the plant-breeding division. The little room occupied by East and Love became virtually the headquarters of the Hopkins' corn-breeding project and the other plant-breeding experiments then being conducted by the University of Illinois. East welcomed the responsibility. It was soon evident to Love that East believed opportunities had been overlooked by Hopkins and Smith—opportunities which if fully explored might open up new and much more rapid means of developing the new kind of corn sought by the men at the University of Illinois.

East showed Love the records of the chemical analyses he had run for three years and pointed out, in the case of the high protein lines, two things which seemed to him of major importance which Hopkins had steadfastly refused to recognize. One was that all of the highest protein lines were descended from a single one of the 163 ears selected by Hopkins at the beginning of the project. The other was that the yield of these high protein strains of corn had dropped constantly as the percentage of protein increased.

Love's close contact with Gene Funk's corn breeding gave him a well-rounded background to understand the problems outlined by East and to enter into discussions looking to their solution. To East this relationship with Love was a real inspiration, for it was the first time since he began working on the Hopkins project four years before that he had the confidence of a person who was both sympathetic and qualified to judge the problems at hand. For example, Love became the first to agree with East that the Hopkins' corn-breeding project was doomed to failure as an experiment to introduce to Illinois farmers a new kind of corn unless some means could be found to prevent decreasing yields in the high protein- and high fat-producing lines.

East was especially interested in devising some means of making full-scale use of the occasional unusual ear, such as the one to which all of the high protein lines could be traced, and still avoid the penalty of decreased yields. Together East and Love outlined an experiment for the purpose of studying the effects of inbreeding or close breeding, an experiment which they hoped would point to some new method that would preserve the advantages of the unusual ear and at the same time avoid the curse of low yield. So it was that these two young men, fledglings in the science of plant breeding, peered into the realms beyond the known, reaching for the star of hybrid corn.

The plan which East decided to take up with Hopkins at the first opportune moment provided for a detailed study of inbreeding of corn. East realized that the close breeding being done on the Hopkins' corn breeding project produced much the same effects over a period of time as inbreeding. This was not the first time that East had sought to probe the mysteries of inbreeding. Two years before, when he had asked Hopkins for permission to have an experimental plot on the University's farm, East had begun an inbreeding project of his own. Unfortunately, shrivelled kernels appeared on some of his ears, and he dropped the entire project after two years, believing that his material had been contaminated with pollen from sweet corn. East talked to Dr. Hottes about the unfortunate development, and Hottes had in his possession for many years a few of the ears bearing the shrivelled kernels that East had brought to him for inspection.

There was, however, inbred corn already available for the experiment which East and Love proposed to make. This corn had been inbred by Hopkins as a sort of check-study in connection with Hopkins' corn breeding program. Although it was never mentioned in any of the university papers, bulletins, magazine or newspaper articles reporting upon the Hopkins' corn-breeding project, an inbreeding program was carried along in connection with it under Hopkins' direction for a decade or more. Scanty and time-bleached records at the University of Illinois make it difficult to establish the exact year when this inbreeding work began, but the program had assumed definite and stable proportions by 1901. Careful records of the work were kept from that year on so that by the time East and Love were discussing the matter, some of the corn had been inbred as much as four times.

So that it would be a simple matter to keep the inbred corn apart from the Burr White in the protein and oil breeding plots, yellow Leaming varieties were used in the inbreeding work. Interestingly enough this decision to use corn of different colors accounts more than anything else for the fact that the first successful hybrid was to be a Burr-Leaming strain, a yellow-white hybrid.

Inbreeding work was carried on by Hopkins for purposes of comparison. He wished to know exactly how much the yielding capacity of corn declined under continuous inbreeding, how much the general vigor of corn decreased as the inbreeding advanced, as well as the answers to a number of other questions. The procedure used in the inbreeding plot was a simple one. A few rows of Leaming corn had been planted in the beginning. Some of the most hardy plants were "selfed" (self-pollinated), and in the fall after harvest the ears of all selfed plants were shelled together and the inbred plot for the following year was planted with this seed. Particular plants were selected again for selfing, the resulting seed was shelled together, and the process repeated the following season.

Most of the actual selfing in the Hopkins inbreeding plots was done by W. T. Craig, who joined the staff as an untrained field technician in 1900. A young man who had had actual farming experience, Craig learned rapidly from Smith and Hopkins. After 1901 he had complete responsibility for making all hand pollinations connected with the Hopkins corn breeding work until 1913, when he left to continue his plant breeding work at Cornell University. So complete was Craig's supervision of the inbreeding work that the inbreds that came from it might logically be associated with his name as well as that of Hopkins or other members of Hopkins' staff.

Between harvest time in 1904 and planting time in 1905, East, abetted by Love, worked up the necessary courage to go to Professor Hopkins and talk the matter over frankly. East pointed out that all of the high protein lines traced back to a single ear among the original 163 used by Hopkins to start the project nearly ten years before and that high oil-bearing strains traced back to a very few ears. He pointed out that yields were going down so rapidly in the high protein and high oil corn that unless ways could be found to reverse this trend, the project would be robbed of any practical value.

Then East described the plan by which he and Love hoped they might uncover means of solving the difficulties. He proposed that a full study of the effect of inbreeding be made; that they start developing pure lines by inbreeding; and then use them in all manner of ways to discover, if possible, some way of taking greater advantage of these remarkable ears —such as the one to which the high protein corn strains traced back—and at the same time avoid the problem of reduced yields. East made a strong appeal and Hopkins was impressed. While he did not permit himself to agree openly with East, he unquestionably knew that much of what East said was true, and he agreed that in 1905, instead of mixing the seed from their inbred ears, East might plant them ear-to-row to see if there were significant differences which might offer opportunity to carry further the suggestions made by East.

Another event of importance occurred during this same winter. The American Breeders' Association held its annual meeting in Urbana, a tribute to the research work that was being carried on under Dean Davenport's administration at the University of Illinois. E. H. Jenkins, who had been named director of the Connecticut Experiment Station in 1900, came to the conference especially to get a first-hand impression of the plant-breeding work that was attracting so much attention at Illinois. Jenkins was acquainted with Hopkins and, while attending the Urbana conference, he asked him to recommend someone who might head a special plant-breeding program at the Connecticut Station. Hopkins suggested Eddie East and arranged a dinner conference for Jenkins and East.

Knowing how puritanic Hopkins was in his personal habits, Jenkins came to the dinner wondering if the young man who had earned Hopkins' recommendation would be as straight-laced as his director. Things progressed pleasantly during the dinner served at an off-campus hotel in Urbana. After the meal, Jenkins pulled from his pocket some of his customarily large cigars and offered one to East, who, to his surprise, replied, "I always like a good cigar after dinner."

Jenkins told East that Hopkins had recommended him for a position which was expected to be created at the Connecticut Experiment Station within the next year as a result of some special funds having been left to the station for research work. East expressed interest in the position, and before the evening was over Jenkins told the younger man that he was favorably impressed and would notify him as soon as plans at Connecticut matured.

Thus Edward H. Jenkins of Connecticut met young Edward Murray East of Illinois and laid the foundations of an important lifelong friendship that was to mean much to both men. Under Jenkins' leadership, encouragement, and advice, East was to establish himself firmly as a leader among plant breeders. He never ceased to be appreciative, and when Dr. Jenkins died twenty-five years later, East wrote an impressive tribute to the man whom he had first met over the hotel dinner table at Urbana on a February evening in 1905.

That spring in 1905 East laid out and directed the planting of the first corn-inbreeding plot of its kind. Each inbred ear of Leaming corn was planted ear-to-row in a plot that included open pollinated Leaming for check material. Most of the inbreds had been selfed either three or four times.

East, Love, and Craig watched their inbred plot constantly. From the time the inbreds began coming through the ground, Hopkins' young assistants fancied that they could see differences between the various ear-to-row plantings. By the time the grand growth stage had been reached at mid-summer, there could be no doubt about it. Some of the inbreds were a foot taller than others, and there were differences in leaf structure and general plant characteristics. In general all of the inbreds were remarkably uniform in comparison with the open pollinated corn in the check rows. Craig made selfs in each of the inbred rows during the pollinating season, selecting a few outstanding plants in each row for inbreeding.

East was so impressed with the research possibilities of the special inbred plot that he had Mrs. Flora Sims, who did photographic work of the University, take pictures as soon as the corn had reached its full height. Mrs. Sims, in 1905, thus became the first person to make photographic records of the comparison between inbreds and the open pollinated corn from which they had been selected. Unfortunately, East was not present on the day that the pictures were taken and consequently does not appear in any of them. However, both Craig and Love were shown in various pictures taken in the inbred plot. In one of these photographs Mr. Craig stood by an inbred holding a card reading "LEAMING—HAND-POL-LINATED—THREE YEARS IN-BRED." In another Mr. Love stood by an inbred holding a card which read, "LEAMING—HAND-POLLINATED—FOUR YEARS IN-BRED."

Professor Hopkins, by now so busy with other problems in the University's Department of Agronomy that he seemed to be losing interest in his corn-breeding project, didn't even find time to get out to the University farms and see the in-bred plot until mid-summer. These were the years when Hopkins was building his reputation as one of the nation's foremost authorities on soils, their use and development, and it is understandable that his interest had to slacken at other points. In the meantime, East and Love were week by week becoming more certain that important things were to be learned in their inbred plot. They had plans for exploring the possibilities which would take two, three, even five years.

Then came the tragic disappointment. Hopkins visited the plot, inspected it, and ordered the work discontinued. He said that he could not see any important differences between the inbreds nor could he see any significance in this kind of work, and that next year they would return to the practice of planting the inbred plot with mixed seed from all the ears of inbred plants.

Actually, Hopkins' decision was only an admission that to him the corn-breeding project, for all its early successes, had failed. Others since have wondered whether Dean Davenport might not have intervened and saved the project or if things might not have gone differently had Louie Smith not been in Europe getting his Doctor's degree that year of 1905. It-might-have-been speculation is interesting, but the truth is that the program was in fact as well as in name the "Hopkins' Corn Breeding Project." In the early years it had made sensational progress because of Hopkins' brilliant direction, and in later years it failed to achieve its ultimate objective of giving Illinois farmers a new kind of corn because of Hopkins' own limitations as a plant breeder and his inability to accept inspiration and aid from others.

In 1907 Dr. Frank Smith, head of the University's Department of Zoology, and Dr. Hottes went over the records of the Hopkins' corn-breeding project year by year from its beginning to see whether it substantiated or rejected some of the new concepts about the influence of heredity. They discovered as East had some years before, that all of the high protein ears traced back to a single ear. Neither of them knew at this time that East had discovered and called the same thing to the attention of Hopkins.

Hopkins' failure to appreciate the possibilities in the inbreeding project laid out by East convinced both East and Love that they could not expect to do effective plant-breeding research under unsympathetic leadership.

East had been in frequent communication with **Dr. E. H. Jenkins** of the Connecticut Experiment Station ever since their visit at the Urbana hotel during the February conference of the American Breeders' Association. For a few weeks Jenkins had hoped to secure East's services immediately. However, Jenkins' plans encountered difficulties which he recognized would prevent East coming in time to begin work before the planting season of 1905, and on March 6 he wrote East: "It now seems probable that we cannot at present take another man on our staff, because of extra demands on our funds in another direction and because of some uncertainty regarding the action of our legislature. This is a disappointment to me, and I was anxious to get the new work started. It is, I hope, only postponed for six months or a year, however. . . If you are not under another engagement next fall or winter, it is quite possible that we may try to persuade you to come here."

Matters moved more rapidly for **Dr. Jenkins** than he had hoped in March, and in midsummer he wrote young East, "Acting under authority of the Board of Control, I offer you a position on the scientific staff of this Station. . . Our object in inviting you to join us is to have you engage at once in the study and practice of corn breeding in Connecticut, with the end of securing more valuable crops. . . I wish you to take the management of the work—planning of the experiments, etc.—on yourself, subject only to my general oversight and direction in matters of station policy and to the financial conditions of the station. You will be responsible to no other of the station staff in planning and executing your work. . ."

The words of **Dr. Jenkins** had unusual significance in view of East's relations with Hopkins during the summer of

1905. East's reaction to Jenkins' invitation was immediate and favorable. He wrote Jenkins, "Your note and letter of recent dates have been received. I merely wish to acknowledge them with this, hoping to write you fully as soon as I have consulted with Dr. Hopkins who is at present away. I wish, however, to thank you for your kind offer, and to say that unless some unforeseen obstacle intervenes, I shall be glad to accept your proposition, and in view of this shall not entertain proposals elsewhere. . . Mrs. East will be very glad to get back to the eastern states, which have been her home with the exception of four years. Since you were here . . . I have been trying to make myself as familiar as possible with Connecticut, its geology, geography and your own station work, with the idea that if I should ever go there it would save time, and if I should not it would be good for me anyway. So I already begin to feel somewhat familiar with your past work, rules of government, facilities and equipment."

Love, Craig, and others on Hopkins' staff were so familiar with the plant breeding work that Dr. Hopkins approved of East's leaving on September 1. Shortly after his arrival in Connecticut, East and Dr. Jenkins went over every phase of the project designed to give Connecticut farmers higher producing and consequently more profitable corn. The work done under the Hopkins' corn-breeding project was discussed in detail, and East also told Jenkins of the inbreeding work that had been done in connection with the Hopkins program but of Hopkins' refusal to permit his staff to make a full study of the possibilities of corn inbreeding.

Dr. Jenkins showed special interest in the experiment launched at Illinois by East in the spring of 1905 for the purpose of studying the effects, as well as the possibilities of inbreeding in corn, and he suggested that such a program be laid out and carried on in Connecticut. Immediately East saw that several years of hard and delicate work could be saved if he could get hold of a few kernels of seed from the Hopkins-Craig inbred corn developed at the University of Illinois which he had planted ear-to-row in the inbred plot the spring before.

East felt that considering the difficulties he had had with Professor Hopkins over the handling of the inbred material, Hopkins would probably refuse to answer a request from him for any of the material. Unquestionably he thought of asking Dr. Jenkins to write Hopkins, feeling sure that Hopkins would not turn Jenkins down. The trouble with such a plan was that Hopkins was really not sufficiently familiar with the inbred material to be very helpful, and anyway it would be at best an unhappy subject to him. In the last analysis East realized that the one person at the University of Illinois most capable of giving him intelligent aid in securing the best inbred material from the Hopkins inbreeding plot was his former assistant and trusted confidant, H. H. Love.

The inbred plot had been harvested at the University of Illinois before Love received the letter from East reporting that in Connecticut East was to have opportunity to carry on corn inbreeding research work with the blessing and full support of Director Jenkins. East pointed out that the work could be advanced by several years, if he could secure a few kernels of seed of each of the most promising inbred lines that had been grown in the 1905 inbreeding plot. East ended his letter by pointing out that if he could secure these inbreds from Urbana, the inbreeding experiments which he and Love had hoped to conduct in the next several years at the University of Illinois could go on at the Connecticut Station without a single season's interruption. This was a great and tense moment in the story of hybrid corn. Little did East know, when he wrote to Love, how much depended upon his getting those inbred lines from Hopkins' laboratory—the first corn inbreds of their quality ever developed anywhere and the only ones in existence at that time.

Hybrid corn growing vigorously and standing erect, unaffected by storm, disease, or insect hazard

A widely used strain of open-pollinated corn on the same farm under almost identical conditions

High degrees of resistance to particular insects have been
developed in certain hybrids. These two strains were subjected to severe chinch bug attack. One was practically
wiped out while the other gave a good yield of corn

Love's interest in the possibilities of the new approach to corn improvement and his high personal regard for East made him receptive to the petition of his former associate. He realized that in view of the controversy which had centered over the special inbreeding work it would be unwise to ask Hopkins' permission to send the inbred material to East. So without mentioning the matter to anyone, Love went to the plant-breeding laboratory where the ears of the Leaming inbred lines were stored and removed a few kernels from several different ears, labelled and described them adequately, and sent them to East. East never did reveal the help he received from Love, and East's possession of the Hopkins-Craig inbreds was not explained until forty-one years later. East, however, did on numerous occasions afterwards express his appreciation to Love personally for this help and pointed out that his aid did result in advancing the work with corn inbreeding by many years at the Connecticut Agricultural Experiment Station.

There is a certain justice in the Hopkins-Craig inbred material having moved from Illinois to Connecticut, there to be molded into the Leaming inbreds which were more than ten years later to be combined into the famous Burr-Leaming double cross, the first successful strain of the new hybrid corn. Especially fitting is it that Cyril G. Hopkins should make some tangible contribution to the coming of the new kind of corn. For all his limitations as a plant breeder, which became so evident as his corn-improvement project progressed at the University of Illinois, Hopkins' work and that of his institution will ever stand as the connecting link between the ageless practice of corn improvement by selection methods and the modern plant-breeding achievement we know today as hybrid corn. Hopkins set out after an entirely new objective in corn, a grain that should have qualities never before associated with this great American crop. He was the first to breed corn on a field scale, first to make wide use of the pedigree in corn improvement. His program aroused an intense interest in the possibilities of breeding better corn in Edward Murray East, the man whose role was to be a determining one in making hybrid corn possible in our time.

CHAPTER IV

Land of the Sleeping Giant

FOR EDWARD MURRAY EAST, moving from Illinois to Connecticut meant leaving one world and entering another. In New Haven, he found bonds between the past and present were everywhere close at hand. The Connecticut Experiment Station, founded in 1875 and the oldest institution of its kind, was then as now located on the former estate of Eli Whitney, famed inventor of the cotton gin. One of the experiment station's important buildings was once an impressive home on the estate of Whitney, who just a century earlier used his Yankee ingenuity to perfect in his New Haven factory the mass production method which transformed the industrial North fully as much as his cotton gin changed the old South.

Still to be seen along the route from the Connecticut Station to its experimental farm at the foot of the Sleeping Giant [1] is the site of the old Whitney gun factory, where America's world-renowned mass production system was born.

Almost immediately, Jenkins suggested that East write a bulletin for the Connecticut Experiment Station outlining the possibilities for immediately developing better strains of corn. "The Improvement of Corn in Connecticut," by Edward M. East was the first page title of the bulletin issued in January, 1906, and it constitutes an interesting evaluation of the work done at the Illinois Experiment Station and

[1] The Sleeping Giant is a picturesque range of mountains named by the earliest colonists. The mountains are today in a state park.

39

of the things East had learned at twenty-six during his association with the Hopkins project.

Said East to Connecticut farmers, ". . . the profitableness of a corn crop depends on two sets of conditions or forces; the first of which, environment, is external to the plant; and the second, heredity, resides within the . . . corn germ itself. Here are powerful factors in crop production ready to act for or against us, with or without our knowledge or control. It is the province of the corn breeder to obtain knowledge of and to bring these factors under his control." Perhaps no better creed has ever been written for the corn breeder.

East quoted Luther Burbank, who had already won wide fame in plant breeding, as saying, "Cultivation and care may help plants to do better work temporarily, but by breeding, better plants may be brought into existence, which will do better work always, in all places and for all time. Plants may be produced which will perform their appointed work better, quicker and with the utmost precision." The standard of perfection for the new hybrid corn had already taken shape in East's mind.

Then with an air of confidence, East offered Connecticut farmers a modified version of hybrid corn that would increase yields as much as ten bushels an acre and at the same time improve the quality. He urged the adoption of a modified form of the Hopkins ear-to-row corn breeding plot, in which two varieties of corn not closely related would be crossed by detasseling one of the parents. For evidence he referred to his work in Illinois, "In an experiment at the Illinois Experiment Station, by detasseling alternate rows of a breeding plot, a cross was forced upon the detasseled rows . . . and it was found that the crossed rows yielded in the second and third years an average of about ten bushels per acre more."

This publication was the first in which East was free to express his own convictions and in it he chose no middle ground on which to stand. Instead he threw in his lot with the hybridists whose ranks had hardly yet begun to form. From that time forward East never questioned the basic concept that hybridization could be employed by plant or animal breeders to increase immeasurably the supply of food and fiber.

Although East believed for a time that he was the first to discover the possibilities of utilizing hybrid vigor in corn by making varietal crosses, actually its advantages had been a matter of record for nearly a half century. This concept probably originated about the time of our Civil War in a suburb just outside London, England, when Darwin made crosses between unrelated potted corn plants grown in a greenhouse. The idea probably crossed the Atlantic Ocean in a letter from Darwin to his friend, Asa Gray, of Harvard University. One of Gray's students was William James Beal, who, in the early eighteen-eighties, became the first man to utilize hybrid vigor between unlike corn families for the sole purpose of increasing yield. Beal's work attracted wide attention in the corn belt experiment stations, and a decade later Morrow and Gardner of the University of Illinois duplicated Beal's experiment and proved to themselves that the hybrid vigor resulting from crosses of unlike parents offered marked opportunities for increasing corn yield and quality. This work was done only two or three years before Hopkins launched his epic corn breeding program.

While East did not know at the time he recommended varietal crosses to Connecticut farmers before the planting season in 1906 that the idea had such a long and solid history, he continued to urge this method of hybridization as the most practical and of the greatest promise until the new hybrid corn had evolved. It is easy now in looking back to see that the varietal cross was the half-way step between tedious trial and error methods of the Indians and the selectionists, and the modern science of hybrid-corn breeding. The varietal

cross provided for purifying the parentage and crossing unlike strains to secure a limited degree of hybrid vigor, that
mysterious result which could be depended upon to increase
sharply not only the yield but the quality of corn.

In adopting the varietal cross, young East had divorced
himself from the corn selectionists and moved into the new
and uncharted realm of corn breeding. The varietal cross
was never widely used because farmers, with justification, refused to exchange their simple job of selecting seed corn for
the exacting, complicated job of maintaining a corn-breeding
plot. However, the varietal cross became a standard of measure with Edward Murray East, and he steadfastly refused
to concede any practical significance to the new hybrid corn
until it had demonstrated a clean-cut advantage over the
possibilities of good varietal crosses.

Some of East's contemporaries later accused him of
losing interest in corn inbreeding and hybridization in favor
of varietal crossing. Actually, from the time he came to
Connecticut, as his 1906 bulletin so clearly indicates, until
hybrid-corn principles had been established, East never
recommended anything but use of the varietal cross as the
quickest means of improving corn. During his experiment
station career, East was always two kinds of person. On
the one hand he had the problem of being practical and offering the farmers for whom he worked something of immediate value. On the other hand he was a research worker,
probing endlessly all the other possibilities that occurred to
him. The objective of this research was to find better means
of improving plants than those he was then recommending to
farmers. He could be tremendously enthusiastic about some
of his research projects, as in the case with inbreeding corn,
but his enthusiasm was limited to the realm of research, something that others were not always careful to detect.

So while recommending to Connecticut farmers the varietal cross as the best method of securing certain and im-

mediate improvement in their crops, East laid plans for working extensively with his inbreds secured from Illinois. He planted them for the first time in the soil of Connecticut in May of 1906, wondering no doubt how they would fare so far away from their native land.

The young scientist was agreeably surprised to see how his inbreds thrived in Connecticut. It is doubtful that East ever fully recognized what an important bearing the marine type of climate found in southern New England had upon his corn inbreeding work. One of the things which had prevented successful development and study of corn inbreds in the Midwest was the tendency to drouth, storms, and violent fluctuations of temperature. A. D. Shamel at the University of Illinois had undertaken a corn inbreeding experiment before the turn of the century, but the less vigorous inbreds were withered in a mid-summer drouth, and in 1905 Shammel concluded that no possibilities for improving corn existed in the approach by inbreeding. Gene Funk began a systematic corn-inbreeding project in 1902, but as successive years of inbreeding reduced the vigor of his plants, they were unable to survive the drouths and other natural weather hazards of the Midwest climate. Although this inbreeding project did not succeed, and Funk set aside aggressive action on breeding, he did not lose faith in more effective methods of controlled breeding that ultimately were to be developed. Only by starting with tremendous numbers of plants were Midwest hybrid-corn breeders later able to discover and develop inbred lines capable of surviving.

The gentle marine climate along the coast of Connecticut provided East almost greenhouse-like conditions under which to work with his frail inbreds. During the next ten years, although East and his associates never worked with more than a few dozen plants in any one inbred line, few inbreds were lost or even impaired by climatic adversity. Actually there is no other place in the United States where the environmental and economic factors favored this type of work as they do in southern New England.

So the inbred corn developed under Hopkins' direction by W. T. Craig grew exceptionally strong and vigorous in the season of its first planting in New England, and young Mr. East harvested good quantities of seed from each of nearly a dozen of his Leaming lines that fall.

After taking one season to determine how his inbreds would react to the new environment, East set about to begin making hybrid crosses. The season of 1907 was the third in which he had observed the inbreds as separate lines and the seventh time his corn had been selfed. By now he was completely familiar with the various inbreds, knew them like a fond father knows his children. He could see marked differences between them, but in general he noted that all of them were smaller and less vigorous than the Illinois Leaming corn from which they came. His inbreds were impressively uniform, and after seeing them in the early part of the growing season, East was more than ever sure that he was ready to begin making hybrid crosses.

In late July and early August of 1907 he made his first single cross hybrids, top cross hybrids—crosses between inbreds and open pollinated corn most widely used in Connecticut—and crosses between two strains of open pollinated corn. For East the making of hybrids between inbred lines was a project entirely without a precedent. So far as he knew nothing of the sort had ever been done before in all the ageless story of corn. He had never talked to anyone who had employed inbred strains of corn to make hybrids, and in the botanical publications of that time there was no record of such crosses ever having been made.

The next season East grew his new hybrids in a carefully planned proving plot in which the corn was planted in rows three and one-half feet apart. According to East's later account in *The American Naturalist,* he arranged the proving plot so that each hybrid would be grown with the lines which entered into it growing on either side. The hybrids were planted five kernels to the hill, but the inbred lines that entered into them were planted at the rate of four kernels to the hill. East saw that every weed was removed before it had any chance to compete with his corn, and he insisted that the plot be cultivated on a time-clock schedule so that his yields were naturally all higher than would have been secured under practical farm conditions.

Results were electrifying. While the hybrid crosses between different strains of open pollinated corn were not impressive, adding only 3 to 9 bushels to the yield, one of the top-cross hybrids between a Leaming inbred and Connecticut Leaming open pollinated corn yielded at the rate of 142 bushels an acre. The Leaming inbred entering into this hybrid yielded at the rate of 62 bushels an acre, and the Connecticut Leaming open pollinated yielded 121 bushels an acre, a gain of 21 bushels an acre for the hybrid.

But the big news was from the single cross hybrids in which both of the strains entering into combination were Leaming inbreds. The best one of them yielded at the amazing rate of 202 bushels an acre, a gain for the hybrid of fantastic proportions, even though one inbred entering into the union yielded at the rate of 62 bushels an acre and the other inbred yielded at the rate of 65 bushels an acre. This single cross hybrid yielded almost 100 bushels an acre more than the best Connecticut open pollinated corn in the plot.

In January, 1908, East went to Washington, D. C., to attend the annual meeting of the American Breeders' Association. Dr. George Harrison Shull, a scientist of the Carnegie Institution of Washington whose branch, The Station for Experimental Evolution, was located at Cold Spring Harbor, Long Island, was one of the speakers at the conference. Shull's address revealed that he had been conducting corn inbreeding experiments somewhat similar to those of

East. As soon as East returned home, he discussed the Shull address with Director Jenkins and then wrote the Carnegie scientist for a copy of his manuscript so that it might be studied further. Shull complied promptly, sending East his own personal copy and asking that it be returned. Jenkins stopped in at East's office just after the plant breeder had finished reading Shull's paper closely. East, in a jubilant mood, told Dr. Jenkins that Shull had supplied substantiating evidence for all of the important things which East and Jenkins had observed along with some new ideas about the importance of inbreeding and crossing of corn.

One of the things which impressed East most was Shull's conclusion that inbreeding was a mechanism by which the corn breeder could select out of open pollinated corn a great variety of the simpler pure types representing the various characteristics to be found in native corn. East was aware that by inbreeding, the corn breeder had a chance to select for particular characteristics, but he had not been able to explain the process so clearly as Shull. Referring to this and other matters of interest in Shull's paper, East wrote the Carnegie research worker on February 12, 1908, "I am returning under separate cover the copy of your paper on corn breeding, which you so kindly let me have. I have had a copy made which I shall keep. Since studying your paper, I agree entirely with your conclusion, and wonder why I have been so stupid as to not see the fact myself."

Shull replied to this letter from East, saying, "I am glad to find that your extensive experiments in corn breeding might have led you to the same conclusion as that at which I have arrived, and that you are going to base your experimentation to some extent upon this view. I am convinced that there is a wide open field here which has not been touched upon heretofore."

In more recent years East's former students and associates have speculated many times over this statement to Shull in which he professed not to have been aware of this important function of the corn-inbreeding process. This attention was undoubtedly focused on it in his own privately conducted corn-inbreeding experiments at the University of Illinois. Certainly it was his belief that variation, and consequent improvement, could be found within and between inbred varieties which led him to propose complete reorganization of Hopkins' inbreeding work in 1905. Probably the most logical explanation is that East recognized there was great variation in corn and that while he had used inbreeding to secure a separation of the innumerable subtypes, he had not been so impressed as had Shull with inbreeding as a quick, sure, and calculable method of securing this separation.

East was so impressed with Dr. Shull's work that he made a special trip to visit the Carnegie scientist the next June in order to check carefully on the work done by the Cold Spring Harbor scientist. Shull described his inbreeding and crossing procedure as the "pure-line method of corn breeding," and suggested that it might bring to farmers a new kind of corn, more productive than any that had been known before. East, with his realistic practical experiment station background, differed with Shull.

This clash of opinion between the two men was to endure for several years. East disagreed with Shull on the importance of inbreeding and crossing inbred lines into hybrids for two reasons. First, East and Shull were thinking at this time of developing techniques which could be handled on the individual farm, and East knew from hard experience that if farmers were reluctant to accept his relatively simple plan for producing varietal crosses, they could never be expected to adopt the tremendously more complicated job of developing inbreds or even producing seed corn when they were supplied with the inbred lines. Secondly, even if by some miracle the farmers would adopt the plan, he considered that the disfigured, dwarfed inbred ears could never yield enough seed to make practical the widespread use on large acreages of single cross hybrids between inbred lines of corn.

His first paper on the subject of inbreeding appeared in 1908. It traced the work he had done from the days at Illinois and discussed the development of inbred lines and what could be expected from making single crosses between them. East declined to predict that hybrids between inbred lines of corn had any practical significance. The same year East wrote another paper in which he endeavored to apply for the first time the Mendelian principle to corn breeding.

CHAPTER V

Unexpected Help

MANY TIMES, especially in very recent years, the contributions of Dr. George H. Shull have been called to the attention of the public. Dr. Shull has received more recognition than all of the other early hybrid-corn makers combined. None other than the magazine *Science* has referred editorially to him as "the originator of hybrid corn." *Life Magazine* has described Dr. Shull as the man who "developed hybrid corn whose seed sales now total $75,000,000 annually in the U. S." While it is unfair to refer to any one man as the originator of hybrid corn or the person who developed this priceless method of corn improvement, Shull's contributions came at such an opportune time that we need to make a closer acquaintance with the Carnegie botanist and his classic experiments with the maize plant.

When George Shull gave his address before the American Breeders' Association in Washington, D. C., on January 28, 1908, something most unusual was revealed. Only two men at that particular time were working seriously with the mysterious job of inbreeding corn, and they were conducting their research less than one hundred miles apart—each entirely unaware of the other's efforts.

There has been a tendency ever since to link the two men together in their contributions to the development of hybrid corn and to conclude, or at least infer, that they did the same things at so nearly the same time that the work of one merely confirmed the conclusions of the other. Nothing could be much farther from the truth.

Actually, the significant thing about the relationship between Shull and East during this important period was not the similarity but the acute differences in their work, in their thinking, and in their evaluation of their work. The letters exchanged by the two men in the months immediately after they met—a period when they were anxious to win one another's confidence—emphasized several points relating to corn breeding upon which they were in agreement; but practically all of their later correspondence and publications bearing upon the subject call attention to their very fundamental disagreements. This disagreement was the most fortunate development in their acquaintanceship, since it kept the possibilities of corn breeding uppermost in their minds over a considerable period of years. Had they quickly reached full agreement, the entire matter might easily have ceased to be a topic of continuing interest.

So intense were the disagreements between Shull and East, it is to the credit of both men that they kept these differences from becoming an open and heated debate, one that might have impaired their relationship with one another as well as with mutual friends and fellow scientists. Being aware of this possibility and the consequences it could impose, Shull and East entered into a gentleman's agreement in 1910 by which they agreed between themselves never to permit their own personalities to precipitate feelings which might obscure the discussion, consideration, or advancement of the corn breeding principles upon which both had worked, at least until such time as these concepts had either been generally accepted or completely refuted.

East died in 1938 without ever breaking this self-imposed silence. Shull waited until 1942, when he justly judged that the issues over which he and East had differed so many years ago had been removed from the realms of controversy. The

new hybrid corn had by that time won a permanent place
on any roll of honor written for American agriculture in the
twentieth century. On June 13, 1942, Shull wrote to Prof.
J. C. Cunningham in answer to questions which the Iowa
State College historian of maize had raised about the early
work Shull had done on corn inbreeding:

"The correspondence between Dr. East and myself shows
that my proposals came to him as an entirely new concept,
which was recognized by him, however, as clearing up experiences of his own which had puzzled him. He and I agreed
between us that we would not enter into any personal controversy about priority, in order not to impede the progress of
the hybrid corn program. Now that nothing can stop that
program, there can be no further justification for preventing
historical truth and accuracy from prevailing. This takes
nothing away from Doctor East, as there can be no doubt
that there would have been a still greater lag between the
proposal of my 'pure-line method' and its full fruition had
he and his students not jumped in so vigorously and effectively to promote it."

This agreement not to discuss the matter of who did the
first work or who was the first to discover and appreciate
the possibilities of improving corn by developing inbred lines
and crossing them into hybrids had the effect of rather completely disassociating Shull with the matter for more than
two decades. Shull did almost no more writing or speaking
about corn breeding after the Shull-East agreement was
reached, while East was then only at the beginning of a
career which was to make him the author or co-author of
practically every important publication dealing with the
subject for years to come.

In papers written up to the time of the understanding,
East not only pressed the fact that his work with corn began
in 1900, some years before Shull's experiments were started,
but on the other hand he credited Shull by referring to the

Carnegie man's work and also by quoting him freely. In one major publication written just about the time the agreement was reached, East referred to Shull's conclusions about corn breeding, giving full credit even to the point of quoting Shull's own summary of his discoveries. However, from the time the Shull-East agreement was reached, East never again in any of his many papers, pamphlets, or books dealing with corn breeding pressed either his own part in this very early work, nor did he ever again credit Shull with having made any contribution to the new hybrid-corn concepts. In this way the Shull-East agreement worked out to East's advantage in so far as public recognition was concerned. Since he was doing the writing, the natural thing was to associate East more closely with the early work than Shull.

As the new hybrid corn became big news to millions of people, there was naturally a rising popular interest in the persons who had done the early work. By the time this public interest in hybrid corn was approaching its peak, Shull was the principal living person who could logically be closely associated with the very early work of crossing inbreds, East having passed away the very year that the new hybrid corn wiped away any question about the prominence it was to take in American agriculture.

The fact that East was gone and Shull was alive soon produced a reversal in the trend which had tended to minimize Shull's part in the early work with hybrid corn. Instead there came to Shull an entire series of recognitions in the form of magazine and newspaper articles as well as medals, citations, and awards. This development caused Shull in more recent years to be referred to as the man who developed or originated hybrid corn—something that can with justice be said of no man. This is well substantiated in tracing Shull's own work with corn.

George Harrison Shull was born and reared in southern

Ohio, and the story of the Shull family is one of those epics which would be unlikely to happen anywhere except in America. His parents, Mr. and Mrs. Harrison Shull, farmed on shares and raised a daughter and six sons, five of whom climbed over the shoulders of the eldest brother to "*Who's Who*" achievements in the fields of science, art, literature, and teaching.

When he was eighteen years old, Samuel, the eldest brother, knew that going to high school was out of the question—he was too poor, and there were no high schools in the area; but he determined to acquire at least an elementary understanding of several subjects including botany by getting the best college textbooks of the time and teaching himself. George Harrison was a lad of ten years at the time, and he took such a great interest in his elder brother's studies, especially the accompanying field work, that within two or three years Samuel turned the books over to him. When George was sixteen years old, another brother, John William, suggested that he make his love of plants the basis of a career instead of just an interesting avocation.

Later, with further help and encouragement from Sam, as the brothers always called Samuel, young George Shull worked his way through school. After teaching country school for two years to earn more money, Shull entered Antioch College of Yellow Springs, Ohio, now well known as the home of Kettering's "green grass boys" who were put to work there by the General Motors research wizard to attempt to unlock the secret of green plants' ability to capture and store the sun's energy. Shull was not only Antioch's star student but also its janitor at twenty cents an hour.

Shull was graduated from Antioch College in 1901 at twenty-seven and transferred to the University of Chicago to do graduate work, singling out for special study such subjects as botany, taxonomy, ecology, physiology, and bi-

ometry, the latter subject being the key that opened the
door to his career as a plant breeder.

One of his teachers, Charles B. Davenport, was so impressed with Shull's work that when he was made director of
the new Carnegie Institution for Experimental Evolution, he
invited Shull to become one of the scientists on his staff.

Shull was so far along with his graduate work when this
opportunity came that the University of Chicago faculty
agreed to take one of his recently completed papers as a
thesis if he could pass the doctoral examinations. He declined the thesis offer, but instead completed another paper
upon which he had already made a good start. This left
him only thirty-six hours to study for the doctoral examinations, on which he did well enough to be granted his Ph.D.
degree, *magna cum laude.*

On May 1, 1904, Dr. Shull arrived at Cold Spring Harbor,
Long Island, New York, where the new Carnegie station was
to be situated. He was the first scientist to arrive on the
ground. The first thing he had to do was to remove young
spruce trees from what was to be his experimental garden.
The plot, which had previously been a vegetable garden, had
not been used for years, and some of the trees were fifteen
feet tall.

Recalling it now, Shull says, "One of my first jobs was to
buy a horse and hire a man to drive him. You see, just as my
life started on a primitive scale, so my scientific career
started on a primitive scale, certainly from scratch."

By the time all of the preliminary responsibilities were
cleared away, it was too late in the season to begin garden
experiments, but early in the fall, Shull set about to plan
for the planting to be made in the spring of 1905. His problem was to study the effect exerted by heredity on the development and functions of plants or animals, and he chose
to make the study with a plant that could be grown quickly
and easily. He selected corn as the plant, and the number of

rows of kernels on the ear as the changing characteristic to
be studied.

There has been considerable interest and controversy over
the question of the origin and nature of the corn which Shull
used in his classic experiments. Recently Dr. Shull re-examined his records, including his diary, and it appears certain that the corn was a native white variety selected from
corn raised as a farm crop on the experiment station grounds
in the season of 1904. Dr. Shull's diary for May 14, 1904,
says, "Sowed buckwheat, corn and sorghum," and on May 27,
"Kelly cultivated the potatoes, corn . . ." Then the diary
for November 7, 1904, refers again to this corn, adding
". . . counted the rows on the ears of white dent corn raised
in Carnegie garden this year."

Next May Shull made an ear-to-row planting from each
of his selections. He planted from eighty to one hundred
hills from each of the ears, and the corn that grew in his
Long Island garden that summer had the appearance of any
ordinary fields of open pollinated corn. At pollination time,
Shull selected one plant, and one plant only, in each of the
rows for inbreeding. The remainder of the season was so favorable that every one of his selfed plants matured a good
seed ear.

Shull did his most important work with corn during the
next two seasons of 1906 and 1907, using such small plant
numbers as to inject into the whole experiment the element
of a miracle. Although Shull continued his corn plantings until 1916, he enlarged but little upon the observations made
during the two golden years of 1906 and 1907 when he observed and concluded wondrous things.

In 1906 he grew his corn children representing one generation of inbreeding, made second-generation selfs as well
as making hybrid crosses between several of the inbred
strains. In 1907 he grew the hybrid crosses as well as the
second generation inbreds. He made additional crosses and

another generation of selfs, a practice that was continued each season until 1916.

Here is what Shull observed. In 1906 and 1907, the inbred corn produced a wide variety of types, many of them very unlike the open pollinated corn with which he began the experiment. In general the inbred corn was not so tall or vigorous as the original open pollinated corn with which he began, becoming progressively inferior in the second generation of selfing. Some of the hybrid crosses between inbred strains were even taller, more vigorous, and higher yielding than the original open pollinated corn with which he began the experiment.

Here is what Shull concluded. Every plant in an open pollinated field of corn is a chance-born complex hybrid with practically no two of them genetically alike regardless of their visible similarity; each plant is made up of innumerable simpler pure types, or biotypes as the plant breeders call them, which can be separated from one another by inbreeding. When, by inbreeding, the simple pure lines or biotypes are separated, the resulting corn plants become smaller and less vigorous because of the absence of the stimulation which comes from combining many biotypes in the genetic pattern of any number of corn plants. There was increased vigor when the inbred corn was crossed into hybrids, bringing together into the new hybrid strains a greatly increased number of biotypes.

That is what George H. Shull did, observed, and concluded in the two years of 1906 and 1907 during which he at no time saw corn that had been inbred more than two generations; nor saw hybrids of inbred strains in more than one season; nor had more corn than could be grown in the vegetable garden of any corn belt farm family. Scientists and laymen alike continue to marvel that anyone could make so little material yield so much information in so little time.

Clearly, no adequate explanation is possible that does not take into account Shull's genius for botanical observation, his great native capacity, and the fine training which enabled him to understand and appreciate what he saw.

Shull made the first public statement about his experiments with corn in an address given before the American Breeders' Association, as we have already noted, in Washington, D. C., on January 28 and 29, 1908. In his paper, entitled "The Composition of a Field of Maize," Shull pointed out to his audience the opportunity of breaking up open pollinated corn into its simpler pure types, advocating the making of every possible cross between them so that the ultimate selection might be based wholly on the ability to produce desirable hybrids that would yield for the farmer a new kind of corn never seen before. Reduced to the simplest form, Dr. Shull told the plant breeders: We are going to grow hybrid corn regardless of what we do; the question is whether we are going to use our newly found knowledge of heredity and grow corn hybrids of our own choosing, or are we going to go along as the Indians have for thousands of years, depending upon the chance hybrid combinations the winds happen to present to us?

Inbreeding and crossing of the resulting simpler pure lines into hybrids of our own design was the mechanism, Shull pointed out, by which we could have a new kind of corn of greater promise than any that had been developed before.

Before closing his remarks that January afternoon, Dr. Shull suggested that continuing hybridization might be necessary so that the farmer could each year raise first generation hybrids made directly from the same inbreds, saying, "The problem of getting the seed corn that shall produce the record crop of corn . . . may possibly find solution, at least in certain cases, similar to that reached by Mr. Q. I. Simpson in the breeding of hogs by the combination of two strains which are only at the highest quality in the first generation, thus making it necessary to go back each year to the original combination."

In recent years Shull's 1908 address has been many times described as being so new and revolutionary in its concepts as to represent a "Bill of Rights" for the new science of plant breeding. Actually Shull's remarkable experiments with corn were chiefly of value because they supplied additional and easily understood evidence to support the observations and conclusions of his contemporaries. Shull himself made this unmistakably clear in the final sentences of his Washington address:

"In conclusion I wish to say that the idea that in breeding maize we are dealing with a large number of distinct elementary species or biotypes is not presented here as a new idea, for DeVries, in his little book on 'Plant Breeding' presents this view, and Dr. East in a recent bulletin from the Connecticut Station has indicated the great complexity of the corn breeder's problems owing to the concurrence of these elementary species and fluctuating variations. I have aimed simply to point out how my own experience in corn breeding supports the same view. I think, however, that the suggestion here made, that continuous hybridization instead of isolation of pure strains is perhaps the proper aim of the corn breeder, is new, and it is this view that I wish to submit for your consideration."

Later Shull discovered that even the possibilities of continuous hybridization for the production of improved varieties of corn had been suggested only a few years before by Morrow and Gardner, two botanists of the University of Illinois who had published their conclusions in Bulletin No. 25 of the Illinois Agriculture Experiment Station.

Shull planted his corn in his Long Island garden in the spring of 1908, and then left on a trip to Europe, placing the responsibility for carrying on the work in the hands of his lifelong friend and associate, Charles L. Macy. On board ship en route to London, Dr. Shull met Miss Mary Julia Nicholl, daughter of a civil engineer who helped build railroads across our western prairies, forming an acquaintance that later led to marriage. Shull returned in time personally to supervise the harvest of his corn material.

The American Breeders' Association held its 1909 winter meeting in Columbia, Missouri, the last week in January, and Shull accepted an invitation to deliver another paper based on his corn-breeding experiments. Realizing that there would be many persons present from the agricultural experiment stations of the corn belt states, he prepared an address to emphasize the practical opportunities which he felt were to be found in his conclusions based on his experiments with corn.

The Columbia paper, entitled "A Pure-line Method in Corn Breeding," showed plainly the influence East had exerted upon Shull since he had spoken in Washington the year before. In the early part of his address in Columbia, Shull presented his "pure-line method" as more practical than those plans for corn breeding being used at the Connecticut, Illinois, or Ohio Experiment Stations. Time was to prove that Shull was justified in this contention, since the plans then being used at the Connecticut, Illinois, or Ohio stations never achieved acceptance, and certainly Shull's "pure-line method" was no less practical than theirs.

Evidence of doubt in Shull's mind about the practical possibilities of his "pure-line method" appeared in the closing paragraph of the Columbia address in which Shull said, "I am not prepared at present to say what will be the probable cost of seed-corn when produced by this method, nor can I surmise what relation this increased cost will bear to increased yield that will be produced."

Obviously these were considerations that were vital to any practical application Shull's "pure-line method" might have.

These were the considerations which East had in mind when he rejected Shull's proposal the summer before as having few, if any, practical possibilities. These were the considerations which have until this day prevented the single cross hybrid from being used on large-scale acreages of field corn.

Immediately after Shull finished his Columbia address, he mailed a copy of it to East, who in his February 4, 1909, response to Shull in a letter reiterated his belief that it lacked practical possibilities, saying, "From the experience I have had in pedigree breeding, I feel that the method I have outlined (the varietal cross) will be much more practical than the one you have outlined in your paper. I wish you could have a little experience trying to get the farmers to take up anything in the least complex."

Shull continued his campaign to win acceptance for his "pure-line method" in the corn belt by presenting another paper before the American Breeders' Association late the same year of 1909. The association moved its winter meeting from the usual January date to the early part of December so that it could be held in connection with the National Corn Exposition in Omaha, Nebraska, an event attended by foremost corn farmers and agronomists from not only the United States, but from a number of foreign countries.

Mrs. Shull accompanied her husband to Omaha. Together they spent their first day at the Omaha Exposition arranging a complete exhibit of the inbred and hybrid cross ears gathered by Shull in his garden a few weeks before for just this purpose. This was the first exhibition of corn hybrids developed from inbreds ever to be presented to the public, and it attracted untold curiosity from both scientists and farmers attending the exposition.

The next day, December 10, Shull made his third talk before the American Breeders' Association in twenty-two months, describing his observations and conclusions. The first part of his address was devoted to a rousing defense of his "pure-line method" of corn breeding and a restrained attack upon such persons as G. N. Collins of the United States Department of Agriculture who described "inbreeding as 'particularly dangerous' when applied to corn."

Shull again pointed to the work of Dr. East as largely substantiating his own conclusions, taking particular care to emphasize that East had independently done similar work and reached similar conclusions. "Dr. East and I have both performed many experiments which have led us to place great confidence in the practical importance of the discoveries . . . Dr. East and I by the application of the newer biological conceptions have arrived at practically the same method. . . It may be true, as Dr. East says, that the pure-line method is 'more correct theoretically but less practical . . .' "

Shull finished his Omaha address with a masterly review of the possibilities for his "pure-line method," placing as he had the winter before in Columbia, Missouri, great emphasis upon the immediate practical application of his corn breeding suggestions. Aided by his fine exhibit, Shull made a much greater impression than he had at any previous time.

Dr. N. E. Hansen, noted plant scientist from South Dakota, was so greatly impressed that he rushed to the rostrum after Shull had finished, shook his hand, slapped his back, and said, "You have all the other corn breeders skinned a mile." What Hansen meant, of course, was that he could clearly see that in the battle between corn breeding and corn selection, corn breeding would come off decisively the winner. The South Dakota horticulturist was in a good position to judge impartially, since corn was not at that time an important crop in his state and he was, therefore, not handicapped with a bias for or close association with the selectionist methods of corn improvement.

And Hansen was not the only person impressed. Many others showed a deep curiosity about the work Shull had been doing, and especially were the agronomists of the Nebraska Agricultural Experiment Station interested. Almost before Dr. Shull had finished speaking, Montgomery and Kiesselbach of that station were making plans to give corn breeding a definite trial. At last Shull had earned a serious trial for his "pure-line method" of breeding corn, and the developments that followed deserve close examination.

Interest in Shull's work at Nebraska's station stemmed back to his first addresses given in Washington and Columbia which had been heard by E. G. Montgomery, then the leading personality behind corn improvement in the developing western corn belt. Montgomery laid out a small experiment in inbreeding so that the first selfing of corn was done at the Experiment Station in the season of 1908. Montgomery continued the inbreeding project in 1909, assisted by the new member of his little department, young Kiesselbach, who had been helping with the experimental work since 1907. Then, benefiting from the enthusiasm engendered in this pair by the chance to meet and hear Shull at the Omaha Corn Exposition, the small project undertaken by Montgomery blossomed in the season of 1910 into a full-fledged program to develop the total possibilities of Dr. Shull's pure-line methods of corn breeding.

It is highly worthy of note at this point that R. A. Emerson, of the Horticulture Department in the Nebraska Agricultural Experiment Station, had at the same time become engrossed with technical studies in the genetics of corn. He also heard and met Shull in Omaha, and this, apart from the work to be undertaken at Nebraska, had special significance. Mr. and Mrs. Emerson had dinner with Dr. and Mrs. Shull, affording Emerson a better opportunity to get acquainted with Shull and his concepts. Emerson continued to work with corn genetics in Nebraska, then spent a year studying with Dr. East at Harvard, and immediately began his long and illustrious career as a geneticist and teacher at Cornell where practically all his work centered on corn. His work there in corn genetics has pointed the way far into the future, and his students have had an important bearing upon the development of the new hybrid corn.

However, Montgomery as well as Emerson soon left Nebraska, and with the close of the 1911 season, the corn breeding project was left under the supervision of T. A. Kiesselbach, who has been attending to it ever since and has for three decades been recognized as the foremost authority on corn in the great Missouri River Valley, now one of the outstanding corn-growing areas in the country.

Kiesselbach was among the first to realize that the score card means of picking the best corn had little value. At the time of the National Corn Exposition where Shull spoke, Kiesselbach had written off the "pretty ear" corn show, and with a number of progressive associates subscribed to the characteristically pithy slogan, "fine feathers don't make hens lay and fancy points don't make corn ears yield."

From the moment Kiesselbach sat there in Omaha and heard Shull give his masterful presentation on corn inbreeding, he never doubted that it would some day be found useful. "I heard Shull talk in Omaha," he recalled recently, "and I was impressed, amazed, challenged, enthused. It was an ear opener for persons who had been ear selecting. Shull told of his experiment in which the poorest hybrid outyielded the best open-pollinated variety by ten bushels an acre."

The past must always be linked to the present, and the work with inbreeding corn at Nebraska was no exception. Not far from Lincoln there lived the man who always preferred to sign himself merely "R. Hogue." His corn had given high grain yields in co-operative experiment station tests throughout east central Nebraska. Hogue Yellow Dent was one of the most productive open pollinated varieties, and it was logical that Montgomery and Kiesselbach should select it to supply the material with which they would work in the new inbreeding program.

The inbreeding progressed well in 1910, 1911, and 1912. The plants became smaller and more uniform with each successive selfed generation. Kiesselbach made the first crosses between inbreds in 1912. These were grown in the 1913 season, the first corn hybrids from inbreds ever to grow under the bright Nebraska sun, first ever to grow in all the corn belt, first ever to grow anywhere west of the Land of the Sleeping Giant in Connecticut.

The yield of some of the hybrids was distinctly superior, but the advantages of the new corn ended right there. In general field performances, especially in its ability to stand up until harvest, which is so important during Nebraska's frequent windy days of early fall, the new hybrids were not the equal of commonly grown standard varieties of open pollinated corn. More work would be required to select the proper pure lines which transmit these other desired characteristics which would further increase the yield. This effort was supplemented in 1914 by starting the selection of inbred lines from the strong-stalked variety, Nebraska White Prize.

Winters and summers fashioned themselves into years during which Dr. Kiesselbach was invited to speak of the new hybrid corn in every corn-growing section of the Missouri Valley. He did much to pave the way for popular acceptance of the new corn beyond the Missouri River in the next twenty years. But progress in hybrid corn breeding on the University of Nebraska experimental farms came slowly—first, because of inability to secure hybrids from the Hogue variety with outstanding characteristics of field performance, and second, because of the weather. Breeding plots and yield tests were wiped out completely by withering drouths in 1918, 1919, 1926, and again in 1930. Early in the thirties irrigation equipment was installed on the experimental farms, and from then on progress became more rapid. Kiesselbach and his staff maintained their faith in the new hybrid corn through all those years and eventually developed hybrid corn breeding and hybrid corn demonstration programs that have had an important part in bringing the farmers of Nebraska to the point where today they plant approximately ninety per cent of their cornland to hybrid corn—a factor that has raised Nebraska corn production so greatly that the state usually ranks third in the Union in this important respect.

Had Kiesselbach's early inbreeding and crossing work with the Hogue lines been more successful from the standpoint of all-round field performance, the main path of hybrid corn development might well have run through Nebraska and spread from there through the other American corn-growing areas. Had this happened, it would have greatly added to the importance of Shull's work and crowned with unparalleled success his campaign to win the acceptance for his corn-breeding concepts among the corn belt experiment stations which he so earnestly attempted to achieve.

As things did develop, the inability of the Nebraska Experiment Station in the early years to develop hybrids which could be of use to corn farmers snuffed out the last opportunity of Shull's making a direct contribution to the development of hybrid corn. It meant that the Carnegie scientist's efforts to secure acceptance had failed for two reasons, first, because his "pure-line method," although embracing much of the technique used by hybrid corn breeders today, was not sufficiently complete to be practical; second, because the agronomists to whom he appealed proved for the most part to be sterile ground on which to sow new ideas about corn improvement. That generation of experiment station agronomists would have to pass and be replaced by another not wedded to the old order of things in corn development before even the hybrid corn we have today could be accepted. George Harrison Shull knocked on the door of an empty house.

Shull's work with corn breeding was practically completed when he finished his address at Omaha. He continued to

grow and study his inbreds and crosses until 1916, but gradually he came to see that the "pure-line method" of corn
breeding had greater theoretical than practical values. In
1913 Shull went to Europe, accompanied by Mrs. Shull and
his eldest son, for a period of study. He was accorded the
honor of making a number of addresses before some of the
leading botanical societies on the continent. At the University
of Göttingen he delivered an address in German, and it was in
this paper that he coined and first used the word *heterosis*,
which has since been accepted by hybridists to mean the
phenomenon of the increase in vigor which results from
crossing corn inbreds. But all thought of his "pure-line"
method of corn breeding having any practical application
slipped more and more from his mind.

On January 5, 1914, Shull wrote from Germany to H. K.
Hayes at the Connecticut Station, "I never believed that my
pure-line method was practical. It was scientifically essential
for the solution of the particular problem I had in hand, of
course." On April 22, 1914, Shull wrote to George M. Allee
of Newell, Iowa, president of the Iowa Agricultural Experimental Association, a farmers' group co-operating with the
Iowa Experiment Station, "I consider the pure-line method
of theoretical rather than practical interest."

Strange words from the man who four years before stood
confidently in front of the members of the American Breeders'
Association in Omaha and advocated the adoption of his
pure-line corn breeding plan on the grounds that it was less
complex and more productive of results than any other
method of corn improvement then in use at the leading
centers of corn development in the United States.

There was, however, no weakening in Shull's faith in the
value of hybridization. His letters from Germany merely
attest the fact that he was by this time aware that the
particular method of hybridization which he had proposed
was not practical. Another letter written also from Germany

in January, 1914, proved that Shull was merely renouncing his particular proposal for corn hybridization and not the concept of hybridization itself. In it he urged E. D. Funk, the noted Bloomington, Illinois, seedsman, to undertake experiments of his own to see how hybridization could be made most useful. As we shall see later, Shull presented the case so convincingly that Funk endeavored to follow up the suggestion.

Although East had discovered for himself most of the things reported by Shull about corn, yet it had a stimulating effect upon the Connecticut Station corn breeder. Shull's conclusions dramatized the problems and opportunities of corn breeding for East as they had never been before. Until he met Shull, East's work with corn breeding suffered from the isolated position he occupied, the penalty that must always be paid by those who venture out alone into unexplored realms. East had been wrestling with his new corn breeding concepts for several years, meeting nothing but a reaction ranging from indifference to outright rebuff.

We need only consider the encouragement East drew from his association with Love and Jenkins to be able to appreciate what Shull's work meant to him. Shull sealed off the possibility of East's ever having to retreat and give up his vision of giving America better corn by harnessing the power of hybridization. The two men differed over the best means of using this power, but the two great scientists stood shoulder to shoulder on the great underlying concept that hybridization properly applied could give us corn and other plant and animal servants vastly superior to any that had ever existed before.

Shull's work as a corn breeder flashed like a great comet through a still darkened sky, leaving a little of its luster to strengthen the hearts of each receptive mind touched by its glorious light.

CHAPTER VI

New Hands on the Oars

THE YEAR 1909 was one of those crucial periods in the story of hybrid corn when all of the forces carrying the development forward suddenly seemed suspended, threatening to halt on dead center. Shull's battle to prove the practical benefit of hybrids of inbred lines came to an indecisive end that year, and for a time in the spring of 1909 it appeared that East might be lost to the cause of hybrid corn.

Early in the year Dr. East received an unexpected and entirely unsolicited invitation to join the faculty of Harvard University's Bussey Institution. The young scientist had come a long way since the days when he was a somewhat bashful, soft-spoken, hollow-cheeked chemistry student at the University of Illinois. As he matured under Director Jenkins' friendly and encouraging leadership, he developed a remarkable capacity to challenge and impress people even in a very short acquaintance. This newly developed ability helped win him a call to the faculty of one of the country's foremost universities. He was but twenty-nine years old when he accepted the Harvard position.

Strangely, the recommendation of East had come to Harvard over the ocean from the noted English geneticist, William Bateson of the University of Cambridge. Bateson had met Dr. East briefly while delivering a series of lectures on the Yale University campus, only a few blocks from the Connecticut Experiment Station. He was so keenly impressed

with the young plant breeder that when he was queried a
few months later by the Harvard faculty, who undoubtedly
expected a suggestion of someone from the British Isles or
Europe, Bateson urged the consideration of their fellow-
American from the Land of the Sleeping Giant.

His new position imposed upon East a real challenge,
considering that it was the first teaching he had ever done
and that it was to be done in one of New England's' most
advanced educational institutions where standards for faculty and'students were exacting.

Both East and his director, Dr. Jenkins, were aware that
under ordinary circumstances East's going to Harvard
would mean the end of his plant breeding program at Connecticut. Director Jenkins was especially concerned, realizing
that it would be impossible with his limited budget to engage
a successor of East's ability. Moreover, Jenkins was not
sure that there was another plant breeder and geneticist in
the country who could match the capacities of Edward
Murray East. In addition, Jenkins felt the impending loss
keenly in a personal sense.

Jenkins and East were both resourceful individuals, and
together they devised a plan which would skirt all of these
difficulties and at the same time create new opportunities
both for the Connecticut Experiment Station and for Dr.
East. Under the terms of the plan which Dr. Jenkins adopted,
he and East were to select some promising but untrained
younger man who would handle the plant breeding program
under East's direction. Technically the arrangement provided that the new man would do the Connecticut Station's
plant-breeding work from May to November and then be
given time during the winter months to go to Harvard and
work toward his doctor's degree with Dr. East.

The arrangement enabled East to continue his direction
of the corn breeding work at the Connecticut Station, in one

degree or another, for nearly ten years after he became a member of the Harvard faculty. This was the decade that established the Connecticut Experiment Station as the cradle of hybrid corn.

Few decisions in all the years of corn development deserve to be placed beside the one which Dr. Jenkins made when he urged East to continue as director of the plant-breeding program of the Connecticut Station. The arrangement set in motion powerful forces to advance the cause of hybrid corn — forces which would not have come into play even Had East remained at Connecticut.

It created the opportunity, even made it necessary for East to draw around him other men and acquaint them with his revolutionary ideas about plant breeding. This was the beginning of the organizing of a new group of agronomists and scientists who were eventually to push out into every experiment station in the country. With them would go new hybridizing concepts that would assure the success not only of hybrid corn but of a long list of hybridized plants and animals now giving our farmers tremendously increased food-producing ability.

It was not that East willed it so, but that circumstances, which to be sure he had much to do in shaping, dropped the mantle of destiny about him. Jenkins' plan created an opportunity for East to project his plant breeding concepts all over the United States. The force of East's vision was so great and East's teaching of it so effective that today almost every plant breeder of note is a former student of East's or has been stimulated by one of East's students. This explains why East rather than Shull was the dynamic force that gave hybrid corn to America. Shull appealed with a partially ineffective plan for corn hybridization to his contemporary generation of agronomists who, like Moses of old, were not destined to enter the promised land. East developed a new generation of agricultural experiment station leaders who gradually replaced the old guard approached by Shull.

Herbert Kendall Hayes, whose name is known around the world for his outstanding plant-breeding work on Thatcher wheat, was the first of the East converts. Hayes became the first of the new cult of plant breeders who were to sweep aside all opposition to these new concepts first advanced so ably by East and who were to eventually hold most of the important plant breeding positions in the agricultural experiment stations of the United States. The contributions of Hayes to the development of the new hybrid corn have been, perhaps, more obscured, but only a little less important than they have been in the field of wheat breeding.

Hayes was reared on a small Connecticut farm, attended the Massachusetts Agricultural College, and was working on a tobacco-breeding project for the United States Department of Agriculture in northern Connecticut when he heard that East and Director Jenkins were looking for someone interested but not necessarily experienced in plant breeding.

In May, Hayes visited New Haven and met East and Jenkins. Characteristically, East decided on their first meeting that Hayes was the logical person to handle the assignment of working out the plant-breeding projects organized and outlined by himself for the Connecticut Station. Although East was not to leave New Haven until September, Director Jenkins suggested that Hayes start to work as soon as possible.

So in July the name Hayes was added to the roster of staff workers at the Connecticut Experiment Station. East, who was so ill most of the summer that it appeared he was on the verge of a nervous breakdown, decided to live out at the experimental farm, near his work, thinking that the stay in the country might improve his health. The plots were located on a tobacco plantation near Bloomfield, Connecticut, fifty miles north of New Haven. So Hayes' first assignment was to report to the experimental farm and spend the summer working with East.

"I didn't know that such a thing as a chromosome existed when I went out to the Experimental Farm that summer to be with Dr. East," Hayes recalled later. "East was really a very sick man much of the time. The crowing of the roosters and the mooing of the cows would wake him up when it first began to get light, often as early as three or four o'clock in the morning. This worried him, but he would get up very early so we could get the plant breeding work in the field done before it became too hot.

"After the sun was bright and hot, East would tire easily. He would work up to the limit of his capacity, and then we'd have to seek out a shade tree and rest. His body was tired, but his mind would go on working. Dr. East seemed to like me from the first, and he would take up those paper sacks a plant breeder uses to cover corn tassels and silks in a hybrid corn breeding plot and draw out and diagram for me the genetic explanation of the things we were doing. By the end of the summer," concludes Hayes, "I had had as much work in genetics as I would have obtained at any college in a full year's course."

East and Hayes worked with several different plants, but it was corn that they discussed in greatest detail. East told his apprentice about his work at the University of Illinois, how he had come to Connecticut to work with Jenkins in order to be free to carry on studies in self- and cross-pollination, which he deemed absolutely necessary to determine the basic principles of practical corn breeding. East imparted to Hayes his own great conviction that corn could be tremendously improved, if only the necessary techniques could be discovered, and soon Hayes had developed an intense interest in corn breeding and a determination to help East continue this branch of his research.

As soon as the experimental plots of the 1909 season had been harvested and the data properly recorded, Hayes went to Harvard's Bussey Institution to become one of Edward Murray East's first graduate students. Together they fashioned a student-teacher relationship that molded an important precedent for scores of students who were to work with East. In a surprisingly short time the reference "a student of East's" became a title of distinction, almost a measure of achievement in itself, and a password that has opened many a door to outstanding accomplishment in the years since.

This deserves examination because the chance of America having the blessings of hybrid corn in our time hinged almost entirely upon this relationship between the young Harvard teacher and certain of his students. This influence was vital not only to working out a practical technique for hybrid corn, but it was just as important in spreading the concept of hybrid corn throughout the plant-breeding centers of the country.

Every great teacher from Socrates down to the present has had his own particular formula for stimulating his students to successful enterprise, and Dr. East was no exception. Ralph Singleton, now a plant breeder at the Connecticut Experiment Station where he has made some outstanding contributions, especially in the development of sweet corn hybrids, was one of Dr. East's students in the mid-twenties. His relations with Dr. East were typical, and of them he said recently:

"East was in Europe at the time I arrived in Boston and I did not meet him until about Christmas. Meanwhile I had heard considerable about him, and all of his students had a great admiration for him, although, I believe, most of them were just a little afraid of him too. He was somewhat austere, although down deep he was most friendly and interested not only in the work his students were doing but also in any personal problems they might have. In many ways Dr. East acted very much as a good father to all of his students.

"During my first year at Harvard, I did not have too much money, a condition common to many of East's students through the years. East was always sure to know about such things, and on one occasion he loaned me, at his own suggestion, twenty-five dollars to tide me over a particularly tough situation. At the close of my first year, I suddenly found it necessary to have an operation, and it was Dr. East who made arrangements for me to go to Massachusetts General Hospital. He visited me more than once and on one of these visits he mentioned that they wanted someone to go to Cuba for a year to make botanical collections. I was selected for this job—such was the charm of a good word from Dr. East in his field of science."

From work with Dr. East on quantitative inheritance in corn, Hayes became interested in the influence of inheritance on the protein content of corn. Material was secured from the University of Illinois, where selection for high and low protein content had been going on since the beginning of the Hopkins' corn-breeding project. This classic study, largely carried out by Hayes in Connecticut, was finally published several years later by Doctors East and Jones. Hayes continued his studies of protein inheritance at the University of Minnesota and used this research for one of several papers submitted in 1921 to the Bussey Institution of Harvard as a D.Sc. thesis.

The corn used by Hopkins in the high and low protein breeding program was Burr White. In 1910 Hayes began inbreeding the Burr White corn, and in the next five years he developed from it two or three inbreds. These inbreds were destined to become one-half of the Burr-Leaming double cross, first successful strain of hybrid corn. Obviously without Hayes' work with the Burr White lines, the Burr-Leaming double cross would have been an impossibility, and the coming of modern hybrid corn might have been delayed indefinitely.

Actually, the demarcation line between Hayes' graduate work and his plant breeding work at the Connecticut Experiment Station was a faint one. During the winter while he was attending school at Harvard, Dr. East would help him plan the plant breeding work for the following year at the Connecticut Station. East would usually accompany Hayes to New Haven once during the winter and spend a few days going over the material that had been harvested from the experimental plots the season before. He would usually visit the Connecticut Experiment Station a few days, once during the growing season to observe the material in the experimental plots. Although Hayes assumed full responsibility for the Connecticut program after a few seasons, East volunteered to continue as an adviser and acted in that capacity for several additional years.

Of East's leadership during his work at the Connecticut Station, Hayes recalls, "Dr. East was approaching the problem of corn breeding on a very broad basis. We studied crosses between varieties, crosses between inbreds and top crosses (crossing an open pollinated variety with an inbred line). He also used corn as one of the materials for intensive genetic research. East felt certain that by approaching the corn breeding problem from every possible angle, something of practical significance would be discovered."

Early in 1910 East suggested to Dr. Jenkins that there was now sufficient material available in the Connecticut Station's records to issue a publication of a kind never before presented, reporting on what had been learned in their corn inheritance studies. Jenkins immediately authorized the publication, and both East and Hayes began the work of preparation. Since the publication was to deal with work largely done by East before Hayes came, and since

Hayes was working under his direction, the publication might logically have been written by East himself. East, however, invited Hayes to be a co-author, no doubt realizing that later publications which might also be issued jointly would be based more upon experiments conducted by Hayes than by himself.

The publication appeared in 1911 as a bulletin of the Connecticut Experiment Station, entitled *Inheritance in Maize*. It was a 141-page book complete with numerous and dramatic pictures to demonstrate the important role controlled heredity can play in the character of the corn plant. The authors concluded as a result of studies of corn inheritance that "segregation was the important and essential feature of Mendelism." They stated also, "Therefore we believe size characters Mendelize."

This publication was written before East and Shull reached their understanding by which neither of them would press the matter of priority, and in this bulletin East wrote: "Strictly speaking the researches comprised more than five years' work, for several of the pure varieties used as parent stocks had been selfed for the two previous years, so that a number of crosses were made in 1905 with full assurance that as far as most of the visible characters were concerned, the parent strains were pure. There was some further advantage gained in the fact that the writers have been interested in experimental maize breeding since 1900, for without this experience the probable error of the results would be greatly increased."

In all his prolific writings on the subject of corn breeding, East never again mentioned his having done inbreeding of corn in 1903 and 1904, nor did he stress the fact that he had been working with corn breeding experiments since 1900. Since the East-Shull understanding of 1910 was not known, until some years after East's death, there resulted a great confusion in the minds of all who attempted to determine when East actually began his inbreeding work. Because East made this reference only once in this little book written in 1910 and issued in 1911, even the historians of the Connecticut Experiment Station eventually concluded that East was mistaken in this reference.

Inheritance in Maize was an intensive study of many years of the effect of inheritance upon characteristics of seed and plant. Certain phases of the aleurone (corn's protein) color inheritance were studied by Hayes as a special research problem at the Bussey Institution, leading to his receiving a Master's degree in 1911. East was a close adviser, and together they devised an explanation of complementary factors, an explanation for a dominant inhibitor, and one for aleurone color inheritance that is still today accepted as basic. Previously the variations from a 3:1 ratio had been explained as an exception to Mendelian law. Their quantitative inheritance studies of ear length and other characters have been generally considered as a classical early experiment which led to the wide acceptance of ex-·tensions of Mendelism as an explanation for inheritance of characteristics of size, still of fundamental importance in practical corn breeding.

The East-Hayes team continued its expanding plant breeding program in 1910 and 1911. New combinations of inbred crosses were grown during 1911, and Dr. East came down to Connecticut to see the hybrid corn at harvest time. The best hybrid combinations yielded at the rate of 150 bushels an acre. With larger plantings being used, nothing like it had ever been seen before. Against the background of the Sleeping Giant, there stood those Leaming hybrid plants, all the same height, every one with a big yellow ear, and all of them maturing uniformly together. The ears were not only large, but so uniform that they all looked alike.

"From the moment I stood there and saw those East

single cross hybrids in the fall of 1911, I never questioned but that some day we'd be raising hybrid corn," explained Dr. Hayes years later. Photographs taken of these inbreds and single cross hybrids grown in 1911, along with the accompanying data, appeared as an important part of a new publication, *Heterozygosis in Evolution and in Plant Breeding*, issued in 1912 by the Bureau of Plant Industry, United States Department of Agriculture. Hayes assisted Dr. East in this publication of fifty-odd pages which emphasized the importance of hybrid vigor in plant and animal improvement and in evolution.

In this publication East again pointed out that he still did not regard Shull's pure-line method of corn breeding as having any practical application, but that hybrids of standard corn strains, or the varietal cross, did have immediate practical significance. By this time East had discovered that the concept of the varietal cross was not original with him, and he pointed out that varietal crossing "has been suggested time and again without gaining a foothold in agricultural practice. Let us hope that the time is now ripe for a scientific method to be understood, appreciated and used."

The fine work that Hayes was doing at Connecticut had been attracting increasing attention from scientists in other institutions ever since he collaborated with Dr. East in the publications of 1911 and 1912. Late in the summer of 1914 he received an invitation to join the Minnesota Agricultural Experiment Station as a plant breeder.

Hayes reported the invitation to Dr. Jenkins, who proposed that they hold a conference with Dr. East to study the possibilities for securing another person to take over plant-breeding work in Connecticut. The matter was discussed with East early in September. East suggested that Hayes delay going to Minnesota until after the harvesting of the plots was completed and the materials arranged in good shape for a new man to take hold of the job. Dr. Jenkins called on Dr. East again to take over complete responsibility for directing plant-breeding work at the Connecticut Station until he could secure and train a successor to Hayes.

In January of 1915, H. K. Hayes went to Minnesota, where in years to come he would make significant contributions to developing hybrid corn in the greatest of all American corn growing areas—the corn belt. To him belongs the distinction of being the only person who took part in working out techniques of hybrid corn in New England and who then joined the ranks of practical corn breeders in the great corn belt. Hayes was one of the main outlets through whom the principles of hybrid corn established at the Connecticut Station were transmitted to the corn belt.

CHAPTER VII

Yankee from Kansas

ALMOST AS SOON as East learned of Hayes' intention to go to Minnesota, there came to mind the name of a likely candidate for the position of plant breeder at the Connecticut Station. The young man was Donald F. Jones, who had already begun graduate work with East the summer before and who was teaching horticulture and genetics in the College of Agriculture at Syracuse University, New York.

A Yankee from Kansas, young Jones was born of a family deeply rooted in America. His parents were both school teachers, and they lived on a small suburban farm where their sons got first-hand experience in such things as growing corn and raising chickens. A great-grandfather ten generations removed, Kenelm Winslow, came to Plymouth, Mass., in 1629. This branch of the family moved to Maine, where, some generations later, one of the girls married into the Jones family. Ancestors of Donald Jones' mother also came to New England not long after the Pilgrims settled on Cape Cod, arriving at Boston and travelling overland, mostly afoot, over the hundred miles of wilderness with the group of early settlers who founded Hartford, Connecticut.

Jones' grandfather heard the call, "Gold in California," and responded, sailing from the port of Belfast, Maine, to Panama, crossing the famous isthmus on a mule and then sailing on to California. He was disappointed at arriving so late and returned to New England by stagecoach. When the coach passed through the Kansas territory, he was so impressed with the country that he decided to return with his family and settle there. This he did eventually, bringing his wife and children with a group of friends to establish the village of Peace, now Sterling, Kansas.

Donald Jones went to Kansas State College in Manhattan and studied agriculture with such men of vision and enthusiasm as H. F. Roberts and J. C. Cunningham, who later became Iowa's foremost authority on corn lore and literature. Probably Roberts first introduced Jones to the idea of improving corn by developing inbred lines and crossing them into hybrids. Roberts and other professors from Kansas State College had gone to Columbia, Missouri, and heard Shull deliver the second of his three papers before the American Breeders' Association. They gave a report of Shull's talk to their classes, and while most of the students were inclined to dismiss the matter as fantastic, young Jones felt they were being too hasty in their judgment. He might never have thought of the matter again, however, had he not a few years later come across the East and Hayes publication, *Heterozygosis in Evolution and in Plant Breeding.* In the meantime Jones, graduated from Kansas State, had gone to Arizona in 1911, the year before the Arizona territory became a state, to work on an alfalfa improvement program.

The East and Hayes publication came to Jones' attention at an opportune moment, since he had just decided that he needed to do some graduate work and was trying to decide which school to attend. *Heterozygosis in Evolution and in Plant Breeding* convinced him that he should go to Harvard and study with Edward Murray East—another of those crucial decisions which helped give us hybrid corn in our time.

Jones wrote to Dr. East, asking about the possibility of doing graduate work with him and pointing out his need to work to defray the expenses of additional education. East's reply expressed interest in Jones, but in the meantime, the offer had come to Jones to teach in Syracuse University. Jones spent the year of 1913–1914 teaching in New York State and went to Harvard the summer of 1914. When Hayes resigned in the fall of 1914 to go to Minnesota, the young man from Kansas was the first to receive consideration.

Director Jenkins suggested that Jones come to the Connecticut Station, do plant breeding under Dr. East's direction, and continue his graduate work with East at Harvard during the winter. The arrangement was an ideal one for Jones, who wanted more than anything else to have a chance to study and work with Dr. East, and he took up his new duties in February, 1915.

Especially was Jones looking forward with interest to the work on corn inbreeding and hybrid crosses made from inbred lines. He was expecting to see the work on corn hybrids going at full speed and was disappointed and a little shocked when he took up his duties at New Haven to discover that this work was still in the seed packet stage and that nothing of commercial importance had been done on it since East and Hayes had dramatically described the results of their experiments in *Heterozygosis in Evolution and in Plant Breeding* more than three years before.

Hayes had, however, continued to inbreed the East Leaming material, had initiated the inbreeding of the Burr White and some other lines, and had left everything in perfect order so that the work could take whatever direction East and Jones wished in the spring of 1915. East and Jones spent a week going over every phase of the work to be done at the Connecticut Station during the coming year. Jones questioned him especially about the work with corn, and East told him as he had others so consistently through the years that while hybrid crosses between inbreds of corn were interesting and he had placed a great deal of new light upon the breeding of plants in general, especially the cross-

pollinated plants, they were not of nearly such immediate
value as varietal cross hybrids between good closely selected
open-pollinated strains.

East wisely decided that the best course for 1915 would be
to continue the work as Hayes had projected it and give
Jones time to become more familiar with the material, the
concepts, and procedures at the Connecticut Experiment
Station. In Jones' office and laboratory were actual ears of
the beautiful single cross hybrids that East and Hayes had
produced by crossing their inbred lines, and perhaps these
impressive ears kept Donald Jones, during his entire first
season at Connecticut, thinking about the possibilities of
making wide-spread use of the new hybrid corn.

Late the next winter, Jones and East planned the 1916
season. Jones said he was not completely satisfied with East's
conclusion that there was nothing of practical importance
in the corn hybrids from inbred lines. East reaffirmed his conclusion that the known procedures and techniques for hybridizing corn offered little if any possibilities for improving corn
on large acreages, but he did demonstrate his greatness as a
teacher by encouraging Jones to investigate the matter
thoroughly himself. As a result East and Jones planned for
1916 a special crossing plot in which all of the Connecticut
Station's promising inbreds would be combined into single
cross hybrids that would be grown and tested in 1917.

This decision to investigate again the nature of hybrids
between inbred lines proved to be the fork in the road that
led to modern hybrid corn. The factors which made it possible now stand out in bold relief. The Connecticut Station
had the greatest stock of corn inbreds in existence at that
time, inbreds that had been provided by the efforts of Hopkins, Craig, East, and Hayes. East, using the things which
had been learned about corn breeding by himself, by Shull,
and by Hayes, placed before the young plant breeder the
greatest pool of information on this subject available any-

where in the world. Then East brought in the new force—Jones' capacities—by urging the young man from Kansas to investigate the problem fully for himself, and they set up a special corn breeding plot for this purpose. These factors provided the means for discovery of the missing parts of the hybrid corn puzzle—parts that neither East nor Shull had been able to find.

That spring in 1916 Jones staked out and planted the special inbred crossing plot. Growing conditions were favorable during most of the season, and early in the fall Jones harvested the plot. He was impressed with how little seed could be harvested from inbred seed parents. There was no question, Jones concluded; Dr. East was right, there was no use trying to raise corn on a field scale with seed from inbreds. But still there were these amazing single cross hybrid ears in his laboratory. If one could only use them for seed, he thought, there would be no limit to the possibilities for the new hybrid corn.

Plant seed from the single crosses? Now if we could put together two of these single crosses, mused Jones, then we would have plenty of seed, more good seed than farmers ever got from ears of corn before. But what would be the result of mating two single crosses? Would the cross, bringing together four inbred lines, combine the total of the outstanding characteristics of all the four inbreds? Would the hybrid vigor be maintained? Would progeny of such a cross have the remarkable uniformity of the single cross hybrids? Or would the result be a degeneration and a throwback to the original inbreds, giving a miserable looking and worthless result? Well, thought Jones, why not try it?

Jones mentioned the possibility to East, whose response neither encouraged nor discouraged. At least the reaction left no very definite impression upon Jones, which is not at all surprising, because other things during the months from harvest time in 1916 until planting time in 1917 were of all-consuming interest. The climax was reached on April 2, 1917, when President Wilson stood before a tense Congress and nation and in solemnly spoken, carefully measured words urged Americans to "fight for the ultimate peace of the world . . . for the liberation of its people," and ended with his historic demand that "the world be made safe for democracy." Four days later the United States was at war, bringing the Connecticut Experiment Station to grips with a new problem.

Should the Station continue its long range plant-breeding research in time of war or switch its limited energies to some war project as a gesture of patriotism? Would its men like Donald Jones continue to work with corn breeding or expend their energies on something strictly of a military nature, be it nothing more than performing kitchen duty for a tough sergeant on the Marne?

Director Jenkins considered the question in all its ramifications and handed down the decision. The plant-breeding research would go on because most of his experiment station's energies were directed toward greater production of food, the essential material of war. Little did he know that his decision would, a quarter of a century later, take on international importance in a vastly greater war when the existence of America and of our way of life would be hanging precariously in the balance.

So Donald Jones went on breeding corn in the Land of the Sleeping Giant that spring of 1917. In another special plot he planted the single cross hybrids he had made the year before. Two of them were outstanding. One was a cross of two old Leaming inbreds which had been sent to East by Love from Illinois. The other was made up of the two Burr White inbreds developed by Hayes. Still determined to find out what would be the result of crossing a hybrid with a hybrid, Jones decided to use these two—virtually the only two he had at his disposal—in the novel experiment. So early in August the Yankee from Kansas made the first cross between the hybrids developed from inbreds by pulling out the tassels from the Burr White single cross and allowing these plants to be pollinated by the Leaming single cross in this isolated crossing field.

The next spring, in 1918, Jones planted the seed of this double-cross hybrid, and he was soon pleased to see it send up shoots strong, vigorous, and uniform. As the season progressed, there were more favorable signs as the plants attained about the same height and tasselled at about the same day. Jones thought his new double-cross hybrid appeared to be almost as uniform as the single-cross hybrids from which it had been developed.

Then came the final verdict! At harvest time, with the Sleeping Giant as the witness, Jones' double-cross hybrid yielded, not just as well, but better than the best yield of the single crosses that entered into it. The double-cross hybrid yielded at the rate of 116 bushels an acre, a good 20 per cent more than the best Leaming open-pollinated corn adapted to Connecticut. The uniformity of ear height was almost as good as either of the single-cross hybrids. The ability of the stalks to stand was, if anything, a little better.

As is so frequently the case in major scientific achievement, the element of chance played an important role in Jones' immediate success with the double cross. Jones and all the other great corn breeders later learned that only a rare and occasional combination of single crosses will effectively blend into a double-cross hybrid. It easily might not have happened again with single crosses, untested for combining ability, in a hundred, even a thousand trials. Jones might have had to work for most of a lifetime to find a combination that blended as perfectly as did his first cross of the Burr and Leaming single crosses. The flipped coin had come down and stood on its thin edge.

An even more remarkable aspect of the discovery of the

double cross hybrid, however, was that it was accomplished by Donald F. Jones, just twenty-seven years old, who had never before initiated a single corn-breeding operation. The double cross was his very first act of corn breeding; the other work he had done since he had taken the Connecticut position followed the directions and suggestions of East or lines laid out by Hayes.

Anxious for assurance that the first success at making a double-cross hybrid was no accident, Jones went to work in 1918 and made the Burr-Leaming hybrid again for testing in the 1919 season. He continued this test for five successive seasons, in which he pitted his Burr-Leaming double cross hybrid against the best open-pollinated strains of corn to be found anywhere in Connecticut. At the end of this exacting test, the Burr-Leaming hybrid had an average of 83 bushels as compared with 69 bushels an acre for the best of the open-pollinated strains. This meant that the Burr-Leaming hybrid had outyielded the field by 20 per cent, the equivalent of one extra corn crop in the five-year period. It is significant that the national per-acre increase in corn yields from modern hybrid corn has averaged just a little more than 20 per cent, revealing how accurately Jones' first double-cross hybrid indicated what could be expected from the new kind of corn.

Like the "shot that was heard around the world," Jones' discovery of the double cross soon brought about reverberations in the minds of practically everyone interested in corn breeding. Men like H. K. Hayes in Minnesota, Henry A. Wallace of Iowa, and James R. Holbert of Illinois sensed immediately that here was a new discovery that bridged over the difficulties which rendered Shull's "pure-line method" utterly impracticable for wide scale corn acreages.

Donald Jones, however, quickly attached even greater importance to his discovery. He sensed from the first that his discovery of the double-cross hybrid had solved much more than the problem of having to get seed from the small, misshapen, inbred ears. He could clearly see the outstanding qualities of all four of the inbreds that entered into his Burr-Leaming double-cross hybrid. Clearly, the double cross technique would enable the corn breeder in the future to focus in one strain of corn the fine qualities of four inbreds rather than two as in the case of the single cross. This widened the horizon for hybrid corn tremendously.

More than that, Jones was beginning to see an underlying scientific explanation that would remove his discovery once and for all from the realm of chance and put the double-cross hybrid on the firm foundation of solid fact. He was now approaching the end of his graduate course with Dr. East at Harvard, and by applying his newly acquired knowledge of genetics to the breeding of a double-cross hybrid, Jones concluded that all pairing of heredity factors in such a double-cross hybrid is in reality a first-generation hybrid, since there is no opportunity for recombinations to unite similar factors and hence allow weaknesses to appear.

But Donald Jones' mind was racing swiftly on down paths that not even East or Shull had been able to explore. Taking form in his mind was an explanation for heterosis and hybrid vigor as a pooling of favorable heredity from both parents. Neither Shull nor East had been able to explain and interpret the effects of inbreeding entirely in terms of Mendelian heredity. They had remained perplexed by the phenomenon of hybrid vigor or heterosis. They assumed that there was some kind of physiological stimulation resulting from the bringing together of different germ plasms in hybrid combination. This vague hypothesis did not explain all of the facts. It did not stimulate further research.

The student Jones and the teacher East held many a long conference on these new theories. Especially difficult was it for East to agree with young Jones' new explanation of hybrid vigor as due solely to dominance of Mendelian units of heredity. The climax came in a conference held in the Bussey

Building after all the evidence from corn and other plants and the new experimental insect, the tiny fruit fly, had been reviewed carefully. East was convinced; he saw the light which had been beckoning Jones from the realms just beyond the frontier of the known.

As a result, in 1918 Jones wrote his doctoral thesis for East on the subject, "The Effects of Inbreeding and Cross-breeding Upon Development," giving the first published report of his new theory to account for hybrid vigor. A year later he accepted an invitation to write his theory into the book *Inbreeding and Outbreeding*. This book had been outlined by East first in 1912, but East saw that Jones' discoveries were of such great importance that he invited Jones to become a joint author. It was published in 1919. The East and Jones book was favorably received by scientists in all parts of the world and resulted in a complete revision of viewpoints regarding the effects of inbreeding and crossing.

Briefly put, Jones' theory held that there is a tendency for the most favorable traits of an organism to be dominant and the deleterious characteristics to be recessive. Hence, in the first generation after crossing of the simpler pure lines or inbreds, there is a tendency for the good traits to dominate the bad. This idea was not completely new, for it had been expressed by two English geneticists, Keeble and Pellew, in 1910, who explained what happened when two varieties of garden peas, each five to six feet in height, when crossed produced in the first generation plants seven to eight feet tall. Their explanation, however, was too simple to account for most instances of hybrid vigor until Jones elaborated upon it in terms of the newly discovered bearers of heredity, the chromosomes. Jones' handling of the explanation was so clear-cut, so readily understandable in terms of the rapidly increasing body of facts about heredity, that it gained rapid and world-wide acceptance.

While Donald Jones' discovery of the double cross hybrid

as a means of solving the practical problem of producing enough seed for the new corn has been generally recognized, his explanation of hybrid vigor may in the light of history appear as a contribution of even greater importance. This phase of his work also sped the coming of hybrid corn. The new understanding of hybrid vigor, the possibilities for creating and controlling it, was to be responsible perhaps as much as the invention of the double cross for immediate interest and enthusiasm in corn breeders throughout the country.

So impressed was Dr. East with the immediate possibilities for practical use of the new hybrid corn that in 1919 he approached the large Sibley Estate, which controlled 15,000 acres of rich prairie land in Ford County, Illinois, with an offer to develop hybrid corn for use on the Sibley acres. He wrote to the manager of the estate, sent him a copy of the new book by himself and Jones, *Inbreeding and Outbreeding,* and expressed the opinion that within a few years corn yields on the Sibley acres could be substantially increased. Although East asked for only a modest remuneration for his efforts, his offer was turned down, a decision which the Sibley Estate management came to regret before many years. North of Gibson City, Illinois, on Route 47 and the Wabash Railroad, there is a substantial looking gray building on the front of which is the sign, "Seed House of the Hiram Sibley Estate." One cannot view this structure without wondering what sort of place it would have been today had the Sibley interests accepted East's offer, opening the way for it to become one of the earliest hybrid-corn centers in the corn belt.

With the development of the **Burr-Leaming** hybrid, the Connecticut Experiment Station faced a situation never before encountered by an institution of its kind. The station had the inbred lines from which could be developed the finest corn ever grown in Connecticut. Would the Experiment Station go into the seed business so that the farmers of the state could have the advantage of the new kind of corn? Would it supply the single-cross hybrids from which the double-cross could be made available to farmers or seedsmen and urge them to produce their own hybrid seed corn? Or would the station turn over the inbreds themselves to anyone interested?

Circumstances, as much as anything, decided the issue in favor of the experiment station supplying the single-cross hybrids to outside persons and organizations. The first seed for the Burr-Leaming hybrid was produced in 1920 and planted by New England farmers the next spring.

While attending a field day at the Experiment Station Farm, Dr. Jones was approached by George Carter, who had a farm on the sea twenty miles east of New Haven. Carter had followed the research work done at the Connecticut Station closely enough to realize that there might be opportunity here. Before the men had parted, it was decided that Carter would become the first person in America to produce seed of this new double cross for farmers.

The Carter farm had been awarded to the Carter family as a grant from the King of England while Connecticut was still a colony. The grant had been made to permit the cutting of the virgin timber, the "King's oaks," to supply lumber for building ships of His Britannic Majesty's fleet.

After the timber had been cut, the farm was kept in the Carter family, although its location on New England's stormy coast made profitable farming difficult. Carter found it impossible to use horses to plow the rocky fields and cultivate crops, as horses were likely to lunge and snap the harness every time a plow or cultivator struck a rock too deeply imbedded to be moved by the implement. Instead, oxen were used then as they are to this day because the ox is more inclined to stop whenever the plowshare hits some immovable object. As a result, the first seed of this corn of the future was produced with power supplied by oxen. Mr. Carter continued to produce seed of the Burr-Leaming hybrid for several years for farmers in every New England state and as far west as Ohio.

In the popular mind, virtually all credit for hybrid corn has gone to those such as Pfister and Wallace who helped translate the New England scientific discovery into reality, while the decades of brilliant painstaking work of the Easts, Jones, Hayes, and Shulls have too frequently been passed over with such a reference as this: "Hybrid corn rests upon some early interesting research done by Dr. G. H. Shull of Princeton and Dr. E. M. East of Bussey Institution, neither of these men being interested in the improvement of corn as such, but rather in using the corn plant to prove certain theories in their study of genetics."

Lumping together the contributions made by East, Jones, Hayes, Shull, and all the others in the early period, how important was their work? How important is the architect who draws the plan for a new kind of building never seen before? How important is he in relation to the men who build it? Answer that and you know the magnitude of the contribution made by hybrid-corn makers whose efforts were brought to focus in New England.

CHAPTER VIII

An Idea Moves West

THE STORY of hybrid corn is now sufficiently unfolded
to put the earlier years in clear perspective and to
lay bare the links between the research work in New England
and the glory to be achieved later in the corn belt. The daring
corn breeding project directed by C. G. Hopkins at the University of Illinois now stands out in cold relief as the half-
way point between the selectionist methods used by the
Indians and the new science of hybrid-corn breeding, introducing as it did the idea of pedigree breeding of corn and
molding Edward Murray East into the corn breeder whose
mind and personality formed the only continuous influence
during the first two formative decades.

Although Connecticut farmers began using hybrid corn
shortly after the first World War, nearly twenty years were
to pass before the new hybrid came into large-scale use in the
corn belt. Why, one may logically ask, was it so long before
the new hybrid corn gained foothold in the real corn country?

But when we consider all of the issues, the surprising thing
is that the delay was no longer than twenty years.

First among the early retarding forces was the limited
interest in the possibilities of hybrid corn. Dr. Shull professed never to have thought that his inbreeding and hybridizing of corn had any practical importance, and he ceased
growing corn entirely in 1916. The work in Nebraska had
lapsed into a study of principles rather than being pointed
in the direction of any practical application in the foreseeable

future. Guy Collins and C. P. Hartley, of the United States
Department of Agriculture, and A. D. Shamel, of the Illinois Agricultural Station, had experimented with inbreeding
and had convinced themselves that nothing of importance
could come from this type of work.

As a result, during this period from 1915 to 1920, the
possibility of there being hybrid corn in our time rested almost entirely with East and the two men whom he had
schooled at the Connecticut Station and at the Bussey Institution. Jones, Hayes, and East, and they alone, were willing
to risk their reputations as scientists to declare that the new
hybrid corn was potentially so much better that it could one
day displace the open-pollinated varieties then in use. Slender
indeed were the human resources of hybrid corn during its
early years.

Not only were the persons able and willing to advance the
cause of hybrid corn few; to appreciate fully the situation in
the late 'teens and early twenties, we must recognize that
most of the agronomists and agricultural specialists were
arrayed against the new method of corn development.

The degree to which those unable to see the possibilities of
hybrid corn were entrenched in the experiment stations of
the corn belt can be seen in incidents that occurred in almost
every state. In Minnesota, Hayes was prevented from moving the new hybrid corn techniques directly into the Mississippi Valley from New England for nearly five years after
he arrived at St. Paul by his leaders, who were unable to
appreciate its possibilities. At the Indiana Experiment Station, the agronomy department, which logically should have
explored the possibilities of the new hybrid corn, refused to
have anything to do with it, and as a result the work with
hybrid corn in the Hoosier state has been done and is to
this day handled by the Department of Botany. Even the
College of Agriculture in Illinois, where Hopkins first blazed

the corn-breeding trail, was among the last to appreciate what the new hybrid corn meant.

The task of getting the concept of hybrid corn moved out of New England and into the other great corn-growing areas of the country was not merely a job of explaining its great possibilities to eager and open minds. Rather it was a matter of beating down the prejudice of a majority of those directly responsible for corn improvement. Against this wall Shull had battered in vain. It was now becoming evident that the least difficult way to win acceptance for hybrid corn outside of New England would be to recruit an almost entirely new group of capable men, courageous enough to throw in their lot with the new science of corn breeding against opposition that would be encountered almost everywhere.

Another thing that complicated acceptance of the new hybrid corn in the corn belt was the failure of Jones' Burr-Leaming hybrid to give a satisfactory performance outside of New England and New York State. This was naturally something that not even Jones or East realized, or could forecast.

Had Donald Jones developed a new kind of automobile or a razor blade in New Haven, Connecticut, he could have taken his wares to Iowa or California and demonstrated their good qualities effectively. Unfortunately, he did not have that chance with his new double-cross hybrid, since the Burr-Leaming hybrid was adapted to the soil and gentle climate of southern New England, and it failed to make an impressive demonstration at any of the numerous places it was grown in the corn belt.

This meant that Jones, Hayes, and East had the infinitely more difficult job of getting plant breeders to accept the abstract principles of the double-cross hybrid so that they would buckle down to the task of developing adapted hybrids for other corn-growing areas.

The nature of the task ahead was soon clearly defined in the minds of Jones, Hayes, and East. Corn breeders must be recruited in every corn-growing area to inbreed the native corn of that region and produce inbred lines from which properly adapted hybrids could be secured.

Of the Jones-Hayes-East triumvirate, it was Dr. Donald Jones who carried by far the greatest part of the load in recruiting the hybrid-corn makers of the corn belt. Before he finished, his contribution in this phase of the work rivalled his discovery of the double cross and the Mendelian explanation of hybrid vigor.

In addition to his Connecticut Station bulletins and the book he wrote with Dr. East, Jones did a number of articles in magazines. Typical of these was an article done for the May, 1919, issue of the old *Breeders' Gazette*, then the *Saturday Evening Post* of the farm magazines. It gave the first account written in laymen's language of the possibilities of the double-cross hybrid and a review of the corn-breeding work done at the Connecticut Experiment Station since Dr. East came to New Haven in 1905. This article and others like it were accompanied by impressive pictures of the Burr-Leaming double cross and the single crosses and inbreds that entered into it. The explanation under the Burr-Leaming picture in the *Breeders' Gazette* read, "Double crossed corn that in 1918 yielded 112 bushels shelled corn per acre (12 per cent moisture) this being 22 per cent more than the product of the highest-yielding variety so far found in Connecticut and grown in the same field in comparison with it." This made intensely interesting reading in every corn belt state where forty to sixty bushel corn yields were the general rule.

Nor did Jones neglect the scientists and plant-breeding group in his writings during this period. In the November 3, 1920, issue of the *Journal of American Society of Agronomy*, there appeared an article in which Jones gave his full theory

explaining hybrid vigor within the scope of Mendelian principle. He has always regarded this as the most important
writing he ever did to advance the cause of hybrid corn.
Like his bulletins, book, and magazine articles, Jones' papers
in scientific publications helped soften the natural and general resistance to the new hybrid corn concepts. Without
them hybrid corn would have been much longer coming.

The work of Jones abetted by the efforts of Hayes and
East soon produced results. A rapidly lengthening list of men
throughout the corn belt were becoming interested in the possibilities of hybrid corn. Except the work being done in
Nebraska, the forces of activation, information, and inspiration stemmed from the Connecticut Experiment Station, and
Jones was the principal personality in the new movement.

In 1921 the United States Department of Agriculture recognized this when its Office of Cereal Investigations, under
direction of C. R. Ball, invited Dr. Jones to make an extensive tour through the corn belt and other corn-growing
areas to appraise corn-inbreeding work and to encourage the
workers engaged in developing inbred lines. Jones' trip was
the first public evidence of interest in the hybrid-corn
movement by the United States Department of Agriculture.
It was the result of a shift in leadership in the important
Bureau of Plant Industry, a development of great importance
to the cause of hybrid corn.

Jones' trip, the first co-ordinating influence among the
individual corn breeders of the corn belt, marked a turning
point in the effort to make effective use of the hybrid corn
technique in corn-growing areas outside of New England.

Jones made personal visits to a dozen places throughout
the corn belt where he had learned of corn-inbreeding work
being done during the 1920 season or before. He visited
state and federal experiment station workers in Illinois,
Indiana, Ohio, Missouri, Kansas, Nebraska, Minnesota, and
Wisconsin. In addition he visited two individuals who were

conducting private inbreeding programs, Henry A. Wallace of Des Moines, Iowa, and Edgar G. Lewis, of Media, Illinois.

Dr. Jones' tour did much to accelerate corn inbreeding throughout the United States. Many of the places he visited had received the Burr-Leaming hybrid from the Connecticut Station and had been confounded and discouraged at its poor showing. Jones was able to explain the importance of adaptation and inspire a new interest in going ahead with the development of inbreds from proved strains of locally adapted open-pollinated corn.

The tour, sponsored as it was by the United States Department of Agriculture, foreshadowed an increasingly greater interest by the federal government in hybrid-corn possibilities. The days of hybrid corn's complete dependence upon East, Hayes, and Jones were nearing an end.

As we have noted earlier, C. P. Hartley, of the U. S. Department of Agriculture, did a limited amount of inbreeding work with corn shortly after 1900 and came to the conclusion that it offered no possibilities for corn improvement at that time. He remained unmoved by the developments at the Connecticut Experiment Station. F. D. Richey, who had joined Hartley's staff in 1911, had, however, followed the work of East, Shull, and others and began inbreeding corn in 1916. Although he received no encouragement from Hartley, Richey continued to carry on his limited hybrid-corn breeding project.

Warren G. Harding was elected president in November of 1920. Soon after his victory at the polls, he offered the post of Secretary of Agriculture to Henry C. Wallace, editor and publisher of the respected Iowa farm magazine, *Wallaces' Farmer*. Wallace accepted the post, fired by a determination to give the Department of Agriculture a thorough housecleaning. He was especially interested in having the department's corn improvement program become more aggressive. Henry C. Wallace had been much impressed with the new

hybrid-corn breeding work his son, Henry A. Wallace, had
been doing, and the newly nominated Secretary of Agriculture was especially anxious to find out why the Department
of Agriculture had been doing so little, if anything, to exploit the possibilities of this new approach to corn improvement.

At this same time Henry A. Wallace was planning a
business trip to Washington, and his father suggested that
he make it a point to stop in at the Department of Agriculture long enough to form an opinion of the men in charge
of the corn improvement work. Since Henry A. Wallace's
mission kept him in Washington for several days and since
there had at that time been no formal announcement that his
father, Henry C. Wallace, was to be the next Secretary of
Agriculture, the young editor of *Wallaces' Farmer* had an
excellent opportunity to appraise the work of the various men
on Hartley's staff.

Henry A. Wallace was not at all impressed with Hartley's
outlook, but he was surprised to learn that Richey had been
conducting, virtually on his own responsibility, a limited
corn-inbreeding project since 1916. When he returned to
Des Moines, Henry A. Wallace advised his father of his
impressions. As a result, on February 16, 1922, Richey replaced Hartley as Principal Agronomist in Charge of Corn
Investigations for the Office of Cereal Investigations.

Richey quickly shifted major resources to developing hybrids from inbred lines, rather than emphasizing the improvement of open-pollinated varieties as Hartley had done.
Richey's vision of the possibilities of the new hybrid corn was
an important force in its further development.

Jones' tour of places where breeding was being done
marked the end of one era and the beginning of another
in the development of hybrid corn. Until this trip, the Connecticut Experiment Station was the unchallenged center of
hybrid-corn research. Soon after the tour the Bureau of

Plant Industry of the United States Department of Agriculture moved into a position of leadership.

Although Jones' contacts with corn breeders in the corn belt soon withered away, he continued to be regarded among plant breeders generally in America and throughout the world as a leading authority in inbreeding and hybridization of corn. During the twenties, distinguished plant scientists from foreign countries were constant visitors to the Land of the Sleeping Giant to get from Donald Jones a first-hand report of his experiences and concepts. To this day, Jones remains a respected elder statesman in the world of plant breeding, one of his most recent tributes having come from Kansas State College. Jones was presented for the honorary degree Doctor of Science at the June, 1947, commencement by F. D. Farrell, President Emeritus of the institutions, who in his citation said, "Mr. Jones' contributions to the knowledge of heredity, particularly of crop plants, have brought him deserved international fame. As a major contributor to the development of hybrid corn and as the inventor of the specific techniques of hybrid-corn seed production, he has conferred immense benefits upon a hungry world." The degree was conferred by President Milton Eisenhower.

The decade of the twenties was devoted almost entirely to the job of subjecting open-pollinated corn to inbreeding and seeking the outstanding inbreds from which future hybrids could be developed. This proved to be a tremendous job. The chances of finding an outstanding inbred capable of sustaining itself and combining well with other inbreds is extremely rare. Plant breeders have found generally that less than one per cent of open-pollinated material ever yields inbreds of promise. Unfortunately, it was generally believed during this period that it was necessary to self a line from three to five years before it could be tested accurately for superior characteristics and combining ability. In this way corn breeders had to work several years with an inbred line,

Carol Mack, great-great-great-great-granddaughter of the
famous Chief Black Hawk, with ears of Sac and Fox corn
in her left hand and hybrid in her right. The Sac and Fox
planted their last crop on their western Illinois corn lands
in 1831, the year before the Black Hawk War and just a
century before the first hybrid corn was grown in the same
area

An exhibit at the second hybrid corn show on record, held
at Purdue University in 1928, showing the various steps in
developing the new hybrid corn. Inbreds in the bottom compartment are combined to produce the foundation single
crosses in the compartment immediately above. Single cross
foundation hybrids are combined into double cross hybrid
seed, which is planted by the farmer to produce the hybrid
corn shown in the top compartment

usually to find out later that it had no promise. Today many hybrid corn breeders begin testing new inbred lines in prospective hybrid combinations almost from the time inbreeding begins, and if the results of these tests are not favorable, they discard the material and save the years of work that might otherwise have been applied.

The experience of the corn breeders through the years has revealed what a remarkable job of development the selectionists of open-pollinated corn had done. The great majority of our good inbreds, the ones upon which hybrid corn rests today, were derived from the well known varieties of open-pollinated corn. It has been from such open-pollinated varieties as Reid, Funk, Leaming, Kansas Sunflower, Lancaster Sure Crop, and other famous strains that most of the good inbreds today have come. The experience of hybrid corn breeders, searching for good inbred lines, revealed dramatically how greatly present-day American agriculture is indebted to the sturdy early settlers, corn-minded farmers and seedsmen who, by patient and painstaking selection for a century or more, had produced these outstanding open-pollinated varieties.

The superiority of these open-pollinated strains developed in the American corn belt explains more than anything else why no outstanding inbred lines have come from corn imported from lands outside the United States. Repeatedly corn breeders have attempted to get good inbreds from corn grown in Mexico, South America, Europe, or Asia, but up to this time not one important inbred has been developed from corn grown outside the United States. On the other hand, some open-pollinated strains from our corn belt such as Funk's 176A have provided a constant stream of widely-used inbreds.

In this search for good inbreds in the corn belt, the influence and backing of the United States Department of Agriculture soon became a vital factor in the work. The federal department's resources were applied to the job of developing hybrid corn through two of its offices. As early as 1918 and 1919 the agronomists working in Dr. H. B. Humphrey's program to curb corn diseases were launching corn inbreeding projects. F. D. Richey began in the early twenties to organize co-operative relationships with Experiment Stations in most of the corn belt states under which the developing of good inbreds was promoted vigorously. In 1925 the Purnell act provided special funds with which the work of discovering and making generally available good inbreds was greatly accelerated.

Although hybrid corn breeding was being done at a score of places throughout the corn belt during the last half of the decade of the twenties, the major part of the job of developing hybrids for this area was done at seven hybrid corn breeding centers. While collectively the other experiment stations made contributions of great value, it was the hybrid corn research done at seven centers in Illinois, Indiana, Iowa, and Wisconsin that permitted us to have hybrid corn so quickly.

The number of men making sweeping contributions were also very few. There are even today not more than fifty men who have the ability necessary to start from scratch with open pollinated varieties and develop the inbreds and combine them into an effective strain of hybrid corn. When one considers how much hybrid corn is now grown by American farmers, it is immediately apparent that Churchill's classic remark, "So many indebted to so few," might have been coined to describe the work of hybrid-corn breeders.

The story of hybrid corn breeding done in seven centers in the heart of the corn belt, three of them privately sponsored and four of them at government-supported experiment stations, will impart a more perfect understanding of the work to develop the first hybrids to have large-scale use.

CHAPTER IX

New Horizons

D URING THE LAST week of August in 1915, there began
a conversation which, in the light of things to
come, was one of the greatest milestones in the story of
hybrid corn. The place was an office at the Minnesota Agricultural Experiment Station just outside St. Paul. Those
present were H. K. Hayes, who had recently come to Minnesota from Connecticut, and a young man named Holbert
from Indiana.

Twenty-five years old and only a few weeks graduated from
Purdue, Jim Holbert told Hayes that he was turning down a
number of other interesting offers of positions for a chance
to go to Funk Farms in Illinois and undertake the job of developing better corn. Recognizing as both men did that Funk
Farms and its seedsmen were regarded by farmers in several
states as the leading center of corn development in the entire
corn belt, they agreed that it was a difficult assignment.

"How would you suggest that I go about this job of improving corn?" asked young Holbert.

Then Hayes did something that probably no other person
would have attempted to do this last week of August in 1915.
"If I were you," he told his visitor, "I would inbreed the best
corn I could find, develop inbred lines and cross them into
hybrids."

But Hayes did much more than give Holbert advice; he
convinced him. In a single hour, the man who learned about
breeding hybrid corn in the Land of the Sleeping Giant cre-

ated in Jim Holbert's mind a determination to try this radically new approach to inbreeding and crossing, nothing short of amazing considering that the opinion that inbreeding destroys corn had been spread like fog over the corn country by Hopkins and agronomists of other agricultural colleges. As a result, Hayes' advice, given as it was before Jones discovered the double-cross hybrid, was in the popular mind something about midway between witchcraft and sheer folly.

Years later Hayes was asked how he could have had the confidence in corn hybridization, the double cross undiscovered as it was, to stamp its future value so deeply and so quickly into young Holbert's mind. He replied, "From the time I stood there in Connecticut in 1910 and 1911, and saw those East single crosses—the most beautiful corn I have ever seen, every ear so large and looking like the one right next to it—I was sure that somehow, some way and some day a practical use for it would be found. I never doubted from that time on that hybrid corn would come."

Naturally, there was a great deal in James Ransom Holbert's past to prepare him to appreciate and respond to what he heard that August morning, but he always freely acknowledged his debt to H. K. Hayes for the persuasiveness and enthusiasm with which he set forth the possibilities of hybrid corn on that day in 1915.

A month later Holbert had already mapped out and begun work on a corn-breeding project that was without precedent. Even today it remains one of the largest projects of its kind ever undertaken.

This was not Holbert's first acquaintance with Funk Farms and the people who made it an interesting and important place, and a glance at a number of things which had gone before will put the work that he was to do there into better perspective. Reared on an eastern Indiana farm, Jim Holbert's first inclination was to become a teacher, but one year as a rural school instructor convinced him that the

country school was not his field. He had, however, saved
enough money to enter Indiana University the next fall, and
during his year there he decided he was not interested in a
teaching career even at the professor's level.

Work in agriculture, he thought, would interest him more,
so the next year, 1911, he transferred to Purdue, at that
time as it is today one of the leading centers of agricultural
learning and research in America's midlands. Holbert's first
work at Purdue had nothing to do with corn, but he did soon
find himself becoming more and more interested in the work
of the seedsman.

This new interest could be traced in no small degree to one
of his teachers, George N. Hoffer, who was himself to become one of the hybrid-corn makers. Hoffer sensed almost at
once that Holbert was a student of unusual capacity and he
put him to work on a study of seed-borne diseases of oats.
Under Hoffer's kindly direction, Holbert delved so deeply
into the seed-borne infections of oats that his report became
one of the best papers on the subject up to that time, a job
that would have done credit to a graduate student or a fully
trained botanist. This piece of work earned for Holbert an
invitation to join Sigma Xi, honorary scientific fraternity.

In March of 1913 young Holbert told Professor M. L.
Fisher, then professor of field crops in the School of Agriculture at Purdue, of his budding interest in farm seed improvement. He asked Fisher to suggest some seedsmen's organization with which he might seek employment during the
next summer to earn much needed cash for school, and at
the same time learn something about the farm seed business.
Fisher discussed Holbert's request with Dean J. H. Skinner,
close friend of Gene Funk in Illinois. As a result, Jim Holbert
wrote a letter to Mr. Funk and asked for a job as a farm
hand on Funk Farms that summer.

Before the young Purdue student arrived for work, Mr.
Funk had learned from Skinner of Holbert's good record as

a student and of his interest in better farm crops. He and
Mrs. Funk talked the matter over, and when Jim Holbert
arrived early in June, he was not assigned to quarters in the
hired hands' ranch house, but was taken right into the Funk
home as a member of the family, beginning the long friendship with Mr. and Mrs. Funk and their children that was to
explain many things which happened later.

Two or three evenings a week that summer, the Indiana
youth would talk far into the night with Mr. Funk. This was
a remarkable opportunity when one considers that Gene
Funk had at that time close acquaintance with the foremost
agronomists in all the colleges and universities of the Middle-
west, was the president of the National Corn Exposition and
an officer in many other organizations interested in better
American agriculture.

Mr. Funk, regarded as the leading corn seedsman of this
period, told his young listener frankly that the present corn
was not good enough. He would say, "Our corn today is good
when everything is favorable, but if corn disease strikes it,
if we have some dry hot weather, or if it rains too much, then
the corn we have now just goes to pieces. And," he would always conclude, "we need corn with better roots so the corn
will stand up and also take the heat and drouth. We must
have *better* corn."

The seedsman was especially concerned over his inability
to reduce ear rot, stalk rot, smut, and other common corn
diseases. As these evening visits continued through the summer, the older man imparted to the younger his deep and
abiding desire to develop corn into an even better crop. Holbert had impressed Mr. Funk too. During the first month he
had learned enough about corn breeding that he could handle
all of the detasselling work on Funk's own farm. By the time
he left for school in the fall there was no question that the
Purdue student would return the next summer.

So in 1914 Jim Holbert spent another three months in

Funk's home, working with corn. On the day that Holbert left to begin his final year at Purdue, Gene Funk told him, "I've got a job for you when you are through with your work at the university. We need better corn and you're going to help us get it. You are going to be a corn breeder—and a good one." Funk's words made a deep impression upon Holbert, mainly because they pointed to a job he would like and be proud to do.

However, Holbert didn't return to Funk Farms immediately after graduation from Purdue. Instead, he spent the summer of 1915 in Minnesota making a cereal disease survey for the United States Department of Agriculture. He secured the cereal survey assignment through his acquaintance with Dr. John Parker, who was beginning his outstanding career as a small grain breeder.

Before the cereal survey was half over, Parker realized how deeply entrenched was Holbert's interest in working with Funk on corn improvement. Parker was the first to suggest that Holbert turn down the possibilities of a permanent job with the Department of Agriculture, as well as the offers that had come to him during the summer from Experiment Stations for research fellowships, in favor of the position offered by Funk. The time in Minnesota was well spent, however, since Holbert learned many things about plant breeding from Parker that were to stand him in good stead later. It was Parker who suggested that Holbert must not leave Minnesota without first having a conference with H. K. Hayes.

Holbert got to Funk Farms in early September, 1915, just about the time corn was well dented. He sought out Mr. Funk immediately and told him of his conference with Hayes and of his desire to experiment with this method of inbreeding and crossing inbred lines into hybrids. The older man listened almost without comment, although he was surprised by the sudden interest in inbreeding exhibited by "his boy Jim."

Whatever may have been his misgivings, the seedsman gave his young associate authority to go ahead on whatever basis he saw fit, an attitude which in view of Funk's previous experience was significant.

What young Jim Holbert didn't know and wasn't to know until years later was that Funk had inaugurated an inbreeding program of his own in 1902, inspired by the work C. G. Hopkins was doing at the University of Illinois. The inbred corn had fizzled out in three or four years, and Funk had not been sufficiently impressed with the possibilities to continue. Furthermore, he had heard Dr. G. H. Shull in both his St. Louis and Omaha addresses.

While Funk, like most other seedsmen and agronomists, was unable to convince himself that Shull's pure-line method of inbreeding and crossing inbreds into single cross hybrids had any practical significance for large acreage plantings, Shull did exert a marked influence upon corn improvement work at Funk Farms. About 1900, Funk Farms seedsmen had begun developing special corn selections, or "corn families" as they called them. Some thirty of these corn families were propagated on separate farms in order that they might be kept free from contamination with other corn, and they were continuously and rigorously selected for qualities such as freedom from disease and for good root and stalk development. Mr. Funk talked to Shull about the scientist's work, especially the increased vigor that resulted from crossing unrelated corn, apparently raising the question whether farmers would accept such hybrids even if they were superior. Shull replied in a letter written in Berlin, Germany, on January 17, 1914:

"According to my view, it is not the method which you use, but the name of Funk Bros. that has become impressive to the intelligent farmer, and if you should find by careful experimentation that some form of direct hybridization will give higher yields with better quality, and so forth, than your present methods, your statement to this effect would be accepted by your constituents quite as readily as they now accept your statements regarding the value of intelligent selection. . . Your establishment is now on such a solid foundation in the esteem of corn-growers of America that you could afford at least to carry out some fairly extensive experiments to test the value of hybridization methods, and I believe that you owe it to yourselves and to your constituents to undertake experiments along this line. . ."

Ever since Funk had heard Shull speak in Omaha, he had been experimenting with simple crosses between his closely bred "corn families," and his seedsmen had found that increased vigor and higher yields could be secured by this type of breeding. These simple crosses were, of course, closely akin to the varietal cross advocated by East and several other prominent botanists and agronomists during this period.

After receiving Shull's challenging letter from Berlin, Funk decided to launch a corn-breeding program whose objective would be to bring together in one hybrid the good qualities of several of the "corn families." A simple cross between two of the most outstanding of his "corn families" was made in 1914, and then in 1915 the corn resulting from this cross was used as a seed parent with another of the outstanding "corn families" as a pollinator parent.

The seed from this field, representing a combination of three separate and unrelated strains of corn that had been purified by years of continuous close breeding, was sold in the spring of 1916 under the special label "Hybrid Corn." While not hybrid corn as we speak of it now, this hybrid was the first of its kind ever offered to American farmers, and it represented the first effort of a recognized seedsman to utilize on a commercial scale the new hybridizing concept that was first described by Dr. Shull in 1908. While this type of corn breeding was continued for a time on Funk Farms, it did not become a permanent practice. Although better than the av-

erage corn then in use, this hybrid of the Funk "corn families" was not enough better to justify the greatly increased
expense of producing it.

In after years the Funk organization has often referred
to its 1916 type of hybrid corn as the "first commercial
hybrid corn." This reference, while technically correct, has
been misleading because it has not always been accompanied
by the explanation that this 1916 hybrid was a hybrid of
close-bred rather than inbred lines such as are generally used
in hybrid corn today. Actually, there was only the slightest,
if any, direct connection between this type of hybrid corn
distributed by the Funk seedsmen in 1916 and the hybrids
which they were to develop from inbred lines years later.

Unfortunately the connection was not as direct as it might
have been. Had either Funk or his young corn breeder, Jim
Holbert, been able to appreciate at that time what they
really had in some of these closely bred corn families, the
coming of hybrid corn from the crossing of inbred lines as
we know it today might have been hastened by many years.
Actually many of these corn families were so closely bred
that they were approaching the uniformity and performance
of a true inbred, some of them having given yields of as much
as 140 bushels an acre when put into hybrid combination.
Had Funk or Holbert only been able to appreciate the potentialities of some of these "corn families" for use in corn
hybrids, they undoubtedly could have very quickly converted
them into a number of great inbreds. In the light of what is
now known, it is evident that Jim Holbert spent more than a
decade to develop inbreds which were perhaps in some cases
not so good as the close-bred material growing on Funk
Farms in 1915 and for some years before.

As it was, Holbert had to begin from absolute scratch.
The young corn breeder went to work immediately in September of 1915 to collect the material on which inbreeding
work was done for the first time in 1916. Little did he know

then what a long hard road was ahead of him, or how little
he or anyone else understood the problem of bringing the
new kind of hybrid corn to American farmers generally.

While Hayes had imparted to him the possibilities of inbreeding and making hybrids from inbred lines, the University of Minnesota scientist had not told him, perhaps
didn't even know at that time, the limitations of this approach to corn breeding. He hadn't told Holbert that hybrids ·
could much more easily and likely be uniformly poor than
uniformly good, and that for every hybrid that proved to be
superior, a hundred others were likely to be miserable failures.
All this and much more Holbert had to learn the hard way,
and one of the things which enabled him to absorb these disappointments and go right on plodding toward the bright
objective painted so wonderfully, for him by Dr. Hayes in
1915 was the constant encouragement which he received from
Gene Funk.

Parker had impressed upon Holbert that the first job of
the plant breeder is to search endlessly to find the rare plants
that give him a real chance to develop new improved strains.
Consequently, Jim Holbert plunged into what was perhaps
the greatest project of corn inspection ever conducted in so
short a time by a single person. He wanted to find those occasional plants in which were combined all the fine qualities
—heavy yield of sound corn, big, strong, disease-free roots,
and stiff disease-free stalks—that farmers like to have in
their corn.

To find these rare plants, Holbert went to work on a
dawn-to-dark schedule, making a tour of personal inspection
of scores of corn fields in McLean County. In many cases he
inspected every corn plant in fields ranging in size from
forty to sixty acres. It was discouraging business, for he
found so few, so miserably few plants that measured up to the
standards he had established.

Holbert tramped through the fields until the corn was all

harvested, and by then he had literally studied millions of corn plants; but in all he had found only a few more than two thousand ears that he deemed worthy. Determined to get good material to enter in the corn breeding laboratory the next spring, Holbert continued to select corn from cribs, basing his judgment now merely on the soundness of the ear. Funk directed men working in the seed corn processing plants · to save for Holbert any ears that appeared to be especially outstanding for weight and freedom from diseased kernels.

By the first of February in 1916, Jim Holbert had just over five thousand carefully selected ears, and he was already on the edge of an important discovery, something that every other corn breeder who came after him also had to learn, something that in its long-range aspect was of great importance to the coming of the new hybrid corn.

The discovery was not a happy one for Holbert. He had come to Funk Farms in September, five months before, a devout believer in the perfection of the beautiful show corn. While at Purdue he had passed the examination required to become a corn show judge and had received the corn judge's certificate, an object which some friends said he prized more than his university diploma. There was some justification for the quip because it was true that he did have his corn judge's certificate framed and he never did accord that distinction to his sheepskin. For a year or so after qualifying for the corn judge's certificate, Holbert even carried in his pocketbook four or five typical kernels of show corn of the best Indiana tradition, selected for him by none other than Prof. A. T. Wiancko, perhaps the Hoosier state's foremost expert on this type of corn.

In weeks and months of searching for the most perfect corn obtainable, Jim Holbert had come face to face with the shocking fact that it was difficult if not impossible to find in the old show corn high yielding plants with strong disease-free roots and stalks. Instead, the few plants that did meet his rigid requirements had ears of a very different type, being, on the whole, longer, more slender and with kernels that presented a smoother appearance. Even when Funk seedsmen found heavy, solid, and completely disease-free ears for him, they always came from the sheller room where the off-type sound ears were shelled so that the seed could be sold in bags—and never from the boxing department where seed ears of satisfactory show type appearance were crated for shipping directly to customers.

This discovery worried Holbert so much that he waited impatiently for Funk to return from a long winter trip so he could report the startling development. He was further amazed to find that Funk was not greatly disturbed, but instead told him to go right ahead and get started with his breeding work.

During February and March, Holbert subjected his five thousand choice ears to germination tests, and after reading the results he threw away three out of every five for failure to give strong, vigorous germination, because of the presence of seedling diseases, or because the seedlings failed to come up to other standards he had established. This left him with only two thousand ears to enter in the corn breeding plots in the spring.

The germination test, in which Holbert put such faith that for several years consecutively he checked well over one hundred thousand ears in this manner, forced him to acknowledge further the inferiority of the old show type of corn. Most of the relatively few show type ears that he had included in his collection were eliminated in the germination tests. There were, however, a sprinkling of the show type ears that managed to make at least a fair showing in the germinator, and Holbert was still hopeful that they would vindicate his faith in them in the breeding plot during the coming season. He was due for further disappointment, and one year after he began work as Mr. Funk's corn breeder, he was convinced that the improved corn of the future could not come from the old show corn.

For the two thousand ears that survived the germination test, Holbert set up a most ambitious corn-breeding program. In one thirty-acre field he laid out enough rows to grow one hundred or more hills of ear-to-row planting from more than twelve hundred ears, all of which had come from Funk Yellow Dent fields. In other isolated plots, he planned smaller plantings of ears selected in fields of Boone County White, Leaming, Funk's Ninety Day, and Bloody Butcher.

Using an especially patient team of horses, Jim Holbert did the planting himself. Beginning the third week in May, he was favored with good weather, and despite the tedious work of changing seed in the planter boxes every hundred hills and stopping to label the beginning and end of the plantings, the job was completed in ten days.

Although there were dozens of farm hands available that summer, the young corn breeder was taking no chances. He plowed his forty-odd acres of isolated breeding plots himself. By the time of the first cultivation in June, he could see marked differences in some of the progenies.

The object of this intensive corn selection work the first year was to find plants of greatly superior field performance, high yield, and good quality of corn. This is the job plant breeders call "isolating superior germ plasm." After he had secured these outstanding plants, the way would be open, Holbert believed, to begin inbreeding and developing the inbred lines with which he hoped to make hybrids.

Naturally, accurate comparisons of the hundreds of ear-to-row plantings could not be made until harvest time. Had he waited to see the yield data before selecting the material for inbreeding, the first selfs could not have been made until 1917, but Holbert was so anxious to get started with the corn-breeding work suggested by Hayes that in July he decided to begin inbreeding. He selected from the most promising ear-to-row progenies a few dozen plants merely on the basis of their mid-season appearance. In all he chose about one hundred plants and selfed them during the tasselling season of 1916. His impatience was well rewarded, for a number of his selfings proved to have promise in the early years of hybrid corn development and from one of these selfs made in 1916 he developed his great Inbred A, which is still today one of the most widely used inbred lines.

In the fall Holbert harvested his experimental plots, checking each ear-to-row progeny for yield, quality of grain, and condition of stalk. Only twenty, approximately one per cent of the original entries, were enough better than well-adapted open-pollinated corn to attract his attention. Then in the winter each of the ears from the hundred or more hills of these outstanding entries was given the germination test which revealed not only the ability of the seed to grow, but also its susceptibility to seedling diseases. When the results from the germinator were tabulated, just twelve of the original two thousand selections were, in Holbert's judgment, sufficiently outstanding to justify further work.

All of the twelve outstanding selections came from the large field in which had been made the twelve hundred ear-to-row plantings from Funk's Yellow Dent ears. Nothing was harvested in the smaller plots of Leaming, Boone, Funk's Ninety Day, or Bloody Butcher that could compare with the top performers in the Funk's Yellow Dent group.

Shortly after the harvest of the experimental plots in the early fall of 1916, Holbert found out why Gene Funk had not been alarmed when his young corn breeder reported that the old show type corn had failed to qualify as the sound and superior type of corn needed to start the new corn-breeding program. Funk explained to him that a decade and more ago, he had made similar observations and had even gone so far as to place in a moisture-proof container a few ears of the best performing corn which he found during the fall in Funk

Farms experimental plots, continuing the practice for several years. The corn he had placed in the containers, said Funk, was the same general type of corn that Holbert had found to be superior.

Shortly thereafter, Funk invited to his farm home a number of agricultural leaders in the Bloomington area, including Dave Thompson, who was then McLean County's first county agent. Funk took his guests to the upper floor of a seed house nearby and showed them the old carbide cans in which he had sealed the best corn grown on Funk Farms for a period of several years. After he opened them and explained their significance, Funk asked young Holbert to report upon his extensive corn-breeding experiments of the preceding year. Funk pointed out that his observations made over a period of years were substantiated by Holbert's more extensive and carefully planned experiments and that the only conclusion he could draw was that McLean County and corn belt farmers generally were losing vast sums each year because they insisted upon raising the old show type of corn.

Funk was so sure of this that he suggested a performance test in which any farmer in the area could enter his corn in fair competition to determine by careful check the best kind of corn for the area. County Agent Dave Thompson was so impressed with the suggestion that he mapped such a program as a county project, and the performance plot was planted the next year on the Lyle Johnstone farm. The results did confirm Funk's contention that the old show type corn was inferior to other types of corn which had been selected on the basis of performance. As a result of Dave Thompson's performance test, interest spread rapidly in what was soon being called "utility type" corn. Soon the agronomists at the University of Illinois, especially W. L. Burlison and J. C. Hackleman, saw the importance of judging corn on the basis of its performance rather than the appearance of the ears, and within a few years large numbers of farmers in Illinois as well as other states quit using the old show corn in favor of the newly developed utility types, something that did, as Funk had promised, result in increasing substantially the profits from corn.

All of these significant developments were touched off by Holbert's first year of corn breeding—because the results of his carefully conducted experiments substantiated observations made by Gene Funk over a period of many preceding years. As we shall later see, the coming of the utility type of corn had an indirect but important bearing upon the development of the new hybrid corn for the corn belt. In 1917 Holbert began developing a new utility type of corn for the Funk organization. He used as parent stock the remnants of the twelve ears that produced the outstanding progenies to plant his inbreeding plot, and all of the remainder he mixed and put in a seed-increasing nursery.

The 1917 inbreeding plot included ear-to-row plantings of the material which had been inbred for the first time in 1916, as well as the material from the twelve progenies that were being inbred for the first time in 1917. As a result the inbred material harvested in the fall of 1917 included some strains that had been selfed twice and some that had been selfed but once.

The year 1918 brought both encouragement and disappointment for Jim Holbert. This was the season in which he planned to make his first crosses between inbred strains. The inbreeding plot looked especially promising all through the spring and early summer. Holbert was already looking ahead to 1919 and 1920, and he was so confident that he had spoken to Funk about reserving a forty-acre field on Funk Farms for the 1920 season when he hoped to plant hybrid corn on field scale for the first time.

Then adversity struck with full force in the form of a battering July rain and wind storm, and in a few minutes all but one of Holbert's strains of inbred corn were so flat on the ground that there was no chance of securing the cross pollination which would have been necessary to make single cross hybrids on large scale that season. Except for a few hybrids made by hand pollinations, Holbert was unable to do more than continue his inbreeding work and plan for large-scale crosses between inbred strains in the 1919 season. Severe drouth occurred during the summer of 1919 in the area where Holbert's inbred crossing plot was located, and especially hot weather at the pollen-shedding season so severely damaged all but one or two of the inbred strains that Holbert was unable even to secure enough seed for perpetuation of the strains the following year, being forced to use remnant seed left over from planting time in 1918 or 1919.

While Holbert was hampered in his plans to get his hybrids between inbred strains into field-scale production, the adversity which he encountered in 1918 and 1919 was in reality a blessing, as it weeded out much of the inferior inbred material and proved the real worth of some others. Especially was this true of the inbred strain later to be designated as Holbert's Inbred A. This inbred strain stood up in the battering rain storm of 1918 and also came through the severe drouth in 1919 in fine condition. By 1921, when the first of Holbert's hybrids appeared in field scale on Funk Farms, Holbert was depending upon such improved inbred lines as his Inbred A and Inbred L, and as a result his first hybrids were much more impressive than would have been the case had not adverse weather balked his plans to make hybrid crosses on a large scale two years earlier.

Holbert's bad luck with his plans to make large-scale crosses between inbred strains in 1918 was in part offset by the remarkable showing made by the utility corn developed from the remnants of the twelve ears that produced the outstanding progenies from his 1916 experimental plots. This new utility corn, available for testing for the first time in 1918, was so impressive that Funk decided to put it into

large-scale commercial seed production, under the name
Funk's 176A. By 1920 this strain was on its way to becoming
the most outstanding and popular open-pollinated corn ever
developed and distributed by the Funk Company.

Holbert's fame as a hybrid corn breeder has now all but
completely obscured his key role in the development of one of
the foremost strains of open-pollinated corn ever used in the
central corn belt, but for years he was regarded as one of
the authorities on the utility type of open-pollinated corn.
It was fitting that he should be named judge of the first
utility corn show, an event which was held at Galesburg,
Illinois, on January 5 and 6, 1921. Credit for the idea of a
utility corn show belongs to Dr. A. G. Johnson, government
pathologist who suggested the possibilities to E. M. D.
Bracker, then county agent in Knox County, Illinois. Bracker
organized and directed the show, an event that later rivalled
the conventional "show corn" type of exhibition after the
University of Illinois agronomists began pointing out its
value.

One of the most significant things about the development
of Funk's 176A in the light of what has taken place since was
the direct contribution this great open-pollinated variety has
made to the development of hybrid corn. From 176A, Holbert
and other hybrid corn breeders have developed a number of
our foremost inbreds — so many that Funk's 176A is perhaps
outstanding among all of the open pollinates in this respect.
In effect, Holbert had pooled in Funk's 176A the fine qualities he had discovered in that first year on Funk Farms when
he walked hundreds of miles up and down McLean County
corn fields in search of superior corn plants. In this way 176A
became a sort of a reservoir of outstanding germ plasm of
the central corn belt from which could be drawn inbred lines
of wide usefulness.

On August 21, 1918, an experiment station of the United
States Department of Agriculture was established on the

farms of the Funk Brothers Seed Company a few miles south
of Bloomington, McLean County. Jim Holbert left the employ of the Funk Brothers to take charge of the station,
which was located there to help the Department of Agriculture's determined effort to find effective control for corn
diseases that were taking heavy toll of the nation's corn crop.

In the early years of this century, root, stalk, and ear rots,
along with smut and other common corn diseases, were serious
topics among corn farmers. To many it was becoming clear
that while the Leamings, Reids, Funks, Hogues, and others
were developing higher yielding corn, the diseases of corn
were increasing at an alarming rate—whittling many a huge
prospective crop down to a fair or poor yield. Gene Funk
had recognized that disease was now much more devastating
than it had been in the lower yielding strains used by his
father and grandfather. He considered it the number one
menace to corn farming.

The U. S. Department of Agriculture had recognized this
problem in the winter of 1916 by initiating a special investigation of corn diseases under direction of H. B. Humphrey.
The next spring the United States entered the first World
War, and Funk went to Washington on a special wartime
assignment in the Department of Agriculture. While in the
capital, he was largely responsible for securing a special ap-
propriation from Congress which provided for establishing
six more field stations in the corn belt at which corn disease problems were to be studied. The first of these was
located on Funk Farms, partially in recognition of Funk's
profound interest in the problem.

The establishment of the Federal Field Station gave Jim
Holbert opportunities so unusual that they probably were
never duplicated before or since. In the next twenty years
Holbert blended his own tremendous abilities with these re-
markable opportunities. The chance to work with Johnson,
Dickson, Hoffer, Burlison, and a score of others like them

in the leading experiment stations and universities of the country was in itself of great importance, for Holbert had no institutional traditions or loyalties to limit the amount of help and assistance he could accept and use. On the other hand he kept in constant and close contact with the practical farmer's point of view through his relationship with Funk and the men who tilled the rich soil in the central corn belt.

Acting under this unusual stimulus, Holbert not only put to use all the things that had been discovered by East, Shull, Hayes, and Jones before him, but he made a whole series of new discoveries that immeasurably broadened the foundation upon which rests the hybrid corn of today.

The first of these came in 1919. In the new inbred lines Jim Holbert was developing, some were highly susceptible to common corn diseases while others growing in the same field were completely free from the same diseases. Holbert had one inbred in which every plant in the plot was stricken with smut; right next to it was another inbred line completely free from this fungus disease, a dramatic sight considering the hideous black balls developed by smut on corn plants.

Funk was deeply impressed with this sight along with equally significant differences in ear rots and stalk rots, as were all persons interested in corn who visited the United States Department of Agriculture station on Funk Farms in 1919 and the years immediately afterward. These and other demonstrations began to attract an ever-increasing number of visitors to Funk Farms. Corn farmers, scientists, magazine and newspaper editors, and agricultural leaders from all over the United States found their way to Bloomington in the next two decades to talk with Jim Holbert and see the evidence of his progress in corn breeding.

The story of what Jim Holbert accomplished at the Federal Field Station on Funk Farms in the next fifteen years after 1920 could be interestingly told by merely reporting the persons who came to Bloomington and what they said.

As early as 1920 Illinois' Governor Lowden, himself a farmer, came to Funk Farms to see the corn-breeding work.

In 1921, Dr. L. E. Call, Kansas agronomist, came to Bloomington. After chatting with Holbert and hastily visiting the corn breeding plots for an hour and a half, Call prepared to leave, explaining, "I just came to see if you had something here. I see you have."

Donald Jones, on his 1921 round-robin tour, visited Holbert and found the only single cross hybrids mentioned in his report of the trip. H. K. Hayes was with Jones when he came to Bloomington, so that the meeting brought together the three men in the United States who until this time had done the most work with corn inbreeding and developing hybrids from inbred lines. It was the first time Hayes and Holbert had met since their historic conference in August of 1915.

Another of Holbert's early visitors was Dr. T. A. Kiesselbach, noted plant breeder of the University of Nebraska. Kiesselbach was so impressed with what he saw at the Federal Field Station on Funk Farms that he asked to have some of the new single cross hybrids sent to Nebraska so that he might test them in the western corn belt. Seed for these hybrids was sent to Kiesselbach after the harvest of the seed plots in 1921, and the Holbert hybrids grew in Nebraska for the first time during the 1922 season.

One of these single cross hybrids was Holbert's A-by-L, made by combining Inbred A and Inbred L, both of which were inbred lines developed by the young Illinois corn breeder. Dr. Kiesselbach described it as the first significant strain of the new hybrid corn that was grown in Nebraska or that he had observed in the corn belt. "Holbert's old A-by-L was the first hybrid that really brought home to us the great possibilities of hybrid corn. It yielded well, and it stood up so much better than our open pollinated corn that it was just in a class by itself," said the Nebraskan.

Among the most intensely interested of all the thousands

of persons who came to visit Jim Holbert and Gene Funk
through the years were those men who later became the great
private hybrid-corn breeders—men without university or
experiment station connections, who had unbounded faith in
the future of the new kind of corn and who were anxious to
further its development.

Lester Pfister of nearby El Paso, C. L. Gunn of De Kalb,
Illinois, and Henry A. Wallace of Des Moines, Iowa, now
some of the greatest names associated with hybrid corn, paid
Jim Holbert visits that increased both in number and duration through the years as the miracle of hybrid corn unfolded.

Indeed, Holbert's attainments attracted such wide attention that his home town of Bloomington became the mecca
for men interested in hybrid corn. The techniques these men
learned in their visits to Bloomington, the inbreds given to
them from the Federal Field Station, and the enthusiasm for
the possibilities of this new kind of corn imparted to them by
Jim Holbert constituted the greatest single force in the
hybrid-corn movement during the twenties and early thirties
when the question of having hybrid corn in our time was
hanging precariously in the balance.

Although in recent years the Pfisters, the Gunns, and the
Wallaces have gone their widely separate ways, especially
after they became the moving spirits in strongly competing
organizations producing hybrid seed corn for America's
farmers, many of the friendships begun during these visits
to Funk Farms have endured to the present time. Were you
this day to step into the simple but impressive office of C. L.
Gunn, to whom more farmers have looked for hybrid corn
than any other single corn breeder, you would see but three
portraits hanging there, one of a trusted assistant; another
of the president of Gunn's organization for thirty years;
and the third of Jim Holbert. Looking at Holbert's picture
in a reflective mood, Gunn said not long ago, "I've always

thought of Holbert as the head of everything that has to do with hybrid corn in Illinois and throughout the corn belt. I appreciate what he has done not only for us but for the whole hybrid corn development. When Jim Holbert says something, you can depend upon it."

What was true of these well known persons was equally true of dozens of others not so famous. Holbert was never too busy to give them as much time as they sought, conducting an endless number of tours through his breeding plots and explaining the latest discoveries over the dining-room tables of the Illinois and Rogers Hotels in Bloomington. Often Holbert would have guests at breakfast, at noon, and again for dinner in the evening.

Not only did Holbert give unstintingly of his time to all these guests, but many of them ended by helping him and the cause of hybrid corn. Dr. Johnson, who directed from Washington the work at the station located on Funk Farms, early impressed upon Holbert the need for checking the performance of experimental hybrids at the greatest possible number of places and under the widest possible range of soil and weather conditions. Many of the men who came to see Holbert were aggressive farmers, interested in better corn, and when they were ready to go, not infrequently Holbert would invite them to test out a few of the new hybrids on their farms the next year. He was seldom if ever turned down, and the following season Holbert's newest hybrids would have a chance to grow miles away in an entirely different set of soil and weather conditions.

The first of these hybrid corn experiment plots was conducted for Holbert by a good-natured Scotsman, J. L. McKeighan, an outstanding farmer living in western Illinois a few miles southeast of Galesburg. Soon Charlie Holmes of Edelstein in north central Illinois, Ben Moews of Granville in north central Illinois, Claire Golden of Cordova in northwestern Illinois, John T. Smith of Tolono in eastern Illinois,

Frank Garwood of Stonington in south central Illinois, and Richard Best of Eldred in southwestern Illinois were helping Holbert too. Eventually, Holbert had nearly twoscore of these farmer co-operators doing the exacting job of conducting a hybrid corn research plot, without financial reward and spurred on because of their friendship for him and their interest in better corn. This co-operation proved to be one of the decisive factors in the remarkable hybrid corn-breeding achievements of the Federal Field Station on Funk Farms.

During the early twenties, Jim Holbert received help and inspiration from another source that proved of inestimable value to him. He decided to work for his doctor's degree at the University of Illinois, and he was assigned to Dr. Charles F. Hottes, the same man who had taught Edward Murray East twenty-odd years earlier. Holbert reaped an unusual reward in his graduate work, largely because of the almost amazing capacity of Hottes to encourage and stimulate a good student.

Especially helpful to Holbert was Hottes' understanding of all the scientific literature relating to the field of plant physiology. Holbert recalls a conference in Dr. Hottes' office in which he raised a controversial point. Dr. Hottes immediately recalled that the matter had been thoroughly covered in a bulletin issued several years before, whereupon he turned to his office table stacked high with materials of many kinds. Hottes went directly to one nondescript pile of papers, dug down, and produced the bulletin to which he referred.

Holbert continued to carry the full load of his responsibilities at the Federal Field Station while he did the work for his doctor's degree, something he undoubtedly could not have done in so short a time had it not been for Mrs. Holbert, a most interested and brilliant helper. During the final difficult year, Mrs. Holbert did two-thirds or more of a vast amount of laboratory work that went into her husband's thesis and the translating of references published in German.

On this and many other occasions, Mrs. Holbert supplied an important part of the resources which enabled her plant-breeding husband to accomplish so much in so little time. In 1925, at the time Dr. Hottes recommended Jim Holbert for a doctor's degree, he said that he wasn't certain whether the degree should go to Mr. or Mrs. Holbert.

Jim Holbert knew that the science of hybrid corn breeding was just beginning to unfold, and that he must watch every breeding plot, every incident, and every circumstance for clues to as yet unexplored possibilities. An outstanding example of Holbert's constant expansion of corn-breeding concepts began in the fall of 1929 when Professor W. P. Flint, respected entomologist at the University of Illinois, predicted a heavy chinch bug infestation in the 1930 growing season for the Funk Farms area south of Bloomington. Some of Holbert's most highly prized inbreds had in the past been badly damaged by chinch bug attack. So he went to Urbana to talk to Flint about some means of protecting them. Flint said that he knew of no insecticide which could be effectively applied to give protection to corn from chinch bugs. Flint did, however, suggest that Holbert plant his precious inbreds in the center of the largest field of corn he could find on Funk Farms, expressing the opinion that the insects would likely not get into the center of so large a field and might never find the inbreds at all.

Holbert followed Flint's suggestions and made a discovery of the utmost importance. The chinch bugs did find the inbreds tucked away in the center of a forty-acre field of corn, and they found them quickly. There were two amazing developments. Before they appeared on any of the surrounding corn in the field the chinch bugs attacked and devastated one or two of Holbert's corn inbreds. But the chinch bugs didn't attack all the inbreds Holbert had hidden. They let some of them entirely alone. Dramatic as was this situation, Holbert refused to draw any conclusions, but instead attempted to "hide" his susceptible inbreds in a large field of corn again the next year. Again the chinch bugs found and attacked the susceptible inbreds before bothering the other inbreds growing right beside them.

Then Holbert called in Professor Flint and his associate, John Bigger, to confirm his observations. Could it be, they wondered, that inbreds might be developed that would resist insect devastation just as certain inbreds had already been proved resistant to smut and other corn diseases?

Holbert crossed the inbreds that had successfully withstood the chinch bug attack into experimental hybrids and planted them in areas infested by chinch bugs along with hybrids made from inbreds that had been heavily damaged by the insects. Yes, it was true! The hybrids made from inbreds that had resisted chinch bug attack were also resistant. The factors which had discouraged chinch bug attacks on the inbreds could be genetically transmitted from inbred to hybrid.

In 1934, after chinch bug–resistant hybrids were available in field scale, another severe infestation of chinch bugs occurred. Frank Bill of the Bloomington Pantagraph used the Pantagraph's airplane, "Scoop," and flew over a Funk Farms cornfield planted alternately in ten-acre strips to resistant and susceptible hybrids. The aerial photograph showed plainly, to the row, where the resistant hybrids began and left off, and the photograph, undoubtedly the first of its kind ever taken, was circulated widely.

This series of experiences with resistance to chinch bugs led Holbert, Bigger, and others to undertake an exhaustive study of the resistance to insects in corn. As years passed, Holbert developed hybrids with marked degrees of resistance to numerous other insect enemies of corn such as root worm, corn borer, ear worm, Japanese beetle, and weevil. In his exhaustive work on insect resistance, Holbert discovered many things of great significance to the modern science of hybrid corn breeding. First, Holbert found to his regret that there is no such thing as general resistance to insects in corn, but that hybrids highly resistant to one insect such as the chinch bug may be very susceptible and quickly destroyed by another insect such as the corn borer even though both insects attack the stalk. Holbert soon discovered that hybrids highly resistant to a given insect in the area of its best adaptation may actually be highly susceptible to attack from the same insect when the hybrid is grown out of the territory to which it is adapted. Holbert demonstrated that insect resistance in a hybrid is a factor so complex that it is likely to result from a number of inheritable qualities, and that to combine these inheritable traits in a single strain of corn is a job often requiring years of work. This explains why new hybrids with greater and greater degrees of insect resistance are constantly being developed.

Another example of the discovery of an important new concept had its beginning in 1925. Just before the end of summer that year, a blast of cold air moved out of the Canadian northwest and brought to the upper Mississippi Valley and Funk Farms unseasonably cold nights. Always watchful, Jim Holbert detected a strange thing. Some of the inbreds continued to grow despite the cold nights. Others were static and never grew again even after the weather turned warm a few days later.

Why, asked Holbert of himself and others, were some hybrids "frosted" before the weather bureau reported frost? Why had some of his inbreds and hybrids stopped growing when the temperature dropped to forty-five degrees while others continued active even after the thermometer readings dipped down to near freezing?

Just as the question about the inbreds hidden from the chinch bugs in the center of a 40-acre field of corn had led to important discoveries, so did this question about why some strains of corn die with the first cool breeze of fall while others continued to add extra bushels of yield despite temperatures eight to ten degrees lower. A number of Holbert's colleagues and co-workers took part in the exhaustive investigations that followed into the nature of damage by cold. Notable among them was Dr. W. L. Burlison, head of the Department of Agronomy at the University of Illinois. This careful inquiry into the nature of cold resistance in corn added important new working concepts to practical corn-breeding procedures.

Holbert and his colleagues devised and built many pieces of special equipment and worked out many new techniques. In connection with the cold resistance studies, Holbert and Burlison built large cold chambers weighing approximately two tons which could subject corn plants to the same temperature that often occurs naturally in spring and early fall. In this way the cool weather of September or October could be reproduced in July, August, or any other time. This equipment was of inestimable value in the important cold resistance work and the discoveries which came from it.

An example of new techniques first used at the United States Department of Agriculture's Experiment Station on Funk Farms was the stalk rot inoculations by hypodermic injection. This, incidentally, illustrated well the help which Holbert so often received from other scientists, since the man most responsible for the development of the artificial stalk inoculation with diplodia was Dr. James G. Dickson, pathologist at the University of Wisconsin.

Holbert, Dickson, and their associates made extensive and effective use of this new hypodermic technique, injecting thousands of plants each year during the time that the most important strides were being made in developing hybrids with resistance to diplodia stalk rots. Usually the injections were made about ten days after pollination took place. There was found to be a close correlation between resistance to stalk rot following the artificial inoculation and the capacity of a given strain of corn to develop stalks that could stand up even if harvest was delayed until late in the fall. Aided by Dickson's new technique, Holbert was soon able to demonstrate that resistance or susceptibility to diplodia stalk rot was inherited and transmitted in corn plants from one generation to the next and that this characteristic correlated closely with the actual performance of these plants under field conditions over a wide area. By making it possible to produce diplodia stalk rot at will, the artificial stalk rot inoculation technique greatly hurried the development of inbred lines and hybrids resistant to stalk rot. Just as the special cold chambers were useful in inquiring into the nature of cold damage, the hypodermic inoculation technique was equally useful in studying the nature of resistance to stalk rot diseases.

When the Purnell Funds were made available to corn belt experiment stations of the land grant colleges in the late twenties, hybrid corn breeding work was accelerated tremendously. The work of the hybrid-corn breeders' conference, first organized by F. D. Richey, was a further means of speeding up the job of producing enough good inbreds capable of being combined into double cross hybrids to win a decision over open-pollinated corn.

Although Holbert had already developed a large number of inbreds in these early years, he realized that no one man could live long enough to produce all the inbreds needed for all the good hybrids that farmers would want once they understood the advantages of the new corn. From the time that the Federal Field Station was established on Funk Farms, both Holbert and Funk had constantly urged everyone interested to work at the job of developing new inbred lines. By nature and by virtue of his position in a publicly supported experiment station, he was always ready to exchange inbred material freely with other corn breeders. Many of the corn breeders shunned the practice, regarding their good inbred lines as something to be used exclusively by themselves and hoping that their own institutions might some day have enough lines of their own to make satisfactory hybrids.

As a result of Holbert's own work and his willingness to accept inbred material from others in exchange for his own, the first outstanding hybrids in the corn belt grew on Funk Farms. By 1923 there were some promising three-way hybrids, meaning a hybrid developed from three inbreds, available for farm testing. Each year thereafter, experiment stations and co-operating farmers received limited amounts of hybrid seed to be grown under regular farm conditions.

In 1925, the first of the double cross hybrids, one bringing together four inbreds, was released by Holbert. By this time there was enough inbred material available so that the Funk Brothers Seed Company personnel who had followed Holbert's progress closely decided to risk the resources necessary to produce a few hundred bushels of seed of the new double cross hybrid to be made available to central Illinois corn farmers.

By 1927, Gene Funk saw that demand from farmers for the new hybrids was great enough to justify a special hybrid seed corn department. Before the year was over, Funk Brothers Seed Company had engaged Dr. Earl Sieveking, an agronomist trained at the University of Missouri and the University of Illinois, to head the new department.

The hour of hybrid corn's ultimate triumph was near. Sidney Cates, influential agricultural writer of national reputation whose articles appeared regularly in what was at this time America's most widely read and highly respected farm magazine, *Country Gentleman,* was the first to announce in unqualified terms that the success of hybrid corn was assured. Cates had followed the work almost from the beginning. In the summer of 1928 he spent two weeks in the corn belt checking on the progress that had been made.

"The Day of Super-Corn Crops Has Come" was the uncompromising title of Mr. Cates' article in the March, 1929, issue of *Country Gentleman*: "The novel, new-style breeding work of the past decade, a work which has reached the fruition stage, puts corn almost as far ahead of what the best of it was ten years ago as this ten-year-ago product was beyond and above the primitive prototype from which it has been coaxed . . . by unknown savages plus four hundred years of the white man's effort."

Cates knew the hybrid-corn makers were opening the door to a whole new world of plants—perhaps animals, too—for our future farmers. He continued, "And furthermore, what has been so recently done also lays bare natural laws which lead on to no one can tell where.

"The Office of Cereal Crops and Diseases of the United States Department of Agriculture, working through its pathological section . . . is the group which has gone further than any other in doing the basic work for the production of this new departure for the greatest of all American crops. And Dr. J. R. Holbert, at Bloomington, using Funk Farms as his field laboratory is in direct command of the studies. . . This corn breeding started primarily to fight the disease problem . . ."

In this article Cates mentioned that "Funk Brothers will this season have about two thousand bushels of the new seed for sale," and inadvertently brought about the first evidence of public interest in hybrid corn. Dr. Sieveking received mail by the sackful from farmers who had read the *Country Gentleman* article. The letters came from practically every state in the Union and from many foreign countries. The slender supply of hybrid seed corn ready for distribution by the Funk organization was quickly gone even though Sieveking allowed only a small quantity to a person.

Leon Steele, now one of the prominent members of the rising second generation of hybrid corn breeders, began

Root-pruning insects attacked this field laboratory where each row was planted to a different experimental hybrid. The strain on the right gave dramatic evidence of its resistance

Mechanical pickers operating on a farm in central Illinois. The superior stalks of hybrid corn made possible widescale use of mechanical harvesters for this crop

working as a water boy on the Federal Field Station on Funk Farms in the summer of 1926 when he was ten years old. Replying to the question of where he worked—as a small lad on his first job—he usually got some version of the same comment: "So you are working for that crazy Holbert." That, in general, was what the rank and file of farmers who made a living raising corn thought about scientists who spent their time walking through cornfields putting little sacks over the tassels and ears.

This general skepticism was one of the things which delayed rapid acceptance of hybrid corn during the early thirties. The farmers in the vicinity of Funk Farms, for instance, could undoubtedly have boosted their miserably low farm income during the darkest days of the depression years if they had used the new hybrids being released from the Federal Field Station on Funk Farms.

Then in the mid-thirties, Holbert and the other hybrid-corn breeders had a chance to prove dramatically the overwhelming superiority of their new hybrids. The drouths of 1934 and 1936 convinced skeptics as nothing else could have done in so short a time. An example of what happened from Ohio to Nebraska in these drouth years occurred in 1936 on the G. J. Mecherle farm, which was operated by Walter Meers and located nine miles east of Bloomington. Dr. Jim Holbert had one of his numerous hybrid-corn testing plots on the Mecherle farm in 1935. In October he went to study it, accompanied by A. L. Lang, University of Illinois agronomist. Mecherle told those assembled, "This is the farm on which I was born. I've always loved it as no other piece of land on earth. You know, I've tried everything I knew or was advised to do by the boys over at the college, but I've never raised a hundred-bushel-an-acre crop of corn on this old farm. I don't know anything that would give me more personal satisfaction or be of more value in establishing the worth of some of these new cropping practices for farms in this part of Illinois than to raise a hundred-bushel crop of corn here next year."

Lang, the soils scientist, and Holbert, the hybrid-corn breeder, spoke almost in the same breath.

"Why, Mr. Mecherle, there's no reason why you can't do that. All you have to do is to put some extra fertilizer on your land and make a thick planting of some of the new high-yielding hybrids, and there should be no doubt about it."

Mecherle was pleased and a little surprised.

"Well, boys, you write the ticket and we'll do the work. That small field south of the house is due for corn next year. That would be a good place for you to start."

Aware that it would be disappointing to Mecherle and most embarrassing to themselves to fail, Lang and Holbert laid their plans carefully. Lang secured help from the soil physics department of the University of Illinois in making plans for some extra tile on the field, and he worked out a special recommendation for fertilizer. Holbert laid out the field in strips and planted five of the newest hybrids available from his Funk Farms Experiment Station. Just to make the results official, Meers entered the field in the University of Illinois' Ten Acre Corn Growing Contest.

Mr. Meers prepared the seed bed with the greatest of care, and planting was done in mid-May just as the rain stopped. June passed cool and without rain. Then came the test. And what happened during the next month and a half will be remembered not only by Walter Meers, Jim Holbert, and Al Lang, but by all corn belt farmers who faced the elements in 1936.

On the last day of June, temperatures of 95° and above were reported in the Meers' neighborhood. These high temperatures continued until July 3, when the high temperature in nearby Bloomington was 102° and still no rain fell. When temperatures of 105°, 109°, and 111° continued for a week, the Associated Press report from Springfield said, "Corn has reached the critical stage where serious injury will result unless drouth conditions are broken this week."

Instead, temperatures moved higher. On July 15 Bloomington's high temperature was 114°. The destructive heat was in big headlines in every newspaper. The Associated Press account of July 15 said, "A blistering sun beat down on millions of acres of deteriorating fields in the vast Middle West and forecasters saw no relief ahead from the wave of prolonged aridity which has inflicted crop damage that experts now estimate will exceed that of the 1934 drouth . . . deaths for the thirteen day record shattering heat reached a total of more than forty-one hundred persons with most of the fatalities centered in Illinois, Minnesota, Michigan, Wisconsin and Missouri."

Corn was badly hurt in McLean County. Farmers were convinced that their crop had been whittled down to a half or even a fourth of normal size. But the Meers' field looked surprisingly good, although white-fired leaves were beginning to appear at the top of the plants.

The sensational heat subsided a little on July 19 after the nation's death total had reached ten thousand persons and livestock struck down were so numerous as to be uncounted. Still there was no rain, and corn was selling for $1.37 a bushel in Chicago, highest price since the first World War. July and the first half of August passed without a single shower on the Meers' farm. Then on the sixteenth of August, the first break came in the drouth. A half inch of rain was reported at Bloomington. Three days later a real ground-soaking shower fell, and then the new hybrids in Walter Meers' field south of the house began an amazing recovery.

In October, contest inspectors for the university's corn growing contest checked each of the five hybrids growing in the Meers' field. The highest yielding hybrid averaged 121 bushels an acre. Three of the hybrids yielded over the 100-bushels-an-acre mark. The entire contest field averaged 101.30 bushels. The McLean County average corn yield for the year was less than 25 bushels—a stirring testimony to what could be accomplished by careful soil management and the new hybrid corn.

Hybrid corn was making the grade. New and more effective hybrids were emerging from the Funk Farms Experiment Station every year during the middle thirties. Even despite the great improvement in hybrid corn in the years since, some of the hybrids developed by Holbert during this period are still being used. An example is Illinois Hybrid 384. The four inbreds that entered into this hybrid of long usefulness are still regarded the best experiment station inbreds ever developed. Three of them, Inbreds A, Hy, and R4, were developed by Holbert, and the other was St. John's Inbred WF9.

Holbert and Gene Funk had adopted the policy of helping everyone and of accepting help from everyone. It was paying big dividends now. Especially close had been the co-operation between Holbert in Illinois and the men who worked on hybrid corn in Indiana under the direction of his old teacher, Dr. Hoffer. This was logical since the Indiana Experiment Station and the Federal Field Station on Funk Farms were closely associated in the corn disease project of the United States Department of Agriculture. R. R. St. John, appointed by Hoffer, assumed the direction of the Indiana hybrid corn breeding program late in the twenties. St. John shared Holbert's views on the need for close co-operation and free exchange of ideas, inbred strains, and single-cross material. Together these two men developed both inbreds and hybrids in the late twenties and early thirties that would undoubtedly have been beyond the reach of either of them working alone.

St. John had been working since 1932 with an especially promising inbred which he called 38–11. The severe drouth of

1936 proved its greatness beyond question. After studying
the performance of this new inbred in relation to others already in general use, there took shape in the minds of Holbert and St. John an idea for a new hybrid that in the years
since has been used by more farmers than any other ever
developed.

One of the single crosses entering into this new hybrid,
they reasoned, would be made up of St. John's outstanding
inbreds, WF9 and 38–11. The other single cross would be
made up of Holbert's Hy and Jenkins' L317. Here, Holbert
and St. John believed, was the pedigree for a hybrid that
would surpass anything that had yet been developed, and
US–13 lived up to their expectations and more. During the
war years, even though US–13 was an old hybrid by this
time, farmers from New Jersey to Colorado and from northern Tennessee to central Iowa depended on US–13 more
widely than on any other single hybrid.

The year 1937 saw the closing of the Federal Field Station
on Funk Farms which had accomplished the original purpose
for which it was established and much more. The Funk Farms
Station was established to study and combat corn diseases
which, with the development of high yielding hybrids resistant to disease, were no longer a major problem.

Closing the station confronted Jim Holbert with the problem of bringing to an end one career and undertaking another. Soon he found there were numerous opportunities
open to him. Some work had already been done on more than a
dozen specialized research projects, all of which he planned to
publish as soon as the manuscripts upon which he was already
working had been completed and presented. The Agronomy
Department of the University of Illinois wanted Holbert to
join the staff and complete these publications. The chief
drawback to this proposal was that it would have taken
Holbert out of hybrid-corn breeding, the undertaking to
which he had devoted the major part of his life.

Holbert was approached with offers from hybrid seed-corn producing organizations, at least one of which was accompanied by most unusual contract considerations. In the end, Holbert did not accept any of these offers. Instead he went back to his old job with E. D. Funk. True, it was a much bigger job now and he had a more imposing title, "Vice-President in Charge of Research," but the objective was the same—better corn for America's corn farmers.

Although Holbert was by now dean of all the active hybrid-corn breeders in the United States, he was only a little past forty with his most productive years still ahead of him. His return to the ranks of the Funk Company opened up a whole new career. In the newly developing hybrid-seed corn industry, he found himself in competition with the very men he had helped for so many years. On the other hand, he found now that he could use his own vast knowledge of hybrid corn breeding to develop new strains of hybrid corn that would belong exclusively to his company. Because of the location of the Funk Farms Station, most of Holbert's work had been with hybrids adapted to the central part of the corn belt. Now he foresaw the need for hybrids that would serve farmers both north and south of this area.

With characteristic energy, Jim Holbert began laying the foundations for the first hybrid-corn research staff that would eventually be nation-wide in its scope, developing hybrids for southern Canada and Minnesota, for New Jersey and Maryland, for Nebraska and Colorado, and for Louisiana and Texas.

In building this new nation-wide hybrid-corn research program, Holbert called into use his gifts as a teacher. Using himself and his trusted associate of many years, Wright Hardin, as the hub, he began immediately to groom younger men to take over important responsibilities in the new organization. First to be called was Leon Steele, his one-time water boy at the old Funk Farms Experiment

Station who rejoined Holbert not long after he completed his college work in botany. Other younger men—Lewis Falck of Iowa State, Les Hug of Pennsylvania State, O. J. Eigsti of the University of Illinois, L. W. Sears of Purdue, and others—joined efforts with Holbert and Hardin as the corn-breeding work expanded. Today these men who are only now approaching their most productive years hold the promise of continuing for a long time to come the concepts introduced by Dr. Jim Holbert into the new business of hybrid-corn breeding.

Holbert's new hybrid-corn research organization produced results in a remarkably short time as new developments in this type of work go. Within the decade after Jim Holbert began developing his American and Canadian corn-breeding program, an entire series of new hybrids appeared that have become the standard of measure for corn performance in their respective areas of adaptation.

Today, Dr. Jim Holbert goes on adding to his amazing career in hybrid corn. The hybrids which he has developed are grown over a wider area than those of any other corn breeder. He goes each year from the mountains on the west to the sea on the east and from Canada to the Gulf of Mexico, studying the performance of the new hybrids that he and his research staff are continuously striving to develop. He travels more widely, talks to more farmers about their corn-growing problems, and directs more hybrid-corn research work than any other hybrid-corn breeder. Jim Holbert has undoubtedly devoted more hours, weeks, and years to the improvement of corn than any other man of record in all the long history of corn. His lifetime has seen more improvement in corn than in any similar period since corn was discovered by the American Indians. No person has done more to give the present generation of Americans hybrid corn than Jim Holbert.

CHAPTER X

Henry Agard Wallace

HENRY AGARD WALLACE has been associated prominently for many years with issues of national
politics and international diplomacy—and many persons
throughout the nation and the world who feel an almost
personal acquaintance with the famous Iowan have forgotten,
or never knew, that he stands in the forefront of the early
hybrid-corn makers. Without the unrelenting efforts of
Wallace, registered both as a corn breeder and as an editor
of the leading farm magazine in the foremost corn-producing
state, Iowa, the wide use of hybrid corn would unquestionably have been greatly retarded.

Henry A. Wallace's grandfather, who signed his name
just plain Henry Wallace, came to Iowa in 1862 as one of
its pioneer United Presbyterian ministers and earned a
place in the hearts of two generations of Iowans achieved by
few other persons. "Uncle Henry," as he came to be uni-
versally known, and his family were God-fearing people,
puritanical in their living habits, shrewd in their business
endeavors, and utterly fearless in the face of opposition or
adversity. The women who married into the family were of
the same mold, and so to this day the Wallaces are generally
determined, hard working, conservative in their personal
habits, and indifferent to tribulations.

Wallace's grandfather was reared in western Pennsylvania
and made his first trip across the north central Illinois
prairie when he came west to attend the United Presbyterian

Theological Seminary at Monmouth, at that time a small western Illinois town of a thousand persons. Wallace was awed by the agricultural wealth of the prairie, especially its capacity to produce corn. In his classic little book, "Letters To My Great Grandchildren," he wrote of his first impressions of the Corn Belt, "It seemed as if the state was literally full of corn. It was piled up in rail pens, without covering, around the houses and other buildings, and sometimes in the fields. . . The next winter I spent a Sabbath in the country, and sat by a stove burning corn for fuel. . . The town itself was full of corn; corn everywhere. And it was also full of rats."

Uncle Henry Wallace was a man of many attainments. He took up the ministry in Iowa after being graduated from the Monmouth Seminary and continued in that calling until his health forced him to give up the confinement imposed by his pulpit duties and the exhausting task of administering to the needs of his congregation. Needing to be out-of-doors, he turned his attention to farming in Adair County, which is in one of the best of Iowa's prairie sections and about one hundred miles west of Des Moines. His health gradually improved, and he climaxed his career by founding *Wallaces' Farmer* and steering it through its tender years.

National recognition first came to the Wallace family in 1908 when President Theodore Roosevelt appointed Uncle Henry Wallace as a member of his Country Life Commission, which was made up five men including Gifford Pinchot, who later became governor of Pennsylvania. The purpose of this special commission was to make a preliminary survey of rural life in America, and the job was done in such a manner as to attract wide recognition during the years before the first World War. Then Uncle Henry's son, Henry C. Wallace, who carried on his father's work as editor of *Wallaces' Farmer*, was named Secretary of Agriculture in President Harding's cabinet, and only a few years later his son, Henry

A. Wallace, was called to responsibilities of national importance.

Against this background and in this atmosphere was Henry A. Wallace reared. He was born on the Wallace family acres in Adair County, Iowa, on October 7, 1888. As a youth he was so serious and meditative that many of his school associates thought him queer and unsocial. After graduating from the Des Moines public schools, Wallace attended Iowa State College at Ames, thirty miles north of Des Moines. Even during college days his family ties remained close, and after he graduated in 1910 he returned to Des Moines and began working for *Wallaces' Farmer.*

At Ames during school days and after, Wallace made friends who were to be of great aid and inspiration both in his work with corn breeding and as an editorial writer. Perhaps most important was his friendship with H. D. Hughes, the respected Iowa State College agronomist of whom Wallace later said in referring to his early work with hybrid corn, "I should give real credit to Professor H. D. Hughes because of the splendid encouragement and co-operation which he was at all times willing to furnish. I don't know of a more kindly man who understands all aspects of human nature and is yet true to science."

The Wallaces have held corn in a reverence that in an enlightened way equals the devotion in which maize was regarded by the American Indians. After Henry A. Wallace had followed his father's footsteps into the position of Secretary of Agriculture, he returned to his beloved Iowa State College to address a conference of the Corn Research Institute:

"Of all the annual crops, corn is one of the most efficient in transforming sun energy, soil fertility and man labor into a maximum of food suitable for animals and human beings. It is to be regretted that so few of the millions whose prosperity rests on the corn plant should have so little

appreciation or knowledge of it. Even those who work most
with corn display little of the genuine reverence for it which
characterized the majority of the corn growing Indians up
until this century."

Henry A. Wallace acquired his intense interest in corn
while he was still a boy in high school. Professor P. G.
Holden, the great corn evangelist of that time, was lured
away from Illinois by an offer from Iowa State College
made possible by the fact that Uncle Henry Wallace,
through the medium of *Wallaces' Farmer*, volunteered to
make up the difference between what the college could pay
the first year and what was required to get Holden to come.
Professor Holden, in a surprisingly short time, was able to
introduce the old corn show in the Iowa farm country as an
important educational institution.

Holden frequently visited his friends, the Wallaces, in Des
Moines. Several times he was entertained in the home of
Henry C. Wallace, and the intent and keen-minded young
Henry A. became acquainted with Professor Holden and
his interest in corn.

On one occasion, Henry A. Wallace, a boy of sixteen, had
the chance to see Professor Holden judge a corn show, selecting the ten most perfect ears and rating all other entries
in order of their excellence. After Holden's remarks as
judge of the show were given, young Wallace went up to
talk to him, asking among other things how he knew whether
the blue ribbon sample would, if planted the next spring,
produce a better corn crop than the sample which had received last place.

Wallace's father joined in the discussion and listened to
Professor Holden give all the reasons why the blue ribbon
corn was not only of superior quality itself but would, if
planted, produce a better crop of corn next year than the
less perfect ten-ear samples that failed to place in the show.
The elder Wallace, seeing that his son was not entirely con-

vinced with Holden's explanation and in all probability having some misgivings himself, suggested to the youth that he take some ears from the lowest ranking ten-ear samples and plant them side by side the following spring and see what they would do. He mentioned that he would be glad to set aside as much of the ten acres of land he owned (at what is now Cottage Grove and Thirty-eighth Streets in Des Moines) as might be needed for the experiment.

Professor Holden endorsed the suggestion, and so began Henry A. Wallace's first experiment with corn. From it were to come things of much greater importance than Professor Holden or the elder Wallace could have dreamed.

Holden helped young Wallace select fifty ears in all, about twenty-five from the prize-winning ten-ear samples and a like number from the samples ranked as the poorest in the corn show. The next spring, in May of 1904, the high school boy planted by hand in ear-to-row fashion about two-thirds of the kernels from each ear. He had about three acres of corn by the time he had finished the plot in which he pitted Holden's prize-winning ears against the tailenders.

Little wonder that young Henry Wallace acquired a reputation for being different, particularly among associates of his own age. That summer when most high school juniors were working at the corner grocery to earn a little spending money or taking a summer vacation, Wallace was out working in the hot sun tending his corn plot with the aid of a single horse and a Planet Junior cultivator.

In the fall he went to his plot, shucked out each row, weighed the corn from each row separately, and made accurate comparisons for yield. The results were a revelation to Wallace and his father and a great surprise to Professor Holden. The highest yielding corn in Wallace's plot came not from one of the pretty ears in the prize winning entries, but from one of the tailend samples, an ear that was long, broad-kerneled, and which had only sixteen rows of kernels and which therefore could not win a ribbon in a corn show. The yield average of corn planted from all the prize-winning ears was lower than the average established by the ears from the lowest ranking ten-ear samples.

From that day forward, Wallace had no patience with the "pretty ear" corn shows, and he campaigned against them almost continually until they lost their significance thirty years later. After he began working with corn inbreeding and making hybrids from inbred lines, one of Wallace's delights was to take one of his inbred nubbins that had been crossed with another so that when planted it would produce a vigorous single cross hybrid and suggest to the winner of the ten-ear blue ribbon of a corn show that his runty, twisted little ear would, if planted, produce a better crop of corn the next year than the big beautiful ears in his winning corn show exhibit. In the Christmas issue of *Wallaces' Farmer* in 1919, Wallace made such a suggestion publicly, challenging Peter Lux, whose Indiana ten-ear corn sample had just won the grand champion ten-ear honors at the International Livestock Exposition in Chicago. *Wallaces' Farmer* not only made the proposition seriously but suggested that Dr. Louie Smith of the University of Illinois conduct the experiment to see which corn would produce the best crop the next year. The magazine even offered to appropriate money to meet the expenses of making such a test. The challenge was not accepted.

Wallace's repeated, hard-smashing attacks on the corn shows led to their rapid decline in Iowa and the corn belt generally. Although in recent years Wallace has conceded that the corn shows were of more value than he credited to them during the years of their supremacy, he was, from the time of his classic experiment in 1904 until they were discontinued, their bitterest and most capable enemy.

As a senior at Iowa State College in the spring of 1910, Henry Wallace read in the *American Breeders' Magazine* the address Dr. George Shull had presented at Omaha on his pure-line method of corn breeding. With his keen appreciation of the possibilities for corn improvement, Wallace found the idea in Shull's paper interesting. He didn't undertake any experiments of his own right away, but in 1913 he planted a small corn plot in his spacious Des Moines garden.

That summer Wallace did his first corn inbreeding, making a number of selfs. He also made some controlled crosses between Silver King, a Wisconsin variety, and Johnson County White, an Indiana open-pollinated corn, with which he was experimenting. He made these controlled crosses between varieties by detasselling one of them so that the other variety could receive pollen from only one source.

As Wallace's papers and letters written during this period clearly indicate, the inbreeding work done in his garden during the first World War period was nothing more than an inquiry into the nature of this type of work. It served to convince Wallace for a time that the method had little promise; it produced no inbred lines and there was only the slightest relation between it and the hybrid corn breeding Wallace was to undertake later.

Years later Wallace described and evaluated this early inbreeding work when he delivered the Spragg Memorial Address at Michigan State College in 1938. He said, "In 1913 I tried doing a little inbreeding . . . and again reached the conclusion that the process was too laborious. At that time and for several years thereafter, I was experimenting with the crossing of varieties from all parts of the United States. Oftentimes these varieties would cross to produce unusually good results, but when I tried to repeat the result the following year I oftentimes had bad luck. As a result of hard experience, my mind was forced to accept the conclusion that varieties might be uniform with respect to outward appearance and at the same time be tremendously variable with regard to genetic characteristics having to do with yield. By 1919, I had been driven completely in the arms of the East and Shull doctrines."

It was when news of Donald Jones' discovery of the double-cross hybrid reached him that Wallace began to look upon corn inbreeding and hybrids from inbred lines in a different light. On the strength of this new contact from the men who had done the work at the Connecticut Station, Wallace prepared to make a fresh and serious start on corn inbreeding and the developing of hybrids from inbred lines.

Wallace's real start came in 1919, and began when he received the old East and Hayes inbreds from the Connecticut Experiment Station and some inbreds out of Hogue's Yellow Dent from T. A. Kiesselbach of the Nebraska Experiment Station. He grew them and made his first single crosses that summer, and it was these dwarfed inbred ears on which he based his challenge to Peter Lux of Indiana in *Wallaces' Farmer.*

The work done by Wallace remained on a limited scale until 1920 when he arranged for more help and more land and began a large-scale inbreeding project to develop inbred lines from Iowa corn. In May of 1920 he received from F. D. Richey some lines that had been inbred once or twice. One of these lines was a selection from the Chinese corn, Bloody Butcher, which produced an inbred of copperish color very unlike any of the other strains of corn with which Wallace was working.

During all these early years Wallace maintained a close contact with Jones, East, and Hayes, who had made the Connecticut Experiment Station the cradle of hybrid corn. He invited Jones to write an article for *Wallaces' Farmer* describing in detail the work done at the Connecticut Station by East, Hayes, and Jones. This article appeared in 1920 and was similar to the one which Jones had written earlier for *Breeder's Gazette.* Later Wallace visited Jones in Connecticut and Hayes in Minnesota. In 1926 when East con-

ducted a round-table on population problems at the Institute
of Politics at Williamstown, Massachusetts, he invited Henry
A. Wallace to participate as one of the speakers. Some of
Wallace's friends have regarded this as the beginning of
Wallace's active participation in national affairs.

Early in 1920 while chatting with his friend, H. D. Hughes
of the Iowa State College staff, Wallace made a suggestion
of far-reaching importance. He urged the Iowa State Department of Agronomy to collect from all the corn show
exhibitors, both the winners of ribbons and those who had
been defeated, samples of their ten-ear exhibits and plant
them competitively to determine those that were the highest
yielders, the most profitable strains of corn for Iowa farmers.
The suggestion was a direct result of Wallace's deeply
entrenched distrust of the corn shows and of his own experiments with comparative yields of various strains of
corn that had their beginning back in 1904 on the plot in
which he planted Professor Holden's corn show selections.

Professor Hughes thought highly of the idea, and before
corn planting in 1920 he collected from corn show exhibitors
in central Iowa thirty samples, receiving a quart of seed
from each. That fall the harvest of the competitive plot
revealed that there were yielding differences of twenty
bushels an acre, and the long, keen-eyed farmer-selectionist,
Fred McCullogh of Belle Plaine, Iowa, had the top yield of
them all. This was the beginning of the Iowa Corn Yield Contest, later to be called the Iowa Corn Yield Test, which is
still being conducted and is regarded as the oldest corn research program of its kind in existence.

The Iowa Corn Yield Test has made two important contributions to the development of hybrid corn. First, it singled
out the strains of open-pollinated corn that were outstanding
and from which good inbreds could be developed. Later it
provided an excellent means of comparing the new hybrids

with the best of the open-pollinated strains and offered farmers a means of determining which of the new hybrids offered the greatest chance to improve corn production for them.

Hughes collected seed samples from ten-ear corn show exhibitors in the central part of Iowa and conducted a second contest in 1921, but by 1922 the merits of the corn growing contest were so obvious that the Iowa State agronomists invited farmers of all areas to participate. Since there was no way of making a direct and fair comparison between corn produced in southern Iowa and in northern Iowa, the state was divided into districts, and a gold medal was awarded the winner in each of the areas with a grand champion or sweepstakes award going to the winner who had the most outstanding record in his district.

In order that the contest in each of the districts should be carried out fairly, the college at Ames has always received all entries and immediately substituted a code number for the name of the farmer making the entry. In this way even the men who planted, cultivated, and harvested the contest plots had no means of positively identifying the various strains in the contest entries.

In the early years after harvest, samples of the winning strains, still under code number, were always laid out for public inspection in the Iowa State College Armory. This exhibition has been held in connection with the annual Farm and Home Week sponsored by Iowa State College and usually held in February. The names of the winners were not announced until the annual banquet of the Iowa Corn and Small Grain Growers Association, which has always been a feature event of the Iowa Farm and Home Week program.

Wallace entered the first of his hybrids in the Iowa Corn Yield Test in 1921, and although his first entries made a fair showing they were not outstanding. In 1922 he entered them again along with some new combinations. They made a better showing, but they were only a little better than the best open-pollinated strains.

In 1923 the tide turned. That year Wallace entered a strange-looking corn, a single cross which because of its distinctive reddish color he called "Copper Cross." Copper Cross had unusual parentage. One of the inbreds entering into it was East's old Leaming line sent to Wallace by D. F. Jones. The Leaming inbred had been selfed for more than twenty years when Wallace used it in his Copper Cross and was perhaps the most outstanding inbred in existence at that time.

The other inbred in Copper Cross, and the one which contributed the copperish color, was originally developed by F. D. Richey from the open-pollinated corn known as Bloody Butcher and brought to this country from the Orient. Richey did the first inbreeding and had selfed it two years when he turned it over to Wallace. The next year, in 1924, Copper Cross won a gold medal in the Iowa Corn Yield Test, recognized as the highest yielding corn in the important south central section. Even under its code number in the big Armory, spectators had no trouble telling that a new and strange kind of corn had won top honors.

An amusing little incident which highlighted the relationship between hybrid corn research work that had been done in New England and which was now beginning in the corn belt occurred shortly after Copper Cross was announced the winner of a gold medal in the Iowa Corn Yield Test. Donald Jones read of its success in Connecticut, and on the spur of the moment wrote a congratulatory note to Henry A. Wallace.

The letter began by calling attention to the large part the Connecticut Experiment Station had played in the victory of Copper Cross, pointing out that in addition to having supplied Wallace with most of his information about hybrid corn from inbred lines it had also contributed half of the inbreds that had entered into the gold medal hybrid. Jones ended his letter by asking if, in view of the important contributions the Connecticut Experiment Station had made to the development of Copper Cross, Wallace didn't think the gold medal might not more properly have been awarded to the Connecticut Experiment Station.

A week later a small package arrived at Donald Jones' office in New Haven. When he opened it, there was Copper Cross' gold medal won in the Iowa Corn Yield Test. Jones was so embarrassed that it took him nearly a week to compose a two-page letter in which he explained that his original letter was intended only as a humorous congratulation to Wallace and that under no circumstances could, or would, the Connecticut Experiment Station accept Copper Cross' gold medal.

Although amusing to both Jones and Wallace, there was symbolic justice in the first gold medal ever won by hybrid corn over open-pollinated having made the long trip from Iowa to Connecticut to pay its respects to the hybrid corn work done by the men at the foot of the Sleeping Giant. Its journey to New England brought into sharp focus the fact that not only Henry Wallace but every other hybrid-corn breeder in the corn belt who was to make important contributions to the development of the new kind of corn in the Mississippi Valley was in one way or another activated by the work done in Connecticut by the three men—Jones, Hayes, and East.

Copper Cross earned another distinction in 1924 when it became the first hybrid developed in the corn belt to be purchased by farmers of Iowa and elsewhere. Approximately fifteen bushels—all that was available of Copper Cross seed— was sold in the spring of 1924 at the price of $1.00 a pound, or at the rate of $56.00 a bushel. Behind the sale of Copper Cross there was an interesting story.

When Wallace visited the 1923 exhibit of the Iowa Corn Yield Test laid out in the big Armory at Ames, he took with him George Kurtzweil, a friend who was on the staff of the old Iowa Seed Company of Des Moines. Wallace had invited Kurtzweil, thinking he might be interested in distributing seed of the new hybrid corn through the Iowa Seed Company.

The two men went over the exhibits. Two or three of Wallace's new hybrids were outstanding. Wallace was explaining the miracles of hybrid corn when Kurtzweil cut in, "This is all very interesting, Henry, but what I want to know is when can we begin selling the seed?"

Wallace surprised Kurtzweil in his reply.

"Which one of the hybrids you see here would you like to sell?"

Kurtzweil suggested he would like the reddish colored hybrid, since farmers buying the seed could easily distinguish it from their other corn and make more accurate comparisons. Wallace said he had foundation inbred material to plant a one-acre seed plot, and the decision was made to produce the first commercial hybrid seed corn ever grown in Iowa.

The first contract ever drawn for the production of seed for hybrid corn gave Kurtzweil the exclusive right for all time to produce the Copper Cross hybrid, a contract which, although it hasn't been exercised for a good many years, is still one of Kurtzweil's most prized possessions.

Wallace turned the seed over to Kurtzweil. The old East Leaming inbred was used for the seed parent, and the meager supply of the Bloody Butcher line was used as the pollinator parent. Only by very sparse and careful planting was Kurtzweil able to plant the plot that measured almost one acre on a small farm owned by Kurtzweil's father, Mathias Kurtzweil, at Altoona, just east of Des Moines. The Copper Cross hybrid seed was produced in a field just north of the Altoona railroad station, well isolated from other corn.

The first detasselling of commercial hybrid seed corn in Iowa was done entirely by a woman, Ruth Kurtzweil, a sister of George. At that time she was a teacher in Puerto Rico and in more recent years has taught Spanish in Waterloo, Iowa, high school.

She was then staying with her father on the farm at Altoona. From the time the first tassels of the parent plants began to appear on the Leaming inbred, Miss Kurtzweil went up and down, pulling them out. Few fields of hybrid seed corn since have been detasselled with such care and interest. Now that producing hybrid seed corn has become such a tremendous enterprise, Miss Kurtzweil delights in calling her friends' attention to the fact that she once detasselled all the hybrid seed corn production fields in the State of Iowa.

Early in the spring of 1924 there appeared the first advertisement of hybrid seed corn ever published. The advertisement was written by Henry A. Wallace and was included in the spring catalogue of the Iowa Seed Company. The advertisement appeared under the headline, "COPPER CROSS, An Astonishing Product—Produces Astonishing Results." The description read:

"A novelty never before offered by a seedsman. The seed we send you is yellow—the corn you will harvest will be a yellow-capped copper.

"Nearly 20 years ago Dr. East, now of Harvard, began to inbreed an Illinois strain of Leaming. This inbreeding has been continued year after year by the Connecticut Station. The yield has gone down to 15 bushels per acre, and the ears are small and the kernels are misshapen. But when this inbred is crossed with another inbred, and the resulting seed is planted, startling things happen. The yield is trebled, quadrupled, and in some cases increased by seven or eightfold.

"The seed we offer here is a cross of inbred Connecticut Leaming with an inbred Bloody Butcher. This cross has been tried out in comparison with other crosses of inbred strains and has outyielded Reid Yellow Dent grown under the same conditions.

"The Iowa Seed Company is offering Copper Cross—a cross of two inbred strains—as a foretaste of what is coming in the corn breeding world. Ten years from now hundreds of crosses of this sort will be on the market.

"If you try it this year you will be among the first to experiment with this new departure, which will eventually increase the corn production of the U. S. by millions of bushels. The Iowa, Illinois, Indiana, Kansas, Connecticut and Nebraska stations are all hard at work developing inbred strains, and crossing them in the faith that they will eventually find combinations which will outyield Reid corn 20 bushels per acre on good ground. Plant Copper Cross side by side with your home grown, heaviest yielding dent corn in the central part of the Corn Belt.

"It takes long years of experimenting to develop inbred strains of corn which will combine to produce a heavy yield. We are therefore charging $1.00 a pound for the seed this year. We have only a few hundred pounds of this seed—first come, first served."

Kurtzweil's Copper Cross seed, developed by Henry Wallace, was the first hybrid seed corn ever to be advertised in a regular farm seed catalogue; the only other earlier sale of the new hybrid seed corn was the Burr-Leaming double cross hybrid seed sold by George Carter of Connecticut, which was not similarly advertised. Copper Cross was the first hybrid developed from inbreds to be produced and sold in the corn belt.

Some farmers who planted Copper Cross in 1924 continued for years to insist it was the best corn they ever raised, but being a single cross hybrid, it was subject to the weakness which made Shull's pure-line method impractical. Both the high cost of Copper Cross seed and the poor condition of its inbred parent ear prevented the hybrid from being continued or widely used.

Wallace's experiments with corn breeding, begun in garden plots in Des Moines, had been moved by degrees to farms near Des Moines in the early twenties. Mrs. Wallace had traded a southern Iowa farm for forty acres of sandy soil just northwest of Des Moines near the little town of Johnston. Mrs. Wallace and Wallace's father acquired additional land nearby so that by 1928 the land at his disposal amounted to a substantial acreage.

Wallace invited an acquaintance of long standing, Jay Newlin, to take over the direction and operation of the farm at Johnston. Newlin had his first contact with Wallace while a student at a small college in southeastern Iowa when he wrote some articles for *Wallaces' Farmer*. Later he transferred to Iowa State College, graduating in 1917. Newlin went into farm editing work on an Iowa newspaper, but soon he became closely associated with Henry Wallace in work with hybrid corn, and he is still manager of this land owned by the Wallace family.

Another of Wallace's acquaintances, Simon Casady, a real estate man in Des Moines with a farm just outside of the city, took a lot of interest in corn breeding. As early as 1922, Wallace did work on the Casady farm. Henry Wallace used to make a practice during the twenties of taking his family on alternate Sunday afternoons during the growing season to the farm at Johnston and the Casady farm so he could study his corn breeding plots. Copper Cross was developed on Casady's farm.

Some men answer their call tardily, some answer in good time, and some anticipate the call. Henry Wallace in his work with hybrid corn anticipated the call. Years before most agronomists, farm magazine editors or our corn farmers were even fully aware that hybrid corn research had been begun, Wallace already had unlimited faith in its future. From the early twenties he repeatedly voiced his faith in the new method of corn development in his personal contacts, public addresses, and through the columns of *Wallaces' Farmer*.

On January 21, 1921, Wallace spoke before the American Society of Agronomy and traced his interest in corn development from the days of Professor Holden's corn shows, saying of his later work, "When I finished college and started to work on corn improvement, I found that East, Shull, Collins, *et al.*, were much impressed with the possibilities of corn breeding." Before the address was over, Wallace made an uncompromising statement which indicated the extent to which he had come to believe in the possibilities of hybrid corn breeding: "There will eventually be as much need for special purpose corns as there is for special purpose cattle . . . when it comes to the question of the development of special purpose strains or varieties of corn, I am inclined to the view that the most certain and rapid progress can be made by developing pure strains by inbreeding and then combining inbred strains into . . . hybrids."

By the mid-twenties hardly a month passed that *Wallaces' Farmer*, in feature articles or in its widely read "Odds And Ends" column, did not point to the possibilities that Wallace saw in hybrid corn breeding. Wallace travelled frequently to the various places throughout the country where intensive work was being done, and after he had spent a few days with Holbert in Illinois, St. John in Indiana, or Kiesselbach in Nebraska, there would appear in *Wallaces' Farmer* a detailed account of the work being done on hybrid corn breeding at those points. Always apparent in these articles was Wallace's own ever-increasing faith in the new corn.

Typical of his predictions of hybrid corn glory was this statement that appeared in the mid-twenties in *Wallaces' Farmer*: "No seed company, farmer, or experiment station has any inbred seed or cross of inbred seed for sale today. The revolution has not come yet, but I am certain that it will come within ten or fifteen years." Fifteen years later ninety per cent of the corn planted in the entire corn belt was hybrid.

Wallace was so sure that hybrid corn would come that during the early twenties he was thinking about how the seed of the new kind of corn could be produced. He began thinking, as did most others from East on down, of individual farmers producing their own seed. Later he convinced himself that the job might be too complicated for the farmer to do, even the crossing of inbred lines after the corn-breeding job was done.

In his address before the American Society of Agronomy in 1921, Wallace suggested that an association be organized to carry on the breeding work and to enlist the aid of "corn crank" farmers to handle the job of crossing the inbreds into seed the farmer could plant. At this time and on many other occasions, Wallace suggested that retired farmers, even those who lived in town, might make a real contribution to this job. Wallace mentioned in one instance that the retired farmer who had good-sized garden plots in town would have excellent isolation for carrying on small-scale breeding.

As the hybrid-corn dream continued to unfold in the mid-twenties, Wallace finally saw that nothing short of a special organization with men specially trained and with special equipment could expect to provide the seed of the new corn in sufficient volume and of high enough quality to win acceptance for hybrid corn from farmers.

So in 1926 Henry Wallace, aided by his friends, Newlin and Casady, organized the first company ever to be formed exclusively for the purpose of developing strains of hybrid corn and for the production and distribution of the seed. At Wallace's suggestion the new organization was named the

"Hi-bred Corn Company," but a few years later the name was changed to the "Pioneer Hi-bred Corn Company" because the word "Hi-bred" sounded so much like the word "hybrid" which in the meantime had come into very common use.

Mrs. Wallace, who had followed Wallace's work with the new corn closely since the days he used to experiment in their Des Moines garden, now demonstrated her tremendous faith in her husband's judgment and in the future of the new kind of corn. She invested a large part of the money she had received from her family's estate in the new company. She remains to this day the owner of a much greater interest in the Pioneer Hi-bred Corn Company than any other person, and she has been handsomely rewarded for her faith and courage in contributing so much of the resources that made the first hybrid seed corn organization in Iowa a reality.

Investment in Pioneer proved to be a godsend for another of the associates whose eyes followed Henry Wallace's into the future. Casady died a few years later, leaving his wife and children a modest estate that included his stock in Pioneer Hi-bred Corn Company, which at that time and for years thereafter yielded no income or return. Mrs. Casady, however, resisted the temptation to give up the interest in Wallace's organization so highly prized by her husband at the time they sacrificed to participate in the forming of the new company. Her investment in the company now affords her a modest income which her devoted husband had so hoped to provide.

Against the background of today's operations, Pioneer's first seed crop in 1926 was miniature indeed. Wallace had got an extra season of corn breeding work done during the winter by arranging with Clyde Herring, once a senator from Iowa, to grow a winter corn crop in his greenhouse. Much of the energy and resources of the new organization in 1926 and 1927 went into the development of better hybrids.

Wallace was in contact with the other men in the country who were doing inbreeding work with corn and as often as possible he arranged to get anything which they had developed that appeared promising. Wallace realized earlier than most corn breeders that getting good inbred lines was a titanic undertaking and that he needed to enlist the aid of as many other persons as possible. He was in a strategic position to acquire a maximum number of the new inbreds since he travelled widely in his capacity as editor of *Wallaces' Farmer*.

As a corn breeder, Wallace's greatest work was done in making canny use of this material which he gathered from so many places. He carried on an intensive inbreeding program, but much of his time was spent working over inbred lines to fit them for greater usefulness and in combining them more effectively. Wallace developed one inbred that became widely used from a strain of Illinois Twin Ear open-pollinated corn. It became his own T.E.A. inbred. Richey got it from Wallace, and later issued it as Inbred BPI540, the letters standing for "Bureau of Plant Industry."

In the years immediately after the Pioneer company was formed, Wallace and his associates, Newlin and Casady, recorded some important firsts in the budding hybrid seed corn industry by designing buildings and equipment which greatly stepped up the efficiency in the production and processing of hybrid seed corn. In 1926 Newlin directed the remodelling of a chicken house on the farm at Johnston into the first forced hot air corn drier to be used exclusively for drying hybrid seed corn. The structure continued in use until it burned some years later, and its foundation still stands.

Almost as soon as this first drier was built, it was evident that a totally new type of seed corn house would have to be developed to handle the processing of hybrid seed corn in the fall as quickly as was necessary to maintain its highest quality. Casady, who had taken engineering at Leland Stanford University, took an important part in planning this structure. Always a perfectionist, he worked the plans over again and again, and even when the plant was built in 1931 he insisted that it was disgracefully inefficient and that he could design a much better one. This structure designed by Wallace and Casady was the first modern hybrid seed corn drying and processing plant ever to be built.

In the spring of 1928, Raymond Baker, a young agronomist from Iowa State College who was destined eventually to take over direction of Pioneer's corn-breeding job, joined the organization. Since the early twenties, Wallace had encouraged young farmers attending Iowa State College to take his inbred lines and cross them into single-cross hybrids or three-way crosses on their own farms throughout various parts of the state. Many of these young men entered their final crosses in the Iowa Corn Yield Test, usually making the entry under their own name as well as Wallace's, with Wallace paying the entry fee. Baker was one of these Iowa State College farm boys whose efforts gave Wallace a sort of state-wide testing and proving organization for his new hybrids.

Baker met Wallace at the exhibition of the Iowa Corn Yield Test in the early weeks of 1926. He had admired one of the new hybrids Wallace had entered in the contest, and expressed a desire to meet the magazine editor and corn breeder only to find that Wallace was standing but a few feet away. During their first visit, Wallace suggested that Baker take some inbreds and make experimental crosses on his father's farm at Beaconfield in southern Iowa.

Baker stopped in Des Moines on the way home to spend spring vacation at his parents' farm and got the seed that Wallace suggested he plant. Young Baker talked to his father about planting the special seed during May while he was still in school so that he could do the detasselling and carry on the corn-breeding experiment in the summer. His father agreed to do it, but when planting time came he was so rushed that he decided against it without consulting his son at Ames. Baker's mother, realizing how intensely interested her son was in working with Mr. Wallace, interceded and went out to the field herself and did most of the planting of the inbreds in a properly isolated place on the farm. In so doing she pried open the door to a brilliant future for her son as a hybrid-corn breeder.

That summer Raymond Baker did his first detasselling and corn breeding work. In the fall he harvested the hybrid seed, and made preparations to enter the best appearing combinations in the Iowa State Corn Growing Contest the next spring. During the winter Wallace told Baker that the inbred combinations which he had given him to cross had proved to be most unsatisfactory and that he didn't believe there would be any justification for investing the entry fee for very many of them. However, Wallace agreed to enter two of the experimental hybrids.

Baker was so disappointed in not getting a chance to enter some of the other experimental hybrids which he thought looked especially promising that he finally made one additional entry and paid the entry fee himself. Strangely enough, the hybrid in which the Iowa State College student pinned his faith won the highest honors in the southern district of the Iowa Corn Yield Test in 1927. Young Baker had a small supply of seed left, and he entered this hybrid in the 1928 Iowa Corn Yield Test. Again the experimental hybrid outyielded all other entries in the state's southern district.

Baker was in his senior year at Iowa State during the 1927–28 term. Late in the winter Wallace talked with him and suggested that he might like to come to work for Hi-bred Corn Company. Baker, who was tremendously interested in the work and who was also planning to be married soon, decided to drop out of college at the beginning of the spring quarter and accept Wallace's offer. Several years passed before he returned to Iowa State College and took the final quarter of his college work and received a degree.

The first year Baker worked under Newlin's direction on one of the farms at Johnston, but he spent a part of his time helping Wallace plant, harvest and study the hybrid corn research plots. But in the fall of 1929 when Wallace went to Europe to attend an economic conference, he asked young Baker to harvest his hybrid corn research plots and to record and evaluate the data.

From this time on Wallace was moving rapidly toward becoming a national public figure and was never again free to give enough of his time fully to direct his company's hybrid-corn breeding. In 1930, 1931, and 1932 Baker gradually assumed more and more responsibility. This gave the younger man a chance to learn from Wallace many of the things that Wallace had learned through the years by tedious trial and error, and Baker rapidly developed into one of the great hybrid-corn breeders of our time.

When President Roosevelt asked Henry A. Wallace to take the position of Secretary of Agriculture early in 1933, it marked the end of Wallace's active direction of the Pioneer Hi-bred Corn Company both in corn breeding and administrative responsibilities. Wallace's close friend and legal adviser, Fred W. Lehmann Jr., of Des Moines, was named president, and Wallace's brother, James W. Wallace, was made executive vice-president and general manager. Raymond Baker assumed full responsibility for direction of the Pioneer research program. Jay Newlin specialized in seed production and later became manager of the farms, and Nelson Urban became vice-president in charge of sales. These men have worked so effectively that their organization has earned leadership in the new hybrid-corn seed industry.

Lehmann has not only helped steer his Pioneer organization through some very difficult periods during the fifteen years since he took over the helm, but he has exerted a constructive influence throughout the entire hybrid seed industry. During the war years, Lehmann was called to serve as the first chairman of the Hybrid Corn Division of the American Seed Trade Association, and his leadership found solutions to many problems confronting this young industry which was constantly having new and unprecedented demands made upon it.

Baker realized that a tremendous responsibility and a great opportunity had been placed before him. He went furiously to work carrying on the development of better varieties of corn belt hybrids. At the time Henry Wallace went to Washington, the name of his company was little known even among Iowa farmers. As the scope of the work was expanded, Baker began adding other plant breeders to his staff. First to join him was James Weatherspoon, a biological statistician with unusual capacity as a plant breeder. Others joined Baker in rapid succession until today the Wallace organization has one of the largest hybrid-corn breeding staffs to be found anywhere, the more recent members being Perry Collins, Murray Brawner, Melvin Temple, Samuel Goodsell, William Landgren, Karl Jarvis, Ray Snyder and William L. Brown. Baker and his men built well on the foundation laid by Henry Wallace, and the hybrids they have developed have made Pioneer well known and respected in every section of the great corn belt as well as other important corn growing areas of the United States and Canada.

Another important impetus came unexpectedly to the Pioneer organization before Wallace left to take up his responsibilities in Washington and has continued to be a force through all the years since. This element was the influence of Roswell Garst—known to countless friends throughout the western corn belt and far beyond merely as "Bob."

Garst's father was one of the early merchants in Coon

Rapids, located seventy-five miles northwest of Des Moines.
Mr. Garst, a person of boundless enthusiasm, says his father
impressed upon him early in his boyhood that he should never
take "two bites at a cherry."

The Garst family owned the leading general store in
Coon Rapids and a considerable acreage of land. Bob Garst
farmed a few years early in the twenties and then for diversi-
fication, moved to Des Moines and went into the real estate
subdivision business. It was while he was in Des Moines that
he first met Henry Wallace and became interested in the
whole subject of hybrid corn.

About the same time one of Garst's fellow townsmen,
Charles Thomas, was a patient in a Des Moines hospital for
many weeks because an arm and hand had been crushed in a
cornpicker. Garst, whose sympathies have always been easily
aroused, heard about Thomas, and although he had not been
acquainted with the Thomas family while he resided in Coon
Rapids, he became a regular caller at Thomas' hospital room.

Thomas likes to recall Garst's visits and the encouragement he gave. Of it he says, "With a wife and four little
children at home, I used to get pretty far down, but Bob
would come around to see me and raise my spirits until the
future looked fairly bright again. Bob's the kind of fellow
that could convince you that if you had just lost both arms,
you'd have no trouble in making a living at all."

About this same time Garst began visiting Henry Wallace
and discussing with him the possibilities of the new hybrid
corn. Garst quickly saw the new corn's potentialities, and he
asked Charles Thomas if he wouldn't like to go into the business of producing and selling hybrid seed corn. Thomas knew
nothing of the new hybrid corn, but largely because of his
great regard for Bob Garst he said "yes."

Garst proposed to Wallace that the firm, Garst and
Thomas, undertake to produce seed for Wallace's hybrids
and sell them to farmers in the vicinity of Coon Rapids. Wal-

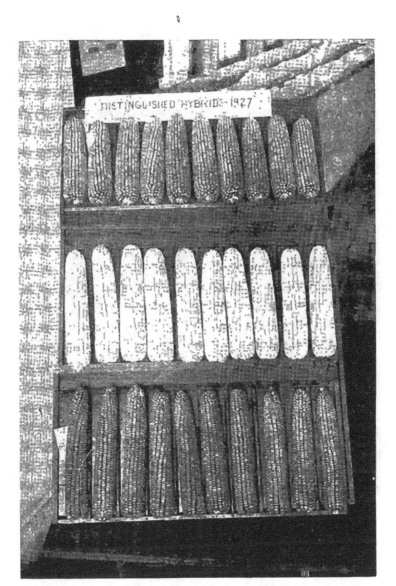

Ears of two yellow hybrids and one white hybrid on display at the 1928 Purdue University hybrid corn show, indicating the remarkable uniformity of ear that characterized even the early strains

The old open-pollinated corn, with many barren stalks,
bends over to meet the new hybrid, standing straight and
strong in spite of the big ears, on a Tennessee farm

lace, who at this time didn't expect his own Pioneer company to supply hybrid seed for farmers as far as seventy-five miles west of Des Moines, agreed, and as a result Garst and Thomas raised their first crop of seed corn in 1930, harvesting fifteen acres that first year.

Not long after Garst became interested in hybrid corn, Nelson Urban, who had been in the commercial printing department of *Wallaces' Farmer* when Henry A. Wallace was its editor, took up the job of sales director for Pioneer. Together Garst and Urban worked out ways of acquainting farmers with the advantages of the new Pioneer hybrids. At first they went out into the farm areas themselves and made every-farm-on-the-road calls until all the seed that had been produced was distributed. Then they began enlisting the aid of key farmers in various communities to help acquaint farmers with the advantages they could expect from the new hybrid corn.

It was difficult introducing the new corn, especially as farmers were bowed down under the most severe depression of modern times. "It took about four years to get a farmer to buy enough of our hybrid seed to plant his entire corn acreage," observed Garst. "The first year he would just buy a small amount, and he'd have good success with it. He would figure that this was an accident, so the next year he'd buy perhaps a bushel of the new hybrid seed. It would do well again, but still the farmer thought it was just something that had happened twice in two years. So the next season he would get enough seed to plant half his entire corn acreage. That year he would really see the difference, so the following and fourth season, he would give us his entire order," explained Garst.

Not even the drouth years of 1934 and 1936 stopped the progress entirely, and then in 1937 farmers in Iowa and elsewhere bought all the Pioneer hybrid seed that was available. In the late thirties subsidiary units were established in

Illinois, Indiana, Ohio, and elsewhere, until the Wallace organization was serving corn farmers the full length and breadth of the corn belt and Pioneer emerged as one of the leading organizations in bringing the benefits of hybrid corn to American corn farmers.

CHAPTER XI

New Victory at Tippecanoe

ANOTHER PART of the epic of hybrid corn took place in the Tippecanoe Country of central Indiana. Purdue University and its Indiana Agricultural Experiment Station are situated at Lafayette, less than ten miles south of the field where, in 1811, William Henry Harrison made himself a national hero when his frontiersmen defeated the Indians in the Battle of Tippecanoe, a victory that opened up the corn lands of the Indiana and eastern Illinois territory.

Indiana's corn farmers in the early years of this century were confronted with another problem almost as distressing to them as the fear of Indian attack that motivated Governor Harrison's march to Tippecanoe. Indiana was by this time a relatively old farming area. More than one hundred corn crops had been raised in some sections of the state, and, especially after the turn of this century, corn yields began to decline under what appeared to be a rising tide of corn diseases.

The older corn grounds of the eastern sections of the United States were all suffering from the same difficulties, and just before America entered the first World War, the Federal Department of Agriculture decided to launch an all-out attack on the problem of corn disease. Because the situation was particularly serious in Indiana, a special field station was located at Purdue University, and later others were opened in Wisconsin and on Funk Farms in Illinois to investigate and, if possible, discover solutions to this very serious problem. In some respects the Indiana station and the work done there constituted the hub of the total attack on the over-all problem of unlocking the secret of declining corn yields on America's old corn grounds. The proving and developing of the new hybrid corn came to be the key to the sweeping successes achieved there in the Land of Tippecanoe.

George N. Hoffer, a botany instructor at Purdue, was appointed in 1917 to direct the campaign against corn diseases at the special Purdue substation. Hoffer, of Pennsylvania Dutch descent, was reared in a small town not far from Harrisburg, Pennsylvania. His father's family traced its lineage back to the famous Swiss innkeeper, Andreas Hofer, who sacrificed his life to fling obstacles in the way of France's Napoleon. Hoffer's direction of young Jimmy Holbert's remarkable study of oat diseases, while Holbert was a student in his Purdue botany class, first focused upon Hoffer the attention that earned him the directorship of the substation.

Hoffer's attention had first been called to the possibilities of hybrid corn by Jim Holbert, who began his inbreeding project in the fall of 1916, but it was not until Hoffer actually made a trip in 1918 to New Haven to visit Jones and saw the amazing performance of the Burr-Leaming hybrid that the real opportunities began to unfold in his mind.

Hoffer's visit to New Haven made such a profound impression upon him that to this day he says, "So far as we are concerned in Indiana, Donald Jones is the father of hybrid corn. I know others did earlier work, but he was the first to give the new kind of corn any practical importance. It was the work he did which convinced us that we must begin corn inbreeding in Indiana."

The one quality of Jones' Burr-Leaming that impressed Hoffer most was its physiological uniformity. During the years Hoffer had been studying corn diseases, Indiana's open-pollinated corn was so lacking in uniformity of quality that it was never possible effectively to measure differences of treatment. The new hybrid corn with its dependable uniformity would, Hoffer saw, open the way to all manner of experiments that could be expected to yield many a precious bit of knowledge about problems associated with the steadily declining corn yields in Indiana.

From Jones, Hoffer secured seed of the Burr-Leaming hybrid, and the first hybrid corn ever to grow in the state of Indiana was planted on the Experiment Station's land in 1919. The hybrid was disappointing in yield and many other respects, but it pleased Hoffer, for it was uniform. Hoffer was convinced that if Jones' Burr-Leaming could be uniformly poor *under Indiana conditions,* other hybrids could be developed that would be uniformly good.

The next year, 1920, Hoffer and his earliest lieutenants, John Trost and B. H. Duddleston, launched one of the largest corn-breeding projects ever undertaken. Into this program went every type and variety of Indiana open-pollinated corn upon which Hoffer and his men could lay hand. When Donald Jones visited Indiana on his 1921 tour of all places in the United States where corn inbreeding was being done, he observed in his official report, "Probably the most extensive work is being done at the Indiana Station in cooperation with the Office of Cereal Investigations, under the direction of Dr. G. N. Hoffer. From two thousand to three thousand inbred strains are now in the second generation."

In 1922 Hoffer added to his staff two men whose work as hybrid corn breeders was, a decade and more later, to focus the attention of hybrid corn scientists and farmers across the nation on the Indiana Experiment Station. One was young Glenn Smith, who was transferred from another assignment at Purdue to specialize on breeding sweet-corn hybrids that would be less subject to the devastating diseases that plagued both sweet-corn farmers and gardeners in Indiana.

The other was Ralph R. St. John, an agronomist and plant pathologist from Kansas who belonged to the same family as the noted prohibitionist, John Pierce St. John, who was elected governor of Kansas in 1879. He was engaged to take Trost's place while Trost was in Minnesota doing graduate work. When Trost returned, St. John remained another year while Duddleston went to Cornell to do graduate work. When Duddleston decided not to return, St. John earned a permanent place on the Indiana staff and eventually took over the direction of breeding work on field corn hybrids.

During the years of work needed to develop inbreds, the early and middle twenties, Hoffer and his men were busy tackling the problem of sagging corn yields in Indiana from other angles. They conducted a long series of experiments between 1921 and 1925 in which Jones' Burr-Leaming double-cross hybrid and the Leaming and Burr White single-crosses were constantly and extensively used as testing mechanisms because of their unprecedented uniformity. H. G. Garrard, working at the Indiana Experiment Station under a fellowship provided by the National Fertilizer Association, also used Jones' hybrids, so that in all the Burr and Leaming hybrids from Connecticut made a direct and important contribution to the Indiana program of hybrid-corn breeding during these early years.

Out of all these experiments came Hoffer's discovery that corn plants are very susceptible to poisoning by iron and aluminum, which are likely to be absorbed from the soil in the absence of sufficient available potash and phosphate. Hoffer found that on poor soils increased amounts of iron and aluminum are likely to be taken into corn plants, and then these plants become easy victims of root and stalk rots. But the Connecticut Station Leaming and Burr hybrids revealed that some corn strains are more nearly able to ferret out needed phosphorus and potash even in relatively poor soil and are therefore better able to resist iron and aluminum poisoning and escape destruction by the fungi causing root and stalk rots. This difference in the capacity of some strains of corn to get extra amounts of plant food even in the poorer soils could, Hoffer believed, mean several bushels an acre increase in yields.

Eventually, the men in Indiana developed what came to be known throughout the corn country of Indiana and far beyond as the Hoffer stalk test for soil deficiencies. By cutting open the stalks and applying the proper chemicals, Hoffer could tell in a few minutes whether iron or aluminum deposits were present in the joints of the plants and what nutrients were lacking in the soil.

News of what Hoffer and his men were doing in Indiana began to circulate throughout the corn belt, and in the fall of 1924 Henry Wallace made a special thousand-mile round trip to the Tippecanoe Country to learn first-hand about the work being done there to develop poor-land corn.

In January, 1925, a detailed account of his visit was published in *Wallaces' Farmer*:

"How can we get the best corn for poor land? G. N. Hoffer of Indiana has the best answer of anyone, so far as I know. Moreover, his methods may also eventually give the highest yielding types for good land. . . Hoffer and Trost made some artificial soils, some of which had plenty of plant food to grow good corn, whereas others were all right except that they had only one-tenth of the normal amount of phosphate; others were supplied with one-tenth the normal amount of potash, and still others were short on nitrates. In each of these artificial soils, a number of inbreds were planted. Most of the inbreds went to pieces. . . The astounding thing, and the one which caused me to go to the bother of making the trip to Lafayette was that one outstanding inbred grew strongly even on the artificially starved soils. It foraged for phosphate and found it even when phosphate was present in only one-tenth of the normal amount in the soil.

"This outstanding inbred—Duddleston's No. 461 (same material from which Indiana's great Tr inbred was derived) of the Indiana Station—gives promise of furnishing one of the foundation strains of a poor-land corn. . . I saw it growing in the field near Lafayette, Indiana, and although the soil was very ordinary it was growing as vigorously as any strain of five-year selfed corn which I have ever seen.

"Hoffer's corn proposition simmers down briefly as follows: corn root rots are serious only when the plants have accumulated iron or aluminum, or both, as a result of the soil being low in such good plant foods as available phosphate and potash. Different strains of corn vary in their ability to choose good plant foods in preference to iron and aluminum. The problem of corn breeding is to find these strains, and Hoffer is doing this. . . The really new contribution which Hoffer has given is the idea of breeding a corn which will do well even though the soil is poor."

While these "poor-land" inbreds did offer new possibilities for raising corn yields on soils of low fertility, Hoffer and his men were interested in them chiefly because they believed that any hybrid able to perform on impoverished land could give a better account than other strains of corn on average or superior soils. In a sense they did their work on soils of low fertility as a means of testing the capacity of their inbreds and hybrids to ferret out plant food, and the ultimate objective was to develop strains of corn that would give superior performance on soils of all levels of fertility.

Hoffer was so much impressed with the progress being made by St. John and Trost that in an address before the National Canners' Association in Chicago he predicted that the new hybrid corn would be so uniform that it would be practical to use machine methods to harvest it, referring specifically to a sweet-corn cutting machine. Hoffer recalls now, "One man at the convention got up and branded me as the world's greatest nature faker in showing pictures of such uniform ears and stalks of corn."

This incident was representative of many that took place during this period, and they are especially interesting to persons today who never had an opportunity to see open-pollinated corn. The hybrids in use throughout the corn belt are now so generally uniform for good standing qualities that it seems odd that the corn of only a few years ago was so likely to lodge and break down in the field that cutting it with machines was not practical.

By 1925, St. John and Trost had made up a number of single-cross combinations from the new inbreds that were emerging from the big inbreeding program begun in 1920. They were now ready to see whether their single-cross hybrids could compete effectively with the open-pollinated corn being grown throughout Indiana. Dozens upon dozens of tests under actual farming conditions would be needed—but who would undertake to conduct such a state-wide testing program for them?

This was the same problem that Holbert had solved by inviting farmers who came to visit him to put out experimental plots and pit his hybrids against their own open-pollinated corn. Wallace solved it in Iowa by inviting students at Iowa State College to plant his experimental hybrids on their farms and report to him their results. Hoffer suggested that the Purdue Alumni Association, many of whose members were farming throughout Indiana, take over as one of its projects this testing of hybrid corn. The alumni organization quickly accepted.

Before corn planting time in the spring of 1926, St. John sent to twenty-five farmers seed for the new hybrid with instructions to plant it in a plot right along with their regular corn fields.

One of these first twenty-five young Indiana farmers to co-operate in making these tests of the new hybrid corn was Claude Wickard, of Camden, Indiana, the man who later became President Roosevelt's Secretary of Agriculture after Henry Wallace was nominated for the office of vice-president. Wickard tested five of the new hybrids that first year. He found that one of them was superior in yield to his own open-pollinated corn.

That fall, St. John wrote to each of the Alumni Association members who had undertaken to test the new hybrids and asked them to select a ten-ear sample by picking the ears from ten consecutive hills of their hybrid corn. He suggested that they bring these samples of the new hybrid corn with them to the Farm and Home Week festivities held annually on the Purdue campus.

Hoffer and St. John had no way of knowing how many of their co-operating farmers would attend Farm and Home Week and bring in their samples, so no preparations were made before the event to receive or display the new kind of corn. When a number of farmers appeared early the first day with their samples of the new corn, Hoffer decided that their specimens would make an interesting exhibit at the regular open-pollinated corn show, famous all over the country for its promotion of the old show type corn.

When Hoffer proposed to the officials in the Purdue University Department of Agronomy, which sponsored the regular corn show, that he would like to have a table in one corner on which to exhibit the samples of their new hybrid corn, he received a prompt and flat refusal. Although surprising, the refusal was rather easily explained. In almost every state the agronomists active at the time when the possibilities of hybrid corn were first explored dismissed the matter as fantastic. In many instances these "old guard" agronomists organized militant attacks to disprove the value of the new hybrid corn. In Indiana one of these situations developed when Purdue's Department of Agronomy, which normally might have been expected to sponsor hybrid corn development, declined to have anything to do with the work. As a result, even to the present time the work with hybrid corn at Purdue is sponsored by the Department of Botany.

After being rebuffed in his effort to put on display Indiana's first hybrid-corn exhibit in the Memorial Union Building with the regular open-pollinated corn show, Hoffer secured a room down on the first floor. All that day additional Alumni Association members who had made the first comparative field tests of hybrid corn in Indiana continued to bring in their ten-ear samples.

By evening the display was so imposing that Hoffer had a large sign painted during the night and erected the next morning at the head of the stairway directing "Farm and Home Week" visitors down to the first display of the new kind of corn. Interest among them was so great and spectators were so numerous at the hybrid-corn exhibit that it proved to be real competition for the main corn show upstairs.

The co-operation with members of the Purdue Alumni Association continued for several years until the question of the superiority of hybrid corn over the old open-pollinated corn was no longer a matter of doubt. The Department of Agronomy steadfastly refused, however, until well into the thirties to permit the new hybrid corn to be entered in their proving plots, in which various strains of open-pollinated corn were tested annually. Finally Harry Reed, at the time assistant director of the Purdue Agricultural Experiment Station, issued an ultimatum to the men in charge of the corn-proving program sponsored by the Department of Agronomy, explaining that unless they permitted hybrid corn to be tested along with open-pollinated corn in their proving plots throughout the state, he would approach each farmer on whose land the proving plots were located and secure permission to plant a plot of hybrid corn at the same location.

Under this pressure the Department of Agronomy accepted hybrid corn in its proving plots. The new kind of corn won sweeping honors in practically all of the proving plots, and from then on hybrid corn came into its own in Indiana. As John Harrison Skinner, director of the Experiment Station says, "We have inoculated Indiana farmers with many worthwhile projects such as ton-litter clubs, onion, potato and tomato clubs, but hybrid corn is one project where the inoculation really took."

The difficulties in Indiana were typical of what occurred in virtually every state in the corn belt, and it is only fair to point out that the agronomists at the experiment station were in most instances protecting what they believed to be the best interests of the corn farmers they served. In Indiana, for instance, the agronomists had worked closely for a generation with a large group of the best farmers in the state, especially those engaged in selecting superior strains of open-pollinated corn. Then suddenly a small group of young men who seemed to have little experience with corn proposed a plan of corn improvement that would sweep into disuse the corn which the agronomists and the leading farmers of the state had spent decades of work developing.

By the early thirties, the time had arrived for the first major payoff in the breeding program launched in the Tippecanoe country of Indiana in 1919 and 1920—and, for that matter, the first great economic contribution made by the new corn anywhere. Glenn Smith, a big, pleasant fellow who grew up in the Mississippi River button-factory town of Muscatine, Iowa, had joined the Indiana staff in 1922 to handle sweet-corn breeding. To this sweet-corn program, to Glenn Smith and the organization with which he worked, to the Purdue Agricultural Experiment Station, and to the

United States Department of Agriculture's Division of Cereal Crops and Diseases was to go the honor of achieving the first really sweeping victory for the movement to hybridize sweet-corn.

In 1923 the Department of Agriculture in Washington sent to the Purdue Experiment Station some 350 samples of various lots of Golden Bantam, the favorite yellow open-pollinated sweet corn, for germination testing. Hoffer's men conceived the idea of using the seed left over from the germination test to start a big program of breeding hybrid Golden Bantam. The major objective was a Golden Bantam hybrid that would yield as well as, or better than, the open-pollinated Golden Bantam and not be so susceptible to corn diseases. Some of the fungus diseases, especially the one known as Stewart's disease or bacterial wilt, were threatening to wipe out sweet corn in the Indiana area, and Indiana, then as now, was important to the canneries for commercial sweet corn.

So in 1923 Glenn Smith organized a special Golden Bantam sweet-corn breeding plot and grew some 350 rows, one row for each of the germination samples sent from Washington the winter before. As he had hoped, striking differences in the various selections became apparent as the season advanced. He eliminated a large number of the least desirable strains at the end of the first year.

Next season, in 1924, Smith made extensive plantings of the selections that survived his first year's culling, and at the pollinating season he did his first Golden Bantam inbreeding. Then began the long years of planting, inbreeding, and eliminating. By the end of the 1926 season, Smith had reduced the original 350 selections down to 6. Still he went on working patiently many a long day under a hot Tippecanoe country sun in 1927 and 1928, selecting only the best plants for further inbreeding in each of his six Golden Bantam inbred lines.

Smith had decided by 1929 that his Golden Bantam inbreds were sufficiently uniform and well established to be
trusted in hybrid combinations, and during the pollinating
season that summer he made his first Golden Bantam hybrid
crosses. They grew in 1930.

The year 1930 brought one of the most destructive epi-
demics of bacterial wilt ever experienced in the Indiana sweet-
corn territory. Glenn Smith's Golden Bantam hybrids grew
that season in a proving plot on the Wilson farm east of
Lafayette, and the bacterial wilt struck there with full force.
Then occurred what other men called a miracle. The wilt
practically wiped out the open-pollinated Golden Bantam
corn planted in the proving plot for a check. The wilt damaged many of the new hybrids, although not all. But there in
the same plot stood one or two of Smith's new Golden
Bantam hybrids that remained as completely unharmed as
though there had been no bacterial wilt in the neighborhood.
These new wilt-resistant hybrids also produced big yields of
fine sweet corn. Glenn Smith didn't say too much about it
that first year. He wanted to be sure. The next season he
planted his Golden Bantam hybrids, and the bacterial wilt
visited the area again with great destructiveness. It was true
—there were those same few hybrids standing up and producing a fine crop of sweet corn while the open-pollinated
Golden Bantam and many of the less resistant hybrid combinations suffered so severely that they would hardly have
been of any value to the sweet-corn farmers.

Then the word got around quickly to all the major areas
producing sweet corn, and experts from far and near came,
saw, and marvelled. One man from Sioux City, Iowa, was so
impressed that he insisted on having a photographer come
out and take pictures showing the open-pollinated Golden
Bantam that had been virtually destroyed by bacterial wilt
and Smith's Golden Bantam hybrid with a good crop of corn
standing right beside it. He explained that his friends and as-

sociates back in Sioux City would never believe him when he attempted to report what he had seen.

Some of the corn canners, however, doubted that Smith's hybrid would win wide acceptance. One sweet-corn processor from Michigan told Smith, "Your hybrid will never be accepted as Golden Bantam sweet corn because our Golden Bantam is an eight-rowed corn with large-sized kernels while your hybrid is twelve-rowed with a moderate-sized kernel."

Glenn Smith's new hybrid was named at a special conference attended by men from many parts of the United States. It was held in Chicago's Stevens Hotel on January 23, 1932. Despite the skeptics it was given the name of "Golden Cross Bantam." Practically every important organization in the country interested in the improvement, production, and processing of sweet corn was present for this meeting—evidence of the interest and hopes pinned on Smith's new hybrid. Besides Smith, those attending this Chicago conference were J. H. Skinner, director of the Purdue Agricultural Experiment Station; K. F. Kellerman, assistant chief of the United States Department of Agriculture's Bureau of Plant Industry; M. A. McCall, chief of the United States Department of Agriculture's Division of Cereal Crops and Diseases; H. J. Reed, assistant director of the Purdue Agricultural Experiment Station; C. G. Woodbury, National Canners' Association, Washington, D. C.; Frederick Clark and G. H. Rieman, Associated Seed Growers, New Haven, Connecticut; Willis L. Crites, Sioux City Seed Company, Sioux City, Iowa; L. A. Koritz, Midwest Canning Corporation, Rochelle, Illinois; Stuart N. Smith, Iowa Canning Company, Vinton, Iowa; and Floyd L. Winter, Hoopeston Canning Company, Hoopeston, Illinois.

Within five years after it was introduced, Golden Cross Bantam had virtually revolutionized the business of canning corn. Golden Cross Bantam put new security in the business of growing sweet corn, largely because the farmer and the processor could count on Golden Cross Bantam to produce a crop when other strains might be damaged by bacterial wilt or other common diseases of sweet corn. Even when conditions were favorable for all strains, Golden Cross Bantam yielded more tonnage, and to top all its other numerous advantages, it was uniform. All the ears in a field of Golden Cross Bantam matured at nearly the same time so that it could be harvested in one or two trips through the field, whereas many trips had to be made through fields to harvest open-pollinated sweet corn. This simplified the processing and gave Americans better quality sweet corn at less cost. Later the uniformity of its maturity and of the position of its ears permitted the introduction of mechanical harvesting equipment for sweet corn.

Within a few years after Purdue released this hybrid, seventy to eighty per cent of all the sweet corn canned in America was Glenn Smith's Golden Cross Bantam. To this day Golden Cross Bantam continues to furnish more sweet corn for canning than all other strains of yellow sweet corn combined.

Glenn Smith, now white of hair, is still working patiently with his Golden Cross Bantam, seeking to introduce additional refinements such as a deeper kernel that will ensure better quality and still greater yield, and placement of the ear a little higher on the stalk so that Golden Cross Bantam can be even more easily harvested by the newest mechanical pickers. Modestly, he says of the remarkable achievement, "Our project was well planned, and I just carried out the work as best I could. Some of it, to be sure, was monotonous, but take the job as a whole and it has been a lot of fun. I shall never cease to be thankful that we had that epidemic of bacterial wilt from 1930 until 1933, for without that bit of good luck we might never have discovered the possibilities of Golden Cross Bantam."

Other major achievements in the Indiana corn hybridization program were soon to follow the discovery of Golden Cross Bantam. By the early thirties, St. John, or "the Saint" as he was so frequently called by his associates, was in full charge of breeding field corn at the Indiana Agricultural Experiment Station. He soon demonstrated a rare combination of great technical skill as a corn breeder, a practical sense of values, appreciation of showmanship, and a great ability to get along with people. To St. John goes major credit for having followed through on the program begun by Hoffer, Duddleston, Trost, and others at Purdue University. It brought the breeding of hybrid corn to a point where the work merited the attention and respect of corn farmers. One of St. John's great contributions during the first half of the decade of the thirties was the development of Inbred WF9, the name being derived from the fact that the particular selection was first found on row number nine on the Wilson Farm. St. John and Holbert made extensive use of this great inbred not only in Indiana and Illinois hybrids; it has since made an important contribution in hybrids used in practically every state of the central corn belt.

During the late twenties and early thirties, St. John of Indiana and Jim Holbert of Illinois worked more and more closely together in a relationship which provided a full interchange of the inbred and single cross material developed at both places. As a result, a number of great new hybrids were soon to be developed both in Indiana and at the Funk Station. An example of these new Indiana hybrids was Indiana 608, into which St. John put his Indiana single cross, WF9 x Tr, along with Holbert's single cross, A x Hy. This Indiana hybrid demonstrated more quickly than all other hybrids its complete superiority over open-pollinated corn in central Indiana, the most important corn belt in the Hoosier state.

In the fall of 1935 in Fountain County, Indiana, the National Corn Husking Contest attracted a crowd estimated by

state police at 125,000. It was described as the biggest sport-
ing event ever held in the United States, as it drew more
persons than even the largest football spectacles.

Henry A. Wallace, Secretary of Agriculture, came unexpectedly from Washington and gave a short address from
the judge's stand before the contest winners were announced.
Dr. F. D. Richey had called St. John the day before the contest and asked him to meet Wallace and himself at an out-of-
the-way point on the New York Central line so that Wallace might avoid meeting the usual favor-seekers that could
be counted on at the announced place of arrival. St. John
stoked his 1927 Buick with all the gasoline and oil it would
hold, which was a considerable amount, and met Wallace and
Richey.

During the journey to the contest field, St. John told
Wallace that for the first time hybrid corn had been raised
on the field to be used for the national corn husking contest,
relating how he had planted half of the field with one of his
Indiana hybrids and the other half with one of Jim Holbert's. St. John, always one to talk with gestures, was driving
his car with a motorcycle police escort at a furious rate of
speed and carrying on a conversation with his companions,
often using one hand to emphasize his point. Then he described the ears of corn in the contest field.

"Why, Mr. Secretary, I tell you, those ears are that long."

Richey and Wallace shuddered at the sight of "the Saint"
taking both hands from the wheel of his speeding car to show
them exactly how long those ears were. St. John rode back
from the contest alone.

Contestants were present from all of the corn belt states,
and they had a field day with the new hybrid corn. Elmer
Carlson of Iowa won. The corn was so plentiful, standing so
well and so easy to husk that he shucked a net load of 41.52
bushels. His tally added more than six bushels to the former
record which had been established in old open-pollinated corn.

Before the national contest was discontinued during the war years, the record had been boosted another five bushels as hybrids continued to push yields upward.

The next year, 1936, brought the great drouth, and it proved another of St. John's new inbreds to be of all-American caliber. One of St. John's proving plots was located on the campus of the Purdue Experiment Station, so close that it could be seen from the office of Harry Reed, the Experiment Station director.

"By the middle of that terrific summer," recalls Reed, "everything in that plot was burned yellow except this one inbred. Its leaves weren't curled; it wasn't wilted. It must have had a water pump in its roots. If it hadn't been for that summer, we'd never have found Inbred 38–11."

The new 38–11 had originally been selected in a corn variety plot of the Reid type in which one important part of the parentage was the famous utility strain of open-pollinated corn, Funk's 176A. This outstanding Indiana inbred is still widely used, entering into hybrids important a thousand miles or more from the Tippecanoe country where it was developed.

By now St. John had to his credit three of the greatest inbreds—Tr, WF9, and 38–11—ever developed in state or federal experiment stations. The story of these three great inbreds is a saga in itself. Much of the field work was done on the old Tippecanoe battle grounds. St. John and his helpers paused many times in their labors to stoop down and pick up a choice flint arrow head. It is impossible adequately to trace the development of these St. John inbreds without calling attention to the co-operation which he received from other persons and other departments. Although the Department of Botany initiated the hybrid-corn breeding program, it had neither land nor farm equipment. St. John always contended that a great hybrid should be named for Daddy Aikenhead and R. H. Wileman, of the Department of Agricultural Engineering, for their help in securing the machinery and equipment needed to process the seed of inbreds and hybrids. A similar tribute is deserved by Frank King of the Department of Animal Husbandry for having made the land available for breeding the hybrid corn. These are examples of the fine co-operation that existed between these various departments, co-operation that made it possible to pay a thousandfold return on the taxpayers' dollars spent for corn research.

Fortified with its own great inbreds and those from other states such as Holbert's A and Hy, Jenkins' L317, and a number of others of great usefulness in the Indiana area, the Purdue Experiment Station soon had an outstanding line of hybrids adapted to the area from Lake Michigan on the north to the Ohio River on the south. St. John worked out many of these new hybrid combinations before he retired to join the breeding staff of the De Kalb organization in 1937. Dr. A. M. Brunson, who in the face of tremendous odds had done a fine corn-breeding job in Kansas during the drouth years, was secured to carry on the work at the Indiana Station. By the end of the decade, Indiana Experiment Station hybrids were being planted on more than half the farms of the state in addition to being used extensively outside of Indiana.

After the Purdue Alumni Association had helped with the testing of the first hybrids, its members turned their attention to the production of the inbred and foundation single cross material needed to produce seed of the Indiana Experiment Station hybrids. Eventually the alumni formed a special organization, the Agricultural Alumni Seed Improvement Association, to take over the job of increasing inbred lines and the production of foundation single crosses. This material was sold to hybrid seed corn producers interested in distributing seed of the Indiana Experiment Station hybrids.

Since this foundation takes no profit, any funds above expenses are disposed of in the form of bequests. In 1946, this organization made a gift of $100,000 to the Purdue Experiment Station, asking that the fund be used to support additional corn research in an effort to increase further Indiana farmers' profits from the state's foremost field crop.

CHAPTER XII

Successful Mission

ANOTHER BIT of ground memorable in the story of hybrid corn is to be found on the Iowa prairie at Iowa State College's experimental farms just outside of the beautiful city of Ames. Here have labored some of the most celebrated of the hybrid-corn makers—Merle T. Jenkins, A. A. Bryan, George Sprague, and others. Here have been developed fine inbreds, including Jenkins' great L317. Here was conceived the hybrid, Iowa 939, probably one of the five most used and best known strains developed during the early years of the new hybrid corn. Here grew the amazing waxy hybrid corn, pointing the way far into the future.

These achievements had their beginning when a young man named Jenkins reported for work at Iowa State College's Agricultural Experiment Station in the early spring of 1922. Merle Jenkins, although born in South Dakota, the son of a highly successful lawyer, had been reared in the fruit and wheat country of Oregon and became a hybrid-corn breeder in Iowa by a series of strange coincidences.

A few months before he finished his work in 1916 at what is now Oregon State College at Corvallis, he took an examination in hope of qualifying for a position in the U. S. Department of Agriculture. When we entered the first World War, young Jenkins volunteered and left for officers' training at the Presidio, the well known military center near San Francisco. Here he received a letter from C. P. Hartley, then in charge of the old Office of Corn Investigations, offer-

ing him a position. Jenkins informed Hartley that he was
now in the army, and Hartley replied asking Jenkins to
notify him as soon as he was out of service. Two years later,
in May, 1919, after serving as an officer in the army, Jenkins
reported at Hawarden, Iowa, just north of Sioux City and
near the South Dakota state line to work with Hugo Stoneberg.

Stoneberg was then in charge of corn improvement being
done by Hartley in the western and northern part of the corn
belt. Jenkins got along well, and late in the summer he went
alone to Piketon, Ohio, to do work on Judge VanMeter's
farm where a corn selection project was being conducted in
which Hartley took a great personal interest. That winter,
as was usually the case for all field workers on Hartley's
staff, Jenkins spent his time at the staff headquarters in
Washington, D. C.

In the fall there had occurred a memorable event that was
to exert a great influence upon Merle Jenkins and upon the
development of hybrid corn. Jenkins joined Stoneberg on a
seed harvesting trip through the northern corn belt. One day
while they were en route to the C. C. Williams farm near
Detroit, Minnesota, about 200 miles northwest of the Twin
Cities, Jenkins and Stoneberg found themselves with several
hours between trains. Although the state experiment stations then had no part in the federal work on corn improvement, Stoneberg suggested that they go out to the University
of Minnesota and have a conference with H. K. Hayes.

Hayes lost no time telling them he had little respect for
the old methods of improving corn through the Indian practices of selection such as were being employed by Hartley at
this time. Instead Hayes insisted that the corn of the future
would be hybrids developed from inbred lines. He told them
of the work E. M. East had done at Connecticut, of his own
work in the Land of the Sleeping Giant, and of Jones' discovery of the double cross hybrid. Hayes made such a strong

case for the new hybrid corn that Jenkins was immediately interested. Of this visit with Hayes in 1919, Jenkins said later, "Dr. Hayes gave us quite a talk about this new hybrid corn. It would be difficult for anyone who didn't know Hayes at this time to appreciate the effect this visit had on me. He was a powerful salesman for hybrid corn in those days. He steamed me up in just that one conference so that I decided to try my hand at inbreeding the next year."

One of the places where Hartley had a corn plot during the 1920 season was the L. A. Barry farm three miles southeast of Oconomowoc, Wisconsin. On this farm located about midway between Madison and Milwaukee in the southern part of Wisconsin, Merle Jenkins did his first corn inbreeding. He made a number of selfs on U. S. Selection 133, a strain of Minnesota 13 selected on the Barry farm under Hartley's direction. Jenkins' acquaintance with U. S. Selection 133 was significant, as he later secured one of his earliest inbred lines, Iowa Inbred 153, from it. When some years later Dr. R. A. Brink of the University of Wisconsin appealed to Jenkins for inbred material to help get Wisconsin's breeding program started, Jenkins sent him approximately one hundred early selections that had been selfed twice. Among them were selfs from Clark Yellow Dent and U. S. Selection 133, and from them Wisconsin corn-breeders developed some very useful inbreds.

During the winter in Washington Jenkins had discussed with F. D. Richey the inbreeding work which, as Hartley's assistant, he had been doing since 1916. The next spring, in April, 1921, Jenkins was given an opportunity to go to the Federal Field Station located on Funk Farms, where he spent an entire year working with Jim Holbert. Here at Bloomington, Ill., Jenkins had a chance to see Holbert's single-cross hybrids being grown on field scale as well as a number of well developed inbreds including Holbert's famous Inbred A.

Jenkins took some of Holbert's inbreds and single crosses to Iowa, where he and L. C. Burnett made some interesting experimental crosses with Henry Wallace's inbred out of Iodent, an Iowa open-pollinated strain. One hybrid involving Holbert's Inbreds A and B and the Wallace Iodent inbred outyielded the best Reid open-pollinated corn in the south-central section of the Iowa Corn Yield Test by thirty per cent.

Henry Wallace commented upon the remarkable performance of this hybrid in *Wallaces' Farmer*. "A foretaste of it [the coming of hybrid corn] was seen in the south-central section of the Iowa Corn Yield Contest last year, when a cross of three inbreds outyielded the nearest strain of Reid corn by thirty per cent. It is safe to say that if this cross had been planted in the Reid Yellow Dent territory in Iowa last year, the average farmer would have had five hundred bushels more corn and the state total would have been increased by 50,000,000 bushels.

"The story of this particular cross is interesting. Holbert, working for the United States Department of Agriculture on the root-rot problem in corn, started inbreeding work with Funk Yellow Dent, finding two vigorous strains which he called his A and B strains. Holbert found that a cross of these two strains yielded unusually well in central Illinois. Jenkins, who worked with Holbert at Bloomington, went to the Iowa station at Ames in 1922, taking with him seed of this cross.

"Burnett tells me that Holbert's A and B cross was crossed on this Inbred Iodent (Wallace's) and part of the resulting seed was planted in the Ames plot of the Iowa Corn Yield Contest in 1923. It outyielded the nearest strain of Reid by eight bushels to the acre, and so in 1924 the rest of the seed was entered in all the plots of South Central Iowa in the regular way, and this time the cross had a lead of more than ten bushels per acre over the nearest strain of

Reid. Moreover, it contained only fourteen per cent moisture as compared with nineteen for the typical Reid Strain."

In February of 1922, Richey replaced Hartley as the principal agronomist in charge of corn investigations for the United States Department of Agriculture, and his first major move was to switch the main direction of the federal program from the further development of open-pollinated corn to an inbreeding project whose objective was to hasten the coming of the new hybrid corn. Jenkins was to figure heavily in Richey's new plans.

Iowa was made the very core of Richey's new program to speed up the research work necessary to developing satisfactory hybrids for the corn belt. Until this time practically all the inbreeding that had been done in the corn belt had been done by Holbert in Illinois, Hoffer's men in Indiana, and Wallace in Iowa. Holbert and Hoffer were in charge of federal programs studying corn diseases and were not connected with the work of which Richey had charge. Wallace was, of course, working on his own and could not contribute directly to Richey's program. Therefore it was not only logical but fortunate that Richey decided to organize a new hybrid corn breeding group responsive to his leadership, a group that would be independent of all hybrid corn work already in progress.

That the hub of Richey's program should be in Iowa was a natural development for several reasons. The new Secretary of Agriculture, Henry C. Wallace, was an Iowa man. He had brought about Richey's promotion to the position held by Hartley because he felt that Richey would inject new life into the federal investigations. Furthermore, Professor H. D. Hughes, Iowa State College's respected agronomist, had been Richey's teacher at the University of Missouri, something that could be counted on to pave the way for effective co-operation at Ames. In addition, Henry A. Wallace, who had befriended Richey, could be counted on to give strong support through his associations at Iowa State College and his connections with *Wallaces' Farmer.* Since no inbreeding work had yet been done at Iowa State College, there was an opportunity to make a completely fresh start, which meant that it would be unnecessary to divide credit with anyone else for the things which might be accomplished.

With infinite care Richey and Jenkins planned the work to be done at Iowa. First, no work would be done with inbred material secured from Connecticut, Illinois, or Indiana—the only three places in the United States where corn was being inbred on a broad and aggressive basis. Second, the open-pollinated material with which Jenkins would work in Iowa was to be selected mainly from the varieties which had made the best records in the Iowa Corn Yield Test. Before planting time some five hundred ears of corn representing a wide range of open-pollinated material had been selected for inbreeding. Richey brought fifty ears of Lancaster Surecrop from his father's farm near LaSalle, Illinois, and from it Jenkins developed a great Lancaster inbred.

Always known as a hard worker, Jenkins applied himself to the job in Iowa with the zeal of an evangelist. He was working with both yellow and white corn, as the great northwestern corn-growing section of Iowa was using white corn at this time. Fortunately, his efforts were abetted by nine consecutive seasons of good weather. During these years he developed an entire series of good inbreds including L289 and L317 from the Lancaster Surecrop supplied by Richey's father; Mc401 from an Iowa Reid type of corn developed by Fred McCulloch of Belle Plaine; BL345 and 349 from Black's Yellow Dent, also a selection of Reid; OS420 and 426 from Osterland, another Iowa Reid selection; CL447 from Clark Yellow Dent; and I205 from Iodent, which was an Iowa Agricultural Experiment Station's selection of Reid.

Of these inbreds one was destined to rank among the greatest ever developed at any experiment station. This was Jenkins' L317, since bred into scores of hybrids used by farmers in almost every important corn-growing area through the central part of the United States and to a limited degree in the eastern and western states.

By 1933 Jenkins had used his inbreds to develop four hybrids for Iowa farmers. Iowa Hybrid 13 was developed for use in the southern part of the state, Iowa Hybrid 939 for the central part, Iowa Hybrid 942 for the north central, and Iowa Hybrid 931 for the northern part of Iowa.

While all of these hybrids were extensively used in Iowa, one of them, Iowa 939, was so widely used outside of the state that it became one of the great hybrids of its time and is still used in several areas. To Jenkins goes the credit for having developed the first hybrid of such wide usefulness in which all of the inbred lines were developed by a single hybrid-corn breeder. The contribution of Iowa 939 is well summed up in a statement by Dr. George Sprague, now in charge of corn breeding at the Iowa Agricultural Experiment Station.

"Iowa 939 was at one time one of the most extensively grown hybrids in America. It was grown from the Pacific to the Atlantic. Even after Iowa 939 was beginning to decline in its usefulness in Iowa, it was still used to plant half the corn acreage in the state of Ohio."

Richey had followed Jenkins' work closely and with great pride all through these golden years of achievement in Iowa, and it was only logical that when he became associate chief of the Bureau of Plant Industry in 1934 he should want Dr. Jenkins as his successor in the position of principal agronomist in charge of corn investigations. So after twelve busy and fruitful years of breeding corn on the Iowa prairie, Jenkins moved to Washington to direct the hybrid-corn research program that Richey had organized.

A. A. Bryan took over the position left by Jenkins. A native of Missouri and a graduate of the University of Missouri, Bryan had since 1922 worked with Joe L. Robinson, Secretary of the Iowa Corn and Small Grain Association, in conducting the Iowa Corn Yield Test. Always an expert in statistical methods, Bryan established the standards for practical corn testing programs, and his contribution enabled the Iowa Corn Yield Test to exert a stabilizing effect upon hybrid corn development, not only in Iowa, but throughout the entire movement.

To Dr. Bryan fell the responsibility of carrying on the work of the Iowa Station during the difficult drouth years. He expanded the search for new inbred material and made a number of other contributions before his untimely death in 1939. Bryan's research evolved the formula now widely used throughout state experiment stations for the number of replications needed to make a sound check of an experimental hybrid's usefulness. Along with Jenkins' method for predicting double cross yields, Bryan's method of replication for plots used to prove hybrid corn has enabled breeders to work much more rapidly and accurately.

Dr. George Sprague came from the Missouri Agricultural Experiment Station to Iowa College to direct the programs for breeding hybrid corn after Bryan's death. Sprague had been reared in Nebraska, had attended the University of Nebraska, and had been urged by his beloved teacher, Professor Keim, to go to Cornell and do his graduate work with Dr. R. A. Emerson. Sprague's first job was at the North Platte Substation in Nebraska, where he bred both small grain and corn. After about five years he was transferred to Washington to work with Richey. Later he went to Missouri to work with Dr. L. J. Stadler.

The best recommendation for the work Sprague has done is that the new strains which he developed at the Iowa Station have been good enough to retire the hybrids developed in the earlier years by Jenkins. With the introduction of the new hybrids released by Sprague during the war years, even the remarkable Iowa 939 has been replaced until it is raised on only a small fraction of the acreage it formerly occupied. Sprague's new hybrids have swept all the other Jenkins hybrids into the discard.

Another breeding project that focused considerable public attention upon the Iowa Agricultural Experiment Station during the war years and after has been the development of a waxy hybrid corn of commercial importance. Waxy corn, a strange mutant from the Orient, was first reported in this country by G. N. Collins of the United States Department of Agriculture, who had received a small sample from a missionary in China in March, 1908. Paul Weatherwax, noted botanist of Indiana University, whose major investigations have concerned corn, in 1922 called attention to the fact that the starch in this strange waxy corn, when treated with iodine, stained a rich violet-red rather than the blue as does the starch of other corn.

R. A. Brink, geneticist of the University of Wisconsin, began investigating the waxy character in corn in 1925. Brink and several of his associates at the University of Wisconsin, including Karl Paul Link, a biochemist, added considerably to both the knowledge and interest in waxy corn. Brink discovered that the waxy carbohydrate was not soluble in water or a ten per cent alcohol solution and therefore was not a dextrin, concluding that the substance was another form of pure starch and named it waxy starch. Brink found that there were numerous differences between the waxy starch and the starch of regular corn, observing that the waxy starch was more like the starch in tuberous plants.

In 1933 the great American corn starch industry was confronted with loss of markets because of the importation of the cheaper tapioca starch, useful not alone in tapioca pudding but in the manufacture of a long list of important products such as gums, mucilages, adhesives, wood glues, and cloth and paper sizings. In October, 1933, Dr. H. E. Barnard of the Corn Industries Research Foundation and Dr. A. P. Bryant, chief chemist and vice-president of The Clinton Company of Clinton, Iowa, visited the laboratories of Professor Link to ask if Link thought there might be a possibility of finding a way to change ordinary starch into a starch with the properties of a tuberous starch like tapioca. Link replied, "This has already been done by nature," and then showed his visitors a sample of waxy corn starch prepared not long before by Link's associate, E. W. Schoeffel. In October, 1937, G. C. Corson and A. J. Munson of the Clinton Company asked Professor Link about the possibilities of growing enough waxy corn so that pilot plant tests could be made, looking forward to production of waxy starch that could be marketed in competition with the imported tapioca.

As a result Brink and N. P. Neal, the hybrid-corn breeder, produced a ton and a half of waxy corn for the Clinton Company in 1938. One bushel of this lot was sent to the noted cereal chemist, R. M. Hixon of Iowa State College, who made exhaustive studies on it during the winter and reported to Link in April, 1939, that his studies confirmed the important conclusions reached by Link, Schoeffel and Brink. Four tons of hybrid waxy corn were produced in Wisconsin for the Clinton Company, in 1939.

Hixon's investigation into the starches of the various kinds of corn was extensive. He had asked the corn breeders at Iowa State College to get him samples of each of the different kinds of corn and in answering this request Byran and his associates had secured a bushel of each of the known types of corn—sweet, pop, flint, dent, flour, and waxy. Using the latest techniques developed in his laboratory and elsewhere, Hixon within a few weeks found that there was no important difference chemically between the starch in the five common types of corn, but that the starch of the waxy corn did differ radically from the cereal starch found in all other types. He found that the waxy starch did closely resemble the tuberous starch such as is found in tapioca.

This was not the first work that Hixon and his associates had done on the waxy corn starch. Interest in this strange type of corn at Iowa State College stemmed from the organization of the Iowa Corn Research Institute in 1934. One of its major objectives became the finding of new uses for corn. As early as 1936 Hixon had expressed the opinion that waxy corn might have commercial value, and the next winter in the greenhouse at the Beltsville Station Jenkins began transferring the waxy corn factors to the inbreds that entered into the outstanding hybrid, Iowa 939. The technique by which this was done permitted Jenkins to retain most of the desirable characteristics of the inbreds and superimpose upon them the waxy factor, which meant that the inbreds and the new waxy version of Iowa 939 maintained almost all of its characteristics except that its starch was like the carbohydrate found in tuberous plants rather than the starch usually found in corn. The external resemblance was so close that it was not possible to tell the difference between regular Iowa 939 and Waxy 939 by appearance. The first Waxy 939 yielded within ten per cent as much as the regular Iowa 939.

This work of transferring the waxy factor to Iowa 939 progressed rapidly, and by 1941 about two acres of Waxy 939 were raised by Iowa State College. By this time the Japanese were sitting astride all the important shipping lanes over which the American supply of tapioca was transported, and with the mounting tension between the two nations, it was decided that as a protective measure Iowa State College should be prepared to provide waxy hybrid

Mechanical harvesting in March with no appreciable loss is made possible by the ability of hybrid corn to stand erect long after the regular harvesting season. This western Illinois farmer was caught by bad weather, left his corn picker in the field all winter, and returned to the harvest the following spring

Charles L. Gunn and his son Ralph, the only father-son team in the hybrid corn-breeder group, with members of a handplanting crew in a De Kalb field laboratory

seed which would enable this country to expand tremendously, if need be, its production of this maize that produced starch of the same quality as tapioca.

This decision was made at Ames late in the fall, and Dr. Jenkins co-operated by devoting a large part of the greenhouse space alloted to his department at the great Beltsville, Maryland, research center to the increasing of the inbred and single-cross foundation material for the waxy corn. So anxious was he that the project have the maximum chance to progress rapidly that he spent Thanksgiving Day in 1941 planting waxy corn in the greenhouse at Beltsville. Greenhouse space at Ames was also used for the same purpose.

Two weeks later the Japs struck Pearl Harbor, and from then on the waxy hybrid-corn program became an all-out war project. Enough seed was produced in the greenhouses that winter so that forty acres of Waxy 939 seed could be grown during the 1942 season. Expansion continued during the war years, and at the end of the war no less than 20,000 acres of waxy hybrid corn were being produced by corn belt farmers. As matters developed it was not the Clinton Company but the American Maize Products Company of Roby, Indiana, that marketed the first waxy corn starch. As a result of Hixon's efforts, this Indiana company followed the necessary experimental processing and was the first to make waxy corn starch available to American industries.

More important than its commercial value is the fact that these waxy hybrids demonstrate what the modern hybrid corn breeder can do in developing special purpose crops from maize. Of these possibilities, Dr. Sprague says, "By changing the nature or percentage of the starch, protein, or oil content there are almost endless possibilities for developing new and special kinds of corn. For instance, an average bushel of corn has an oil content of about four and one-half per cent. If this could be increased to twelve per cent and at the same time retain the yield factors, corn would yield more oil and be of perhaps greater usefulness than soy beans. This, of course, may be a pretty big 'if.'

"The emphasis in the future is going to be more and more," adds Dr. Sprague, "on developing strains of corn for special purposes. I'm not at all concerned about a deficiency of problems. First, the chemist has to do his part in analyzing the problem, then the hybrid-corn breeder will have to do his part in developing plants to fit these new needs. We are now at a point where if industry will just tell us what kind of corn is needed, the techniques which have been evolved by the hybrid-corn breeder offer us an excellent chance to develop a new kind of corn to specification. Corn is so variable that I feel certain that once we fix the new objective clearly in mind, we can get the job done."

CHAPTER XIII

New Empire—in the North

IN NO STATE has the new hybrid corn registered more dramatic effect than in Wisconsin. A line drawn east and west through Lake Winnebago dividing the state about half north and south gives one a splendid opportunity to demonstrate at a glance what hybrid corn has meant here. Before the coming of hybrid corn, little if any cribbing corn was raised by Wisconsin farmers living north of that line. Even corn for silage was a hazardous crop in the northern half of Wisconsin. Today cribbing corn on farms north of the line is common rather than exceptional, and silage corn is a big and dependable crop in that area. Naturally, the benefits of the new hybrid corn have been even greater in terms of extra bushels in the great long-established corn-growing territory in the southern part of the state.

Who moved the Wisconsin corn belt north so farmers previously unable to raise enough grain to feed their live-stock could have the benefits and prosperity that are common to the American corn country? Primarily responsible are a small group of University of Wisconsin scientists— Brink, Neal, Dickson and Wright. Drawing on the pool of knowledge ferreted out by the early hybrid-corn makers, collectively these men went to work and labored tirelessly for twenty and more years until they succeeded in giving Wisconsin farmers a new kind of corn that each year adds an extra fifteen to twenty-five million dollars to the farm family income of the Badger State.

Although E. W. Lindstrom and E. D. Holden did the first corn inbreeding in Wisconsin in 1920, working with sweet corn, it was not until 1923 when Dr. R. A. Brink came to the University that a start was made in the breeding of hybrid field corn. Brink, a Canadian who had been reared in Ontario and had received his early education there, went to Harvard and took his graduate work with Edward Murray East.

In 1922, some months before he finished his work with East at Harvard, Brink accepted an offer of a position in the Department of Genetics at the University of Wisconsin. Realizing that he would be working in a state where corn was an important crop, Brink immediately wondered if hybrid-corn breeding might be inaugurated in Wisconsin. Upon finding during a visit to Wisconsin that little attention had been given the matter, Brink returned to New England determined to learn everything he could about corn hybridization before he began his work in the midwestern state.

At Harvard one of his fellow graduate students was Paul Mangelsdorf, who had much the same kind of position at the Connecticut Experiment Station as H. K. Hayes and Donald Jones had held earlier—a job that involved responsibility for breeding plants at the Connecticut Station during the spring, summer, and fall with an opportunity to do graduate work with Dr. East at Harvard in the winter.

Mangelsdorf was tremendously impressed with the new Burr-Leaming hybrid in tests against the pick of all the open-pollinated strains of corn in Connecticut. A series of continuous tests, begun by Donald Jones in 1918, showed that the new hybrid's yield was consistently twenty per cent higher than even the best open-pollinated corn. In addition, the quality was, if anything, better, and the stalk development of the hybrid was vastly superior.

At Mangelsdorf's suggestion, Brink made a trip to New Haven during the climax of the pollination season in July of 1922 to see at first hand the plant breeding being done there by Dr. Jones and his staff.

"As I think of my visit in the light of what I know now," observes Dr. Brink, "I know it was the very worst time of the year for them to have visitors, but Donald Jones took me in like a long-lost son. He gave me one of those little aprons plant breeders use in the breeding plots during the pollination season, and he took me right out to the experimental farm there at the foot of the Sleeping Giant and let me actually do some of the work myself.

"It was a great opportunity for a young fellow like myself, anxious to learn all I could about corn breeding. Jones and Mangelsdorf had a great demonstration that year of what the new hybrid corn could do. Nowhere else in the world at that time could you see the possibilities of hybrid corn laid out in front of you so dramatically. It was one of those experiences that brought you up short," Brink adds.

Brink was so impressed with Jones' Burr-Leaming hybrid that he asked for enough seed to test it in Wisconsin. The next season the Burr-Leaming hybrid added to its many other firsts the distinction of being the first double-cross hybrid ever to grow in the Bedger State. "It was beautiful," recalls Brink, "except for the smut. It smutted one hundred per cent, but otherwise it was remarkable. Each stalk stood perfectly. Its ears were large, and the over-all uniformity made an impressive sight."

Shortly after Brink arrived at the University of Wisconsin, he suggested a breeding program to develop hybrids of field corn. Professor R. A. Moore, Wisconsin's grand old man in crop improvement, who had himself fathered some of the state's most popular open-pollinated strains, affixed his signature to a memorandum one afternoon early in 1923.

"I'll never live to see anything come from this corn breeding project," he told Brink, "but I'm glad to see you taking an interest in it and this type of work being started."

A few months later Brink wrote to Merle T. Jenkins at the Iowa Experiment Station where he knew intensive hybrid breeding already had begun. Brink pointed out that the corn breeding was getting off to a late start in Wisconsin, and he ended by asking Jenkins to send him any early material which might be helpful in developing corn for Badger state farmers. Jenkins responded generously, sending Brink no less than one hundred lines that had been selfed twice. One of them was a selection from an early Reid-type of yellow dent, the original material of which was supplied for Jenkins' program by an Ackley, Iowa, farmer using Osterlund's open-pollinated corn. From it Wisconsin hybrid-corn breeders developed their great R3 inbred, one of the greatest ever discovered for the northern United States and Canadian corn belts.

On April 4, 1925, the University of Wisconsin's hybrid-corn program was reorganized and made a co-operative undertaking of the Departments of Agronomy, Pathology, and Genetics. Wisconsin's noted pathologist, Dr. James G. Dickson, was by this time taking a great interest in the new project. His own work had often taken him to the Federal Field Station on Funk Farms where he had observed the work being done by Jim Holbert and his staff. Dickson and Holbert worked on a number of pathological corn studies, and through this relationship Dickson came to appreciate the possibilities of corn and the techniques and practices of the successful breeder. Thus Dr. Dickson was able to make an important and immediate contribution to the breeding program in Wisconsin. The fine spirit of teamwork that developed between the three sponsoring departments—agronomy, pathology, and genetics—resulted in rapid progress at Madison in the developing of hybrid corn.

In May of 1926, Norman P. Neal, aged twenty-nine, stepped off an ocean liner at San Francisco after making a six-thousand-mile voyage from his home in New Zealand. Although he had never seen a field of corn, he was to become one of the foremost members of the small group of great hybrid-corn makers.

Neal was interested in pasture improvement work. The very life of New Zealand rests upon a pasture economy. Neal's undergraduate college work had convinced him that by applying the newest concepts of plant breeding, soil improvement, and land management, the pastures of his native land could be developed to a new state of productivity, but he could find no university in either New Zealand or Australia where such a study could be made. He knew that Wisconsin was the great dairy state in America, and he decided to come to the United States and do his graduate work at Madison.

Like most foreigners, Neal was impressed with the vast stretches devoted to corn as he crossed Nebraska, Iowa, and Illinois in the spring of 1926. He arrived at Madison and the University of Wisconsin in June and took a job testing cows during his first summer in America.

In the fall he began his graduate work at the University, and Dr. R. A. Brink was designated as his faculty adviser. Brink told him in detail of the things he had learned from East at Harvard and from Jones at the Connecticut Experiment Station in New Haven.

Neal's interest in corn breeding was kindled by these contacts with Brink, but there is little reason to believe that the New Zealander would have forsaken his interest in pasture study had it not been for another development in the summer of 1927. Wanting to earn money to pay for his graduate work, Neal accepted an opportunity called to his attention by Brink, to work in the corn-breeding plots. This was Neal's first close contact with America's great cereal crop, and he spent the summer working merely as a field laborer.

By fall, however, Neal had shown such interest and aptitude that the interdepartmental executive committee directing hybrid-corn work named the young man from New

Zealand a graduate student assistant for Wisconsin's corn
program. The first position of this type on the program had
been held by P. H. Senn, now on the staff at the University of
Florida.

With the coming of Purnell funds in 1925, making available greater support from the federal government, the work
of breeding hybrid corn was expanded in Wisconsin. All of
the open-pollinated strains used in the state and throughout
the northern United States farming territory were entered
in the Madison breeding plots. These were the years when
the new inbred lines for the north country were being developed, and the work went on ceaselessly and always on an
increasing scale.

In 1931 Norman Neal was given the complete responsibility for executing the Wisconsin corn-breeding program
outlined by the interdepartmental executive committee. During the 1931 season plans were completed for producing the
first Wisconsin hybrid that would be offered for regular farm
use. Neal had made up a number of single and three-way
crosses in 1929 and had tested them in 1930. One three-way
cross was especially promising, and one acre of seed was
produced in 1931. All of the seed harvested was parcelled
out to southern and central Wisconsin farmers for testing in
the 1932 season.

This first Wisconsin hybrid, Wisconsin 550, was so good a
hybrid that corn farmers continued to demand it for several
years, something unusual for the first hybrid produced in a
corn-breeding program.

The time for a full blossoming of Wisconsin's program was
close. In 1933 seven hybrids were released, and seed fields
totalling eighteen and three-fourths acres were used to produce hybrid seed for regular farm use.

Not long after the release of the first hybrids from the
University, Neal and all the persons at Madison concerned
with the hybrid-corn program found a great friend and ally

in a good-natured young man who since 1929 had been on
the staff of the branch experiment stations in the extreme
northern part of the state. A. M. Strommen had been reared
in the northern part of the state, and after attending the
University of Wisconsin he sought and received an appoint-
ment that permitted him to return to that part of the state
which he loves best.

To Strommen fell the task of taking up the work of an
unusually worthy predecessor, E. J. Delwiche. Delwiche, always alert to new developments in agriculture, had read the
reports of the earliest workers with corn hybrids and was
especially impressed with Jones' articles describing the Burr-
Leaming double-cross. He began inbreeding experiments in
1923, the same year that Brink inaugurated the field-corn
breeding at Madison. Delwiche's work was done at the University's branch experiment station at Spooner, Wisconsin,
located in the extreme northwestern part of the state about
one hundred miles northeast of St. Paul, Minnesota. He
worked entirely with an open-pollinated strain, Wisconsin 25,
and from it secured some fine inbred material, although not
enough to make an effective double-cross hybrid.

Then by using material from experiment stations located
farther south, along with inbreds developed at Spooner,
Strommen was in a position by 1939 to release his first hybrid adapted for northern Wisconsin. Previously, much of
the corn used by farmers in this region was scanty in yield,
and some of it closely resembled the corn raised there years
before by the Indians. As the corn-breeding program at
Madison began to produce results, Strommen took full advantage of the opportunity to synchronize his work closely
with that of Neal. By the early forties, he had demonstrated
that the new hybrids could increase corn yields in the
Spooner area from twenty to thirty per cent, and in addition
could afford northern farmers an expanded use for corn and
a more certain supply as well.

Next the University of Wisconsin faced the same problem that had confronted every state experiment station when its breeding program had developed hybrids that could be of value to farmers in general. How could the fruits of hybrid-corn research be made available to farmers; how and by whom would the seed for the new Wisconsin hybrids be produced?

The executive committee, with the counsel of farmers and the seed trade, painstakingly worked out an answer that differed in many respects from that developed in any other state. For many years Professor R. A. Moore had emphasized the need of a maximum of opportunity for the farmers of the state, especially the farm youths, to take an active interest in the work of the state's College of Agriculture and Experiment Station. As early as 1885 Dean W. A. Henry inaugurated a special winter short course, probably the first project of its kind to be undertaken by any American university, that enabled farm boys to come to Madison for a few weeks during the off-season of farm work and study the latest experiments being conducted by the University. Moore had directed this winter short course for many years.

Thinking in terms of this philosophy, the interdepartmental executive committee developed a program by which individual farmers, and especially young farmers, would be encouraged to handle the job of producing seed of the new hybrid corn in Wisconsin. These policies were worked out in the darkest years of the depression, and the executive committee foresaw that production of hybrid seed could give a considerable number of farmers an opportunity for increasing their farm income.

In order to supply these farmers with material, the University of Wisconsin assumed responsibility for growing, processing, and distributing foundation seed stocks. The University also worked out a careful system for producing and processing the hybrid seed grown by the farmers throughout the state. The interest of the ultimate user was protected through a system of official certification of seed which provided for inspection closely supervised by the University of the important steps in the production and processing of the hybrid seed corn. The system was eventually extended to other farm seeds and continues in operation to this day.

The man most responsible for developing this Wisconsin system of seed corn certification was Andrew H. Wright, better known to personal acquaintances throughout several states and Canada as "Andy Wright." Wright not only grasped the full meaning and importance of the University's policy to encourage a greater interdependency between the farmers of Wisconsin and the College of Agriculture, but he worked out the administrative procedures and even devised and invented special machines which would make it possible for the individual farmer to produce seed for hybrid corn of high quality as a small-farm operation.

After the details of the seed certification program were fully developed, the state legislature of Wisconsin wrote the entire plan into state law so that the producers of all hybrid seed corn licensed for sale in Wisconsin could have the same general standards. The plan made it possible for the private producers of hybrid seed who wished to operate in the state to enjoy the same advantages as those who produced the hybrids developed by the University of Wisconsin.

This Wisconsin system has brought about many constructive developments. It has provided Wisconsin farmers with hybrid seed corn of a high uniform quality. It has helped a large number of farmers to participate in the highly technical job of producing hybrid seed corn. Perhaps best of all the Wisconsin system has effectively promoted that closer relationship between the College of Agriculture and the farmers of the state as has no other project ever undertaken by the University.

As the decade of the thirties passed, the corn program in Wisconsin was continually expanded. Inbreds developed with the Purnell funds in the late twenties were now coming into their greatest usefulness, but Neal and Strommen didn't stop there. They drew upon all of the inbred material developed at the other experiment stations, combining it with their own material in every conceivable pattern. Strommen even devised special tchniques for injecting some fine qualities of the inbreds of the central corn belt into his own inbred lines developed at Spooner. Dr. Brink made a survey of the source of germ plasm in Wisconsin hybrids in 1945 and found that only fifty-three per cent of the germ plasm in the entire list of Wisconsin hybrids had been developed by Neal, Strommen, and their associates, whereas forty-seven per cent of the germ plasm had come from breeders outside the state. Dr. Neal never lost an opportunity to pay tribute to the help which his Wisconsin program has received from other state and federal experiment stations.

American and Canadian farmers were quick to appreciate the value of these new hybrids. Each year seed acreage was increased by 1,000 to 5,000 acres, but a dozen years passed before it was possible to build up the supply of the new hybrids to a point where there was a reasonable balance with the demand.

In one war year, 1944, Wisconsin hybrids grew on nearly ten million acres of land in the northern United States and Canada, many of these acres representing land that might not otherwise have been planted to corn. That year farmers in Wisconsin planted more than a score of different strains of hybrid corn developed either at Madison or Spooner on an acreage that represented a 500,000-acre increase over prewar years. In addition, the departments of agriculture in eight other states and in Canada recommended one or more Wisconsin hybrids to farmers of their region. In Oregon four of the Neal-Strommen hybrids were approved, in Colorado five, in Michigan four, in North Dakota four, in New York ten, in Minnesota seven, in Pennsylvania three, and in Maine one. Canadian officials recommended thirteen Wisconsin hybrids to their Canadian farmers.

In the war years, when food was the first requirement of victory, the new Wisconsin hybrids enabled tens of thousands of farmers to grow corn who had never raised corn in volume before. They sent it to the war fronts and the home fronts of the Allied nations as a precious high-energy food like cheese, pork, milk, butter, and eggs. The effect on the Allied cause was like the sudden and unexpected discovery of a new food-producing nation or continent, one which helped tip the scales where total victory and total defeat were balanced.

Now the new hybrid corn developed by the men at Madison and Spooner has been converted into an instrument of peace. This new corn now has as its principal objective the erecting of a more stable and more prosperous agriculture in those regions where only a few years ago the summers were too short to permit farmers to have the full blessings of the maize plant.

The Story of De Kalb

TOM ROBERTS had a problem. He was the county agricultural agent, or farm adviser, of the De Kalb County Farm Bureau. His organization was soon to hold its 1923 summer picnic in the town of De Kalb, and he still had no speaker to deliver the address of the day.

Then an idea struck him. The new Secretary of Agriculture in the Harding cabinet, Henry C. Wallace, must, thought Roberts, go back and forth between Washington and his home in Iowa occasionally. In all probability he travelled through De Kalb on the Northwestern Railroad.

So Tom Roberts, whose friends insist that he was never known to lack resourcefulness, wrote the Secretary of Agriculture, and Wallace accepted. On the appointed day Wallace came. Roberts admits he doesn't remember what the Secretary of Agriculture told the large audience that day, but he does remember almost every sentence of a conversation that took place in his office later while Wallace was waiting for his train.

Charlie Gunn, who took a particular interest in corn improvement for the De Kalb County area, was there. In the course of Wallace's visit Roberts told him of the corn show that the De Kalb Farm Bureau sponsored each winter, and he brought out one of the prize-winning ten-ear entries.

After admiring the corn, Wallace said that in his office in Washington he had some small, twisted nubbins that could produce a bigger yield of corn than would the blue ribbon ten-ear sample. He explained that these small runty ears were a new hybrid corn that in time would enable farmers in the corn belt to increase corn productivity above anything known.

Secretary Wallace went on his way, but Tom Roberts and Charlie Gunn kept right on thinking of what he had said about the future of this new corn. They were confronted by a difficult situation, and this new kind of corn might be just the thing for which they were looking.

William C. Eckhardt, soils expert from the University of Illinois and former associate of Dr. Cyril G. Hopkins, had come to De Kalb County as its first agricultural adviser in 1912. Five years later he helped organize the De Kalb Agricultural Association, whose major function was to supply farmers of the county with good farm seeds. Eckhardt himself had induced Charlie Gunn to give up running a ranch in Colorado to take over the securing, testing, and improvement of field seeds that the new De Kalb Agricultural Association would supply northern Illinois farmers. Much of Gunn's time had been spent developing better corn.

Eckhardt resigned as De Kalb's farm adviser during the first World War to take a position in Chicago, but in 1921 he returned to De Kalb County and established a farm seed business in direct competition with the De Kalb Agricultural Association which he had helped organize only five years before.

Roberts and Gunn realized that this could become a struggle to the death for the De Kalb Agricultural Association, for Eckhardt would naturally draw most of his business from his De Kalb County farmer friends, the same men whom he had previously urged to ask the De Kalb Agricultural Association for farm seeds. They realized that the real battle would center on seed corn, upon which the De Kalb Agricultural Association depended for support more than on any other type of farm seed.

So Roberts suggested to Charlie Gunn that this new hybrid corn might give the De Kalb Agricultural Association a seed corn so much better that it could effectively meet Eckhardt's competition. Roberts' words fell on fertile ground. Gunn not only agreed with him but immediately began making plans to put the suggestion into effect.

At once developments began which were to establish the town of De Kalb on the prairie sixty miles west of Chicago as the home of an organization whose efforts are unmatched in making the new kind of corn available to American and Canadian corn farmers. Built largely upon Gunn's ability as a hybrid-corn breeder and Roberts' rare capacity for directing the production and distribution of seed, De Kalb has come to represent hybrid corn to more farmers than has any other name.

The achievement of Charlie Gunn is without a close parallel in all the story of hybrid corn. Unlike practically all of the other hybrid-corn breeders who received special college or university training, Gunn had only his thorough knowledge of practical corn belt farming and his years of work with open-pollinated corn to prepare him for his career as a hybrid-corn breeder. He was born in 1886 on a farm near McNabb, a small town in the Illinois River valley forty miles northeast of Peoria, Illinois. When he was nineteen, he went to work for Walter Griffith, a close friend of Gene Funk and James Reid, one of the foremost corn show judges of this time and owner of a thriving seed business. Gunn's time during much of the year was spent selecting corn for seed purposes. Griffith would raise all the seed corn he could on his own farms, but when the demand exceeded his own supply, he would locate a good commercial field of his type of corn and select from it ears good enough to be used for seed.

Young Gunn's job was to give each of these ears the "jack-knife" test, which consisted of taking five kernels from each and cutting them open to see if the germ was in good condition. The ears which passed the test were sent to Griffith's customers unshelled and packed in wooden boxes, since many farmers raising open-pollinated corn preferred to pay slightly more to receive the seed on the ear so they could judge more accurately the kind of corn they were to plant. Unshapely ears that passed the jackknife test were shelled and sold as shelled seed for a dollar less per bushel. From his job and his association with Griffith, Charlie Gunn acquired a thorough education in merchandising open-pollinated seed corn.

After working with Griffith for several years, Gunn went to western Colorado to operate a ranch. Chief crops on his ranch were corn, potatoes, wheat, and sweet clover. Gunn introduced sweet clover into that area, and raised it as a crop even though most of his neighbors regarded it as a weed. In 1917, after the Gunns had been in Colorado four years, they came back to Illinois to spend a vacation at McNabb. They also attended a Prairie Farmer picnic at Ottawa. Here Gunn met Eckhardt, the De Kalb county agent, who told Gunn that the De Kalb Agricultural Association had been recently organized and described the work it was intended to do. He ended by urging Gunn to give up his interests in Colorado and join the staff of the new seed organization in De Kalb. Gunn sometimes wonders what his life would have been like if he hadn't attended that picnic in Ottawa that summer day in 1917.

Eckhardt had a keen appreciation even before Gunn came to De Kalb County of the need for improving corn. He had already introduced Western Plowman from Will County, Illinois, a hundred miles southeast of De Kalb. This new strain of corn matured a little too late for the De Kalb area, but it had so many fine qualities that one of Gunn's first assignments was to develop an earlier variety of Western Plowman. His work with Griffith prepared him well for this task, and he laid out a program of selection that within a year or two was showing definite results.

Gunn was not satisfied merely to develop an earlier variety of Western Plowman. He was also determined to have the new strain more resistant to disease. He soon discovered that the corn he had developed was more nearly free from disease and had slender, smooth ears unlike the old, rough show corn. The result was that Gunn developed a high-yielding utility corn that became known throughout northern Illinois as Gunn's Western Plowman. From this strain he later secured one of De Kalb's best inbreds, giving even greater importance to this first open-pollinated corn for the De Kalb Agricul-°tural Association.

When Roberts and Gunn decided that the new hybrid corn might be very useful in meeting the competition of Eckhardt's seed business, they also decided that the breeding should be done in complete secrecy for as long as possible. Gunn realized that developing the new hybrid would be a long job at best. He estimated that at least ten years would be required.

Secrecy would have several advantages. The possibilities of hybrid corn were untried and uncertain, and should the work come to nothing, there would be no necessity to explain the failure. If, on the other hand, the hybrids succeeded, the investigators would gain at least a few years' start on Eckhardt if they worked in secrecy.

As matters developed, the strategy worked perfectly. From the time Secretary Wallace first emphasized the possibilities of breeding hybrid corn until the summer of 1928, only Gunn, Roberts, and Gunns' chief helper, Orton L. Bell, knew of the corn-breeding being conducted. They all participated, doing much of the work on their personal time.

Orton Bell's connection deserves some explaining. He was .

sixty years old and a retired farmer in 1920 when Gunn asked him if he would like to help with some experimental plots which were then devoted largely to improving Western Plowman. Bell proved to be a most trustworthy and discreet assistant to Gunn.

For twenty-five years Bell continued as Gunn's assistant— no mean achievement for a man who began his job at sixty. When he retired in 1945 at the age of eighty-five, Mr. Bell received a gift of several thousand dollars from the organization he had served so well.

Mr. Bell was never sensitive about his age. On the contrary he liked to make a point of it. He put humor and sparkle into many a difficult situation during the tedious years when Gunn was meeting the inevitable disappointments of the hybrid-corn breeder. Bell's standard remarked in such a situation was, "Come on, Charlie, let's get going. I don't want this hybrid corn to be just something for the future. I want to see it in my time."

By the time Roberts and Gunn had definitely decided to begin a program for breeding hybrid corn, the 1924 growing season was too far advanced to make a start that year. The men put the season to good use, however, by visiting state and federal experiment stations where hybrid corn was being bred. Gunn was especially anxious to learn as much as he could about the procedures and techniques which were being used by such men as Hoffer in Indiana, Holbert in Illinois, and Jenkins in Iowa. In the course of these visits, Gunn also collected as much inbred material as was available.

This inbred material given to Mr. Gunn had been developed in central Indiana, central Illinois, and central Iowa. Unfortunately Gunn discovered later that these experiment station inbreds matured too late for the northern Illinois area. Very soon it became clear that it would be necessary to develop his own inbred lines, and with this fact in mind he steadily increased his program of inbreeding until within a few seasons he was working with very large numbers of plants.

In May, 1925, Gunn laid out and planted his first hybrid corn breeding plot on the J. J. Kingsley farm a mile and one-half west of De Kalb. Fred Conners, the operator of the farm, reserved a garden plot of about one acre for Mr. Gunn's use. In it Gunn and Bell planted forty varieties of open-pollinated corn and the inbreds Gunn and Roberts had received from the state experiment stations the season before.

The following year Gunn's inbreeding plot was located on another farm near De Kalb. During the years when the inbreeding work was being secretly conducted, the inbreeding plot was moved to a different farm each year. Each year the inbreeding plot became larger and required more ground.

In each of these early years, Gunn added from thirty to fifty new strains and varieties to be subjected to inbreeding. William Webb, of Plainfield, who had developed the original Western Plowman open-pollinated strain in Will County, Illinois, came to De Kalb to judge the farm bureau's winter corn show early in 1925. He brought with him an ear which he regarded as a standard of perfection for his strain and presented it to Mr. Gunn after the show. From this ear Gunn was able to develop an outstanding inbred. He was so impressed with it during the first two years of inbreeding that he made a trip to Mr. Webb's farm just west of Plainfield and bought a dozen ears, paying fifty cents each. Not one of them ever yielded anything of significance.

By the middle of the 1928 growing season, Gunn and Roberts were convinced that their program was going to yield results, and they decided that the time had come to break the secrecy that had been maintained for more than four years. During late summer and fall, they took the members of the board of directors of the De Kalb Agricultural

Association to see the inbreeding plot and explained its objectives. With but one exception, the members of the board heartily concurred with what had been done. One member of the board, however, was critical of the way the matter had been handled. He resigned.

At Farm and Home Week held at the University of Illinois early in 1929, Gunn had a chance to visit with Jim Holbert and talk over the work they had been doing at De Kalb. Holbert agreed to come to De Kalb the next season and look over the inbred lines and make any suggestions which might occur to him. Holbert did visit Gunn and inspect his hybrid corn breeding plots at De Kalb that summer and each season as long as Holbert remained a federal agronomist, placing at Gunn's disposal everything from his long experience.

Two or three times each season Gunn would visit Holbert in Bloomington and inspect his breeding plots on Funk Farms. One of those unusual individuals who can get along with a minimum of sleep, Gunn would, many times during the early thirties, get up at three in the morning, drive his Model A Ford the one hundred and twenty miles to Bloomington in time to have breakfast with Holbert, spend the day studying his hybrid corn material, and then drive back to De Kalb.

While the advantages to Mr. Gunn and the De Kalb breeding program were obvious, the advantages to Holbert were also numerous. Speaking of this work Holbert says, "My contacts with Charlie Gunn and Tom Roberts while I was working in the United States Department of Agriculture were most stimulating and challenging. First, the inbreds with which Mr. Gunn was working were new to me since they were for the most part lines of his own development.

"Here, as I saw it then, was a golden opportunity to help set up a series of evaluation tests that called for new ideas and new plans which, if proved successful, would advance the practical use of hybrid corn by many years in our important northern Illinois corn growing area. This area, of greatest interest to Mr. Gunn, was between the influences exerted by the Central Corn Belt Experiment Stations and those considerably farther north."

The most discouraging thing to Charlie Gunn from 1925 until 1930 was the very few inbreds that were being developed. Although he had placed from thirty to fifty new open-pollinated entries in his hybrid corn breeding plot in each of these early years, he wrote in his pedigree book before planting time in 1929: "Not enough inbreds yet to make a quadruple cross."

Jim Holbert made a number of suggestions that solved this problem, at least for the time. He proposed to Gunn that he use some of the experiment station inbreds, admittedly too late in maturity, with Gunn's own earlier inbreds and see if the resulting hybrid might not be early enough to use in northern Illinois. Gunn was immediately impressed with the possibilities of Holbert's proposals, and as a result the De Kalb hybrid corn research program was greatly accelerated in 1931. Holbert recalled these developments years later:

"Together we blueprinted the necessary crosses for testing purposes, using Gunn's inbreds and the most promising of all other available inbred lines. Gunn and his assistants did the work systematically, thoroughly and aggressively. Field test results of these hundreds of single cross hybrids and three-way cross hybrids in the 1932 and 1933 seasons were most revealing. These tests gave us reason to believe that a few of the combinations would be definitely better for northern Illinois farmers than the open-pollinated corn they were then using. Tom Roberts, who, although he did not participate in the corn breeding work, always followed every development with keen interest, looked over our tests. Then he looked up and said, 'If you and Gunn have that much confidence in those figures, why not produce them?'

"Fortunately, it was possible to begin production of one of the promising three-way cross hybrids very quickly — possible because Mr. Gunn operated on a basis that was new to me at that time. He always started to increase inbred lines and all single crosses that had even a remote possibility of being useful, at the same time he began testing the experimental hybrids. Mr. Gunn never considered that he had any foundation seed until he could figure his supply in bushels. He just never was a 'packet-quantity' corn breeder.

"Gunn always took advantage of his opportunities promptly and to the fullest extent. I remember one incident which illustrated Gunn's capacities in this respect. En route to do the planting of one of our experimental field plots in Northern Illinois, I paid Mr. Gunn a surprise visit and left with him some one- and two-pound samples of seed of some inbreds and single crosses which I thought might be useful in his hybrid-corn breeding program. Late that afternoon on the way back, I stopped at his office and to my surprise he invited me to go out and see the new isolation plots planted with the seed I had given him only that morning. We got in his car and drove out to see them. They were located in a large area devoted to the growing of peas for the canning factory nearby. The necessary small plots in the pea fields had been disced up, the seed bed prepared and the little increase plots were already planted."

De Kalb's first hybrid seed corn for farmers was produced in 1934. In this very first year Roberts and his De Kalb organization demonstrated their aggressiveness and faith in the new hybrid corn. Under the circumstances a five- or ten-acre field of seed for the first year's production might have been considered by many an adequate start, but not Tom Roberts. That very first year De Kalb planted seventy-five acres which with normal yields would have provided well over two thousand bushels of seed.

Here was a factor coming into play that was to be as great as the hybrid-corn breeding done by Charlie Gunn. Roberts' unquestioning faith in the value of hybrid corn to corn belt farmers, his determination to let nothing stand in the way of bringing the new corn to just as many farmers just as soon as possible was from the first season in 1934 without a close parallel anywhere in the story of hybrid corn. Gunn's research and Roberts' capacity to make this research available in the form of hybrid seed to a maximum number of farmers in an unbelievably short time have made the name De Kalb among the greatest to be associated with hybrid corn.

In 1934 the De Kalb Agricultural Association had no farms of its own on which hybrid seed could be produced. Roberts didn't like to ask any of his numerous friends to take the unknown risks involved in producing the seed, so he turned over practically the entire corn acreage on a farm that he and Mrs. Roberts owned to produce De Kalb's first hybrid seed crop. This proved to be a wise move.

The seventy-five acres of hybrid seed were planted in mid-May. The spring had been unusually dry, an indication of things to come. Ironically, the rains stopped right with the planting of the fields. There was no rain of consequence on the seed field from May 15 until August 15. Gunn and Roberts watched their ten-acre hybrid corn breeding plot and their seventy-five seed production acres swelter and wither under the combined forces of drouth and heat, for the drouth was accompanied by record temperature. By July 10 they realized that unless moisture was provided during the tasselling season, they were going to lose everything. Being unanimous in the belief that good fortune is always on the side of those who help themselves, Gunn and Roberts decided to do their best to provide some of the moisture that nature was so ruthlessly withholding.

Roberts located an old milk truck and pressed it into service hauling water to the small breeding plot and to the large production field. The water was brought from an old gravel pit a mile and a half away. Between July 15 and August 15, when the rain came, the old milk truck worked on an around-the-clock schedule hauling tens of thousands of gallons of water to keep the drouth from overwhelming the new hybrid corn in the De Kalb plots.

These desperate efforts to stave off the effects of drouth and heat met with some victory and some defeat. Gunn managed to save his small hybrid corn breeding plot with its precious store of new inbreds from which would come the great De Kalb hybrids of the future. Roberts hardly made a dent in the job of watering the seventy-five acres in seed production. That fall the harvest yielded a mere trickle of the seed which might have been expected under normal weather conditions. In all, De Kalb seedsmen got only 325 bushels of corn and hundreds upon hundreds of bushels of cobs. The seed was sold at fifteen dollars a bushel to farmers, most of them in De Kalb county.

One might have expected the men at De Kalb to be a little more conservative in planning their seed production for the 1935 season in view of the 1934 disaster. But again Roberts asserted the aggressiveness and willingness to take sweeping chances to achieve a maximum exploitation of the new hybrid corn's possibilities, planting 310 acres to hybrid seed production on a farm near De Kalb. Dr. Merle Jenkins, director of corn investigations for the United States Department of Agriculture, called it the largest field for producing the seed of hybrid corn ever called to his attention up to that time. There have been few as large since.

This large production was devoted to an entirely new

hybrid—another that had come out of the big program to combine De Kalb and experiment station inbreds planned by Gunn and Holbert in 1931. Although there was an excessive amount of rainfall during much of the season in 1935, Roberts' men harvested 14,500 bushels of De Kalb seed of good quality.

This large volume of seed raised a number of problems and resulted in introducing some entirely new concepts into De Kalb's program. Until this large seed crop was harvested, Roberts had been thinking largely in terms of De Kalb County and nearby areas in northern Illinois as the territory to be served by De Kalb hybrids. With nearly 15,000 bushels of the new hybrid seed available, new methods of distribution were called into use. Roberts placed an advertisement in *Prairie Farmer*, the farm magazine that reaches a majority of farm homes in Illinois and Indiana. It was a small advertisement in one color, announcing that De Kalb had hybrid seed corn and inviting farmers to send for it through the mail.

The response to this *Prairie Farmer* advertisement was surprising and in one respect discouraging. Farmers by the hundreds wrote to De Kalb and enclosed cash or checks for a bushel or more of the new hybrid seed. About seventy per cent of the farmers lived in areas to which the De Kalb hybrid was not adapted, and as a result the time of a secretary was required for several days writing the farmers to this effect and returning their money.

This experience wiped out of Tom Roberts' mind completely the idea that his De Kalb organization could limit its development of hybrids to the northern corn belt. "I was convinced from then on," says Roberts, "that as quickly as possible we should have to broaden our hybrid corn breeding program so that we could have hybrids for farmers everywhere throughout the corn belt. We simply couldn't hope to work effectively and efficiently any other way."

Roberts talked to Jim Holbert about the possibilities of adding hybrids to the De Kalb production schedule for farmers farther south. Holbert, whose greatest work had been done in hybrids of this general maturity, proposed that the use of two or three of the newest hybrids that he developed at the Federal Field Station at Bloomington for north central Illinois be considered. These hybrids were produced so successfully that two years later special production areas farther south in Illinois were needed.

The demand for hybrids adapted to areas farther south was so great that Roberts and Gunn decided that their own research staff should be expanded. Recognizing Holbert's achievements in developing hybrids for this general area, it was their hope that they might interest Holbert in leaving the Federal Field Station on Funk Farms and devote his time to the problem of developing De Kalb hybrids for the central and southern corn belt.

At the first opportunity, Roberts approached Holbert to see if there would be any chance of getting his services, or, if not, of his suggesting someone else. Holbert appreciated the invitation, but he felt that his responsibilities to the Federal Field Station would not permit him to accept it.

Instead, Holbert suggested that Roberts and Gunn approach R. R. St. John, whose outstanding work in developing hybrids for the central corn belt at the Indiana Experiment Station had won "The Saint" wide respect and recognition. St. John accepted the position and began work in 1937. Drawing on his keen understanding of breeding techniques for corn and his wide experience with existing inbred lines, some of the most important of which he had developed himself, St. John was able to make an important and almost immediate contribution to the De Kalb hybrid-corn research in the central and southern areas of the corn belt.

In order to get adequate distribution for the large 1935 seed crop, Roberts offered De Kalb hybrid seed to farmers in

the Humbolt area of north central Iowa. This area was selected because all the information available indicated that
the length of season and other factors bearing upon corn
production were approximately the same as they were at De
Kalb, Illinois, and consequently the hybrids that performed
well in De Kalb County would also perform well in the Humbolt section of Iowa.

In 1936 De Kalb produced its first hybrid seed outside of
Illinois or De Kalb County. That year, despite the great
drouth which was more severe farther south, but which didn't
reach as far north as the drouth in 1934, the De Kalb seedsmen produced the astounding total of 90,000 bushels of seed,
all of it hybrids for the northern reaches of the corn belt. In
addition to the area around De Kalb, large amounts of seed
were produced around Tom Roberts' home town of Waterman, Illinois, and at Humbolt, Iowa. This seed was used by
farmers in northern sections of Indiana, Illinois, and Iowa.

Roberts' De Kalb organization was now on its way to
establishing unmatched leadership in the job of giving northern corn belt farmers the benefits of this new kind of corn.
The hybrids developed during this period by Gunn were
proving so much better than open-pollinated corn that the
demand was without precedent before or since. No corn like
it had ever been seen on the farms of those great corn-growing regions of northern Iowa, upper Illinois, and Indiana.
Gunn's hybrids outyielded the old corn on farm after farm
by twenty-five to thirty-five per cent, and they stood better
in the fall, came up better in the spring, withstood drouth
better in the summer. A revolution in corn growing for the
northern corn belt was unfolding on thousands of farms
because of the work done by a few men living in De Kalb.

Plans for increasing the production of hybrid seed corn
cannot generally be safely made until the winter before the
seed crop is to be planted in the spring. By this time, there
is no opportunity to increase the supply of foundation ma-

terial needed for any hybrids in which greatly expanded
volume is sought.

Gunn always managed his program to breed and produce
foundation seed so that he constantly had the greatest possible supply of these foundation seed materials ready to
meet such unexpected developments. Charlie Gunn realized
from the beginning that in successful hybrid-corn breeding,
which gives farmers the kind of hybrids they want and need,
it is not how much inbred and foundation single cross seed
you have left over which hurts, but that it is the inbred and
foundation single cross seed which you do not have that is
disastrous. He refused to make the cardinal mistake of not
having foundation materials that were within the realm of
possibility to produce, and therein is found one of the important explanations to the remarkable job the De Kalb
organization was able to do in providing more farmers with
the benefits of modern hybrid corn during these years in the
middle and late thirties.

In 1937 Tom Roberts geared his organization for a stupendous job of producing seed for hybrid corn. Large new
production centers were added farther south at Monmouth,
in the western part of the Illinois, and at Tuscola to the east,
reflecting the first effort to produce hybrids adapted to
farms farther south in the corn belt. The production centers
in De Kalb County and Waterman in Illinois and at Humbolt in Iowa were organized to produce every last bushel of
hybrid seed corn. The weather at all of the production centers was unusually favorable in 1937, and when the harvesting and processing of the seed was complete, almost a quarter
of a million bushels of De Kalb hybrid seed were in the sack.

Still farmers turning from their old open-pollinated corn
to the new hybrid took all the seed De Kalb and others could
produce and wanted more. In 1938, additional De Kalb production centers were established at Fremont in Nebraska,
Grinell in Iowa, and Lafayette in Indiana, and Roberts was

able to push the total production of De Kalb hybrid seed up to 370,000 bushels. For the first time De Kalb hybrids were offered to Canadian farmers, and thousands of acres of corn land in Ontario were planted in the spring of 1939 with the hybrids developed by Charlie Gunn and his De Kalb staff.

By 1939 the hybrids developed by St. John for De Kalb were beginning to come in volume, and production at the De Kalb centers in central Illinois and Indiana climbed again. Two additional centers for production and processing of hybrids developed for the northern corn belt were opened that year, one at Jackson, Minnesota, and another at Storm Lake, Iowa. De Kalb's total production for the 1939 season exceeded half a million bushels for the first time.

Now the role the men of De Kalb were playing in substituting the new hybrid corn for open-pollinated corn was becoming increasingly clear. In 1935, the first year that farmers planted De Kalb hybrids, only a little more than 2500 acres were planted with the new corn developed by Charlie Gunn. By 1940 well over 4,000,000 acres of American and Canadian corn ground were planted with De Kalb hybrids. Nearly 10 per cent of all the corn produced in the American corn belt was De Kalb corn in 1940. And still it was only the beginning.

In the summer of 1930, Charlie Gunn's ten-year-old son, Ralph, asked his father for a job and got the position of "water boy" at his father's breeding plot. This role was continued two or three years and gradually was transformed until young Ralph Gunn was helping his father, Bell, and others with the routine work at the corn plots.

By the time the youth was through high school, he was taking considerable responsibility and had acquired from his seven or eight years of summer work a thorough understanding of the procedures and objectives of the breeder's work. There still was no particular thought of his becoming a hybrid-corn breeder himself. For the most part he did the work because he liked to be out of doors. His father, believing that youngsters should make up their own minds about the kind of work they do, carefully avoided any suggestion that his son might like to continue working with corn after he was out of school.

Ralph Gunn went to Wheaton College at nearby Wheaton, Illinois, for two years, and when he came home for midterm vacation during his second year, he asked his father whether he thought his chances of being successful as a corn breeder were good enough to justify his making it his profession. Naturally it was a great moment for the elder Gunn, but he gave the young man a restrained reply to the effect that if he got a good, sound education as a plant breeder and applied himself diligently to the work, he could see no reason why he shouldn't get along. After this conference with his father, young Gunn considered all of the agricultural colleges in the United States with a view to doing his last two years of college work where he might specialize in plant breeding. Again his father insisted on taking a minor role in these considerations, and finally the young man settled on Iowa State College at Ames.

At Iowa State College Ralph Gunn did most of his work in plant breeding and genetics with Dr. I. J. Johnson, Dr. E. W. Lindstrom, and Dr. George Sprague. For a thorough and classical background in corn breeding, his choice of Iowa State College would have been difficult to improve. Johnson came to the Iowa State faculty after working a number of years with Dr. H. K. Hayes, imparting to young Gunn indirectly the concepts Hayes had acquired and developed back to the days of his association with Edward Murray East in the land of the Sleeping Giant. Both Lindstrom and Sprague did their graduate work at Cornell with Dr. R. A. Emerson, one of the foremost plant geneticists of his generation. Like Hayes, he had formerly worked with East at Harvard.

After graduation from Iowa State College, Ralph Gunn joined the corn breeding department of the De Kalb organization. For a year he worked closely with his father, and the corn-breeding fraternity had its first father-and-son team. After this, young Gunn took over the direction of one of the important De Kalb hybrid breeding centers located at Dayton, twenty miles south of Fort Dodge, Iowa.

In 1940, Charlie Gunn presented to northern corn belt farmers a new hybrid known as De Kalb 404A, destined to establish itself as the outstanding single hybrid of the first great decade of hybrid corn. Made up of inbreds from two Iowa and two Illinois strains of open-pollinated corn, the new 404A was adopted by farmers so rapidly that within four seasons after it was introduced by De Kalb, it was being planted on 2,500,000 acres of corn land—an acreage equal to half or more of the corn growing area of such states as Indiana, Ohio, Wisconsin, or Missouri.

Gunn's 404A demonstrated numerous remarkable qualities, perhaps the most outstanding of which has been its capacity to give high yields of corn north of the point where such high corn yields had previously been obtained. As a result, it has become a standard remark among farmers and corn breeders alike that "404A moved the corn belt two hundred miles north." This expansion of the area of the corn belt stands as one of hybrid corn's greatest achievements, a development that has given America new strength and new opportunities.

Especially is 404A a tribute to Charlie Gunn, the corn breeder, and Tom Roberts, the man who planned well and pledged his future and the future of his organization that farmers might have the benefits of this new kind of corn.

CHAPTER XV

Fame Comes to El Paso

NOT LONG AGO two fishermen met on a lake in Florida. One was from Chicago, the other an owner of a small resort along the lake's edge. After the weather and the current batch of fisherman's hard luck stories had been exhausted, the Floridan put the usual question, "What's your business?"

The man from Chicago replied that he was working with a hybrid-corn organization.

"Hybrid corn," queried the Florida fisherman. "Let's see, I've been reading about that a good deal lately. Must be a lot better than the old corn. Discovered by a man up in your state, wasn't it?"

"You mean Dr. Edward East? He was originally in Illinois and did some of his first work on corn at the University of Illinois," suggested the Chicago man.

"Don't believe that was the name," the Floridan replied.

"Maybe you're thinking of Jim Holbert of Bloomington, Illinois," continued the man from Illinois. "I believe Dr. Holbert was the first man in the corn belt to work intensively on hybrid corn."

"Doesn't exactly seem like that was his name," mused the native of Florida.

"Could you be thinking of Henry Wallace? He's not from Illinois, but he did come from the neighboring state of Iowa and he did a lot of early work on hybrid corn."

"Nope, I'm certain it wasn't Wallace. Pretty sure it was an Illinois man. A farmer up in Illinois, wasn't it?"

"Oh, you mean Pfister . . . Lester Pfister?" explained the Chicago man.

"That's the guy," shot back the Florida fisherman.

This experience in one variation or another has occurred times without number in the years since the new hybrid corn became a topic for common conversation not only among farm people but urban folk as well, for without any question people have the name of Pfister associated with hybrid corn more than any other. This is true because our magazine, newspaper, and radio editors have given more attention to Lester Pfister than to any of the other hybrid-corn makers, possibly more than to all the others put together.

Typical of the impressions imparted by this tremendous amount of press and radio attention is *Life's* statement, "Largely responsible for the success of hybrid corn is Lester Pfister, corn-hog farmer from El Paso, Illinois."

Statements of this sort have a curious touch of irony about them when the entire panorama of hybrid corn is unfolded and we have an opportunity to see that, of the major hybrid-corn makers of our generation, Lester Pfister was among the last to begin his work. But before the full story of hybrid corn began to come into clear focus, such statements not only carried conviction; they also served to further the cause of the new corn.

The editors found in Mr. Pfister a human interest story of the first magnitude, and the fact that he had worked with hybrid corn was treated merely as an important by-product. With Lester Pfister and his family as the main characters in a "rags to riches" story, the American press and radio gave hybrid corn attention that it would not otherwise have received.

The net effect was to acquaint the public in general and corn farmers in particular with the advantages of modern hybrid corn. St. John, the hybrid-corn breeder from Indiana, said recently, "*Life Magazine's* article on Lester Pfister did more to popularize hybrid corn among corn belt farmers than all the government and university bulletins ever written on the subject."

If anything, Lester Pfister's experiences, his achievements, and his philosophy all taken together make a more significant and interesting saga than any of the magazine writers ever took time to fashion about him. Pfister was born July 6, 1897, on a small farm located a few miles southeast of El Paso, Illinois, a center of Illinois' cash grain district where farmers make a big business of raising corn for sale to corn processors and to elevators located in Chicago, Peoria, Decatur, and Kankakee. His parents were tenant farmers, and his father, John Pfister, died after a short illness induced by overwork when his son, Lester, was but eight years old.

His mother, Emma Haas Pfister, a resourceful woman, settled her husband's affairs and found that she had approximately $4,000 and her own energies with which to rear five children, two sons and three daughters, ranging from six months to eleven years in age. She moved into the town of El Paso and managed to keep the children in school, although the boys quit to go to work before they were graduated from eighth grade.

Lester Pfister quit school in the early spring to go to work as a farm hand at the age of 14, earning $30 a month while furnishing his own board. In the fall a year or so later, young Pfister husked 2,080 bushels of corn at 3 cents a bushel, earning $62.40 in 6 weeks of hard work. He furnished his own board.

In 1915, when Lester Pfister was seventeen, his mother started him and his brother Lloyd, who was three years older, to farming the 128-acre farm of her father, Joseph Haas, who had broken eighty acres of virgin prairie with two teams of oxen. Grandfather Haas had exhibited many of the qualities that were to contribute to Lester Pfister's successes, displaying real capacity as an inventor and the dogged persistence that has characterized his more famous grandson. He had developed and used a corn elevator and a water-tank heater years before such equipment came into general use on Middle Western farms.

Farm prices were rising at the time the young Pfister brothers began farming. Two years later they rented an additional eighty acres. Later, when Lloyd married, they divided their operations. Lester took over responsibility for Grandfather Haas' farm.

From his experience as a farm hand, Lester Pfister had learned that there were great differences in the varieties of corn used on farms in the El Paso community. Even on apparently comparable types of soil, young Pfister observed that different strains of corn varied greatly in yield. Some of it was hard to husk, some easy. Certain strains were much more likely to have rotten ears and more stalk than others, and he observed various other differences.

So almost from the time he started to farm, Lester Pfister began ear-to-row corn testing to determine accurately which strains of open-pollinated corn were most profitable on his land. After M. L. Mosher came to Woodford County as farm adviser, Pfister took the opportunity to go over the records of his ear-to-row tests with him. They held conferences that were to be of much greater importance than either of them realized at the time.

Mosher, too, had been convinced ever since he studied field crops at Iowa State College that farming could be made much more profitable in such states as Illinois and Iowa if the strains of corn in general use could be improved. In 1919, Mosher proposed a dramatic plan for determining the outstanding strain of corn in Woodford County. The plan, to be sponsored by the Woodford County Farm Bu-

reau, would be a three-year testing program, the results of
which would not be announced until after the final harvest
had been completed.

Mosher's testing project was simple enough. The Farm
Bureau invited farmers in Woodford County each spring for
three years to submit samples of the corn they were using.
Each season the corn was planted side by side in large
proving plots. Effort was made to permit all the corn to
grow under identical conditions. At harvest-time each of the
strains was shucked out and weighed. One of the proving
plots was located each year at the Woodford County Farm
at Metamora. In 1919, another plot was conducted on the
Frank Hock farm at Minonk, and in 1920 and 1921 proving
plots were located on the Charles Smith farm at Eureka. The
best of the county's show-type corn was entered, and there
had been much speculation over whether the old show corn
would demonstrate superiority over some of the other distinctly different types.

The work done by Lester Pfister on his ear-to-row proving
plot had so impressed Farm Adviser Mosher that he asked the
young El Paso farmer to take over responsibility for making
the comparisons and preparing detailed reports on each of
the proving plots. It took nearly three weeks of Pfister's time
each fall, but he enjoyed the work and did it faithfully.

Then came the payoff. One winter day early in 1922,
Farm Adviser Mosher called a meeting of all those interested
in the results of the Woodford County comparative corn
tests. This was the first time in all the recorded history of
corn that such a thorough test had been made, and announcement of the results was awaited with eagerness. Henry
Wallace, a friend of Mosher's since college days, came over
from Des Moines to be present for the important meeting,
and most of the 118 farmers who had patiently supplied seed
samples of their own corn for three successive years were on
hand. Practically every entry represented from ten to forty

years of selection from open-pollinated corn by Woodford County farmers.

Mosher gave a full accounting of the carefully prepared reports made by Lester Pfister. The ten outstanding varieties of corn were named, and one of them was the winner by a substantial margin. The winning strain had been entered by George Krug, a farmer in the Minonk community who had never placed any faith in show-type corn and who, for years, had saved as seed the heaviest and most solid ears which he found in his crib, simply selecting them without regard to their looks, whether they were cylindrical or long and tapering, whether they were rough or smooth.

Wallace wrote an article for *Wallaces' Farmer* about the Woodford County comparison test and of George Krug and his corn. He ended by telling Iowa farmers that if they had all planted Krug's corn the previous year instead of their own a million less acres would have been required to produce Iowa's corn crop, and that Iowa farmers would have had as extra profits the expense connected with raising a million acres of corn.

Pfister was so impressed with the results of the three-year testing program that he discarded his own strains of open-pollinated corn and began raising Krug corn.

Demand for Krug's corn arose immediately among not only farmers of Woodford county but far beyond and especially in Iowa, where farmers read Henry Wallace's accounts of the Woodford testing program. As a result Pfister sold more than one hundred bushels of his 1922 crop for seed purposes. Within a few years he was selling more than a thousand bushels of Krug seed each spring, and an important part of it went to Iowa farmers.

In 1924, Lester Pfister was married to Miss Helen Vogel, reared on a farm ten miles from El Paso. They continued to operate Grandfather Haas' farm, on which they raised hogs and Krug corn.

The next year occurred another important milestone. On July 21, 1925, the El Paso farmer began inbreeding the best plants of Krug corn that he could find in his seed fields. Before the pollinating season was over, Pfister had inbred approximately two thousand plants.

Pfister's decision to begin inbreeding his Krug corn was no sudden impulse. His farm was only thirty-odd miles from Bloomington, and Lester Pfister first saw Jim Holbert's hybrid corn on the United States Department of Agriculture Experiment Station located on Funk Farms early in the twenties. He visited with Holbert, Dr. C. M. Woodworth at the University of Illinois, and others. He read everything about the new corn that came to his attention, following with special care the articles that appeared in *Wallaces' Farmer* and the Bloomington *Pantagraph* in which were frequent reports of the early hybrid-corn breeding being done by Henry Wallace and Jim Holbert. Within a few years Pfister had acquired a remarkable understanding and appreciation of the possibilities of the new hybrid corn, at a time when most farmers, even open-pollinated seed producing farmers, were scarcely aware that hybrid-corn development had even begun.

In 1925, Pfister entered his Krug open-pollinated corn in the Iowa Corn Yield Test, and his entry was the high yielder in its district. Although he could not claim the gold medal awarded the Iowa Corn Yield Test district winners because he was not a resident of Iowa, Pfister did go to the Iowa Farm and Home Week held at Ames in February of 1926 to study results of the state yield test.

While in Iowa, Pfister met and visited at length with Henry Wallace, whom he had first met in Woodford County when the three-year corn comparison test results were announced. Pfister told Wallace of his desire to develop inbreds and to have hybrids from his Krug corn and that he had begun inbreeding work during the summer before. Wallace was impressed with Pfister's interest in developing hybrids from Krug corn, but while he was encouraging, he also spoke frankly about the possibilities of success.

"Only one farmer out of ten thousand can develop a really good inbred," cautioned Wallace, "but you have made a fine start and I think you should go ahead with it. Certainly you are working with an outstanding open-pollinated corn, and someone should get good inbreds from it so that the fine qualities of Krug corn can be preserved for future generations."

Pfister stuck doggedly with his inbreeding work through the summers of 1926, 1927, and 1928 before he began making hybrid crosses. He had ruthlessly eliminated the plants among his inbreds that did not represent the finest qualities of his Krug corn, until in the mid-thirties he had left less than a dozen of the original two thousand selfed lines begun in 1925. Some of the years had brought extreme periods of drouth. Chinch bugs, grasshoppers, and other hazards plagued his inbreds in one season or another. Fortunately, Pfister had that keen judgment which told him that these adversities were in reality strokes of good fortune, since they afforded the best possible means of eliminating inferior inbred plants. Even when some of his most favored inbreds were destroyed, Pfister always dismissed the matter with his oft-repeated quip, "Let the weaklings die."

In October of 1932, F. D. Richey, principal agronomist in charge of corn investigations for the United States Department of Agriculture, came to El Paso to visit Lester Pfister and to see what progress he had made with his Krug inbreeding program. Richey was impressed, and asked Pfister if he might have the most promising of the inbreds to enter in the winter greenhouse tests to be made at the United States Department of Agriculture Experiment Station at Arlington, Virginia.

Pfister consented, and Richey grew a crop of Pfister's inbreds from Krug during the winter months late in 1932 and early 1933. One of them, Pfister's 187, Richey found to be outstanding, so he tested it again on the out-of-doors Arlington plots in the summer of 1933. Pfister's Krug inbred was just as outstanding under natural conditions as it had been in the greenhouse.

Richey released this great Pfister inbred to the federal and state experiment stations, issuing it under the same number, 187, given it by Pfister. Quickly the El Paso farmer was given wide credit for having developed it. This inbred was used in many of the first hybrids to be offered by experiment stations to corn belt farmers. In this way the work done by Lester Pfister made a contribution to the general development of hybrid corn by supplying one or two inbreds at a time when there was such an acute shortage of good inbred material.

In 1929 Pfister made the first crosses between his inbreds, and these were grown in the 1930 season. In 1930, he made crosses between his best single crosses, and his first double-cross hybrid grew in the 1931 season. He named his first hybrid "Pfister's 4857," taking the second digit from each of the four numbers which appeared in the pedigree (140 x 187) (159 x 174). Compared with the double-cross hybrids then available, Lester Pfister's first hybrid was a good strain. It was early for the El Paso area, being more perfectly adapted to the corn farming territory about fifty miles north of Pfister's farm where the hybrid was developed.

In 1930, the estate of Pfister's grandfather was settled, and as a result, Lester Pfister decided to give up the farm which he had operated since he began farming in 1915. In that same year, he bought a 160-acre farm located just across the road, paying $225 an acre. Then came the depression, and a few months later comparable land in the community could be bought for $120 or less. In 1932 and 1933,

Pfister sold corn for 26 cents a bushel, oats for 11 cents a bushel, and one lot of hogs for as little as $3\frac{1}{4}$ cents a pound.

Caught between a $32,000 debt and the tragedy of collapsed farm prices, the Pfister's were, like many thousands of farm families during this distressing period, confronted with the danger of losing their property. The St. Louis Land Bank which held the mortgage on the Pfister farm suggested at one time that Lester Pfister take bankruptcy, and as an inducement the bank offered to rent the farm to him for an indefinite period.

At this point the determination of his Grandfather Haas flared up in Lester Pfister. He told the bank that if he had to rent a farm it would be some other farm and that he would instead ask for an extension on his overdue payments of principal and interest and that his family would endeavor to see the problem through to a successful conclusion, high debt or no debt. Bank officials, impressed with Pfister's determination, granted the extension and several thereafter.

Like so many Americans who were bowed down during this tragic period of economic paralysis, Lester Pfister was suddenly old beyond his years. Yet, despite all the hardship, he did not allow his corn breeding to suffer. Probably the only person in all his acquaintances who encouraged him in this was his wife, and her attitude showed real understanding since during much of this time her family was reduced virtually to eating only those things that could be raised on the farm, and had little else to wear but clothing with patches on the patches and cardboard to cover holes in shoes acquired in the days before our agricultural economy collapsed so completely.

Pfister's determination to continue his hybrid-corn breeding even if it meant some neglect of other farm work drew a barrage of withering criticism from many of his neighbors and acquaintances who were still almost totally unaware of the possibilities of hybrid corn. Most of the hybrid-corn makers endured this criticism in one degree or another, but none of them was so beset as was Pfister.

Realizing that the sight of him working in his corn plot, putting hundreds of little paper sacks over tassels and ear shoots would occasion public scorn, Pfister tried for a time to do his corn breeding in the most remote place on the farm or behind a hedge row that grew along one side of his farm. This proved to be poor camouflage, and such remarks as "he must figure to keep the shucks from freezing" and other expressions of ridicule were common talk for miles around. As the general suffering of the depression years increased, people were naturally less tolerant, and some of the neighbors sincerely believed that Lester Pfister's mind had been affected by the general adversity. Naturally, Pfister regretted all this, especially because of the hardship it brought to his children in their school associations.

But he sensed that this was no time for hesitation, and drew comfort from the classic quotation, "On the plains of hesitation bleach the bones of countless millions who, at the dawn of victory, sat down to rest, and resting died."

The dawn of victory was already red in the eastern sky. In 1932, Pfister tested his first hybrid against his Krug open-pollinated corn, and the verdict went to his hybrid by such a margin that he decided to produce some of it for sale in 1933. In all he produced 225 bushels, purchased largely by farmers in Woodford County and in Iowa to whom he had been supplying Krug open-pollinated seed corn. In the 1934 season his hybrid seed crop totalled 665 bushels and was distributed more widely.

In April of 1933, Lester Pfister and his friend, Jim Holbert of the United States Department of Agriculture Experiment Station at Bloomington, had a visit of far-reaching consequences. Holbert came to El Paso to visit Pfister and to suggest the possibilities for new hybrids that might come from Pfister using some of the inbreds developed at the

Funk Farms Station with his Krug inbred lines. In the course of their visit, Holbert even offered to make the trial combinations and test the results in the regular state-wide corn testing program. Pfister was so .much impressed that he immediately gave Holbert an adequate amount of seed of his best Krug single crosses.

That summer Holbert used Pfister's single cross with a number of his own to make up several experimental double-cross hybrids. These were placed by Holbert in the Illinois Corn Performance Tests inaugurated by the University of Illinois in the 1934 season. Despite the severe drouth of that year, two of these experimental hybrids made up of his own inbreds and those from Pfister and entered in the University Tests as hybrids "Illinois 360" and "Illinois 366" were outstanding. In "Illinois 360" Holbert had used with Pfister's Krug single cross his own great single cross, (A x Hy). Holbert's single cross, (A x 90), entered into "Illinois 366" along with Pfister's Krug single cross.

Pfister accompanied Holbert to the proving plots that summer and fall in 1934, and was so greatly impressed that he decided to begin producing the "360" and "366" hybrids immediately. Holbert supplied Pfister with enough seed of his single cross, (A x Hy), so that the El Paso farmer-seedsman was able to produce a considerable amount of seed for the new hybrids in the 1935 season. Therefore, what had in 1934 been the experimental hybrids "Illinois 360" and "Illinois 366" became in 1935 Pfister's 360 and 366. The net result was that the El Paso farmer became the sole possessor of the two greatest hybrids developed up to that time for the central and north central corn belt.

Farmers in the central corn belt from central Ohio to eastern Nebraska quickly discovered that the new Pfister hybrids could deliver so much more corn per acre than did their old open-pollinated strains, that they took every bushel of seed Lester Pfister could produce. Whereas in the second year of his hybrid-seed production in 1934, Pfister had produced only 665 bushels, he distributed 5,770 bushels in 1935, 13,700 bushels in 1936, and more than 37,000 bushels in 1937. These were the epoch-making years when the new hybrid corn was sweeping the old open-pollinated strains into discard and when farmers wanted more of the new hybrids than could be produced. In 1937, the entire Pfister production of 37,000 bushels was sold to farmers who came to El Paso to get it or secured it by mail.

A number of factors combined during the late thirties to create this tremendous demand for the new Pfister hybrids. Most important of these factors was the possession of the two fine hybrids, Pfister's 360 and 366. In addition, Pfister's own contacts with farmers made in his open-pollinated seed business through Illinois and Iowa provided a springboard for getting immediate and widespread distribution. A third and especially important factor in creating demand for Pfister hybrids during the late thirties was the nationwide publicity which Lester Pfister received in newspapers, magazines, and radio broadcasts. This wave of publicity was touched off by the somewhat fanciful article done by the collapsing *Country Home Magizine*, which, in an effort to maintain a hold on rural readers, was catering to the sensational. *Readers' Digest* poured real fuel on the fires by reprinting the *Country Home Magazine* article, which left the impression that this El Paso farmer had virtually single-handedly discovered and unfolded to the world the miracle of hybrid corn. Then followed an ever-widening ring of public attention which included a full length pictorial article in *Life Magazine* and numerous radio appearances, including network attention from NBC on the then popular March of Time program on which Pfister personally appeared.

Lester Pfister capitalized on this unusual demand for his hybrids in a masterly manner and in so doing performed a great service for corn belt farmers. Realizing that it would be impossible for him to produce and process all of the seed of Pfister hybrids that farmers wanted, he appointed associate seed producers in one section of the corn belt after another. By 1943 the parent Pfister organization and its associates were able to provide Pfister hybrid seed corn to farmers in all the principal corn belt states.

Besides doing a thorough job of inbreeding Krug corn and giving personal publicity to the new hybrid corn as no other one person ever did, Lester Pfister made still another contribution. He drew upon the ability, perhaps inherited from Grandfather Haas, to invent, devise, and improve a series of machines useful in the production and processing of hybrid seed corn. Pfister's first love in many respects is his machine shop, and from it came, and are still coming, new contrivances and original adaptations of existing machines to increase the efficiency of producing hybrid seed. One of his first important contributions to the mechanical equipment of the producer of hybrid seed corn was the Jitterbug Grading machine which Pfister designed to sort out by mechanical means kernels of similar size.

Later Pfister developed a detasseling machine which permitted detasselers to ride through the hybrid-seed field rather than do the tedious job on foot. These machines have since been adopted rather generally by other seed producers. Two of Lester Pfister's most recent machineshop achievements have been a tractor-sprayer for applying DDT dust to reduce corn borer damage in his seed crop and a four-row cornpicker. The tractor-sprayer is a gaint of a machine rolling on wheels so big that it passes over the top of corn at full height. The four-row cornpicker was made a reality by putting together two-row cornpickers and synchronizing their action so that they appear and perform as one machine.

Today Lester Pfister still lives on his farm in the same community where he began working as a hired hand at the age of fourteen after leaving school a few weeks before he would have been graduated from the eighth grade. He has acquired 1080 acres of land, including the farm his Grandfather Haas carved out of the prairie with an ox-drawn plow. He still personally directs the handling of the precious inbreds that he so painstakingly developed from his Krug corn. He still manages his Pfister Hybrid Corn Company which supplies "Hybrids By Lester Pfister" to the farmers in the Corn Belt.

Through the years Lester Pfister has taken an increasing interest in the problems confronting corn belt farmers. He is especially concerned about the problem of maintaining soil fertility, which he regards as the foundation not only of a prosperous agriculture but of a prosperous America. "The thing that concerns me most is whether or not we are taking proper care of our soil. In this new hybrid corn, we have one of the most efficient mining machines ever devised by man. This capacity of hybrid corn to mine our soil fertility quickly and convert it into increased amounts of food was a godsend during the great war, but I wonder now that the war is over whether we will map adequate programs to maintain and improve the condition of our soil.

"You know my Grandfather Haas came out here and broke eighty acres of virgin prairie with four oxen and a walking plow. If he had had tractors and power farm equipment and modern hybrid corn, he would have raised a hundred and twenty bushels of corn on every one of those acres. Today we average about sixty bushels to the acre. How much will we be getting sixty years from now? Our biggest single problem is to maintain our soil fertility. Not only the future of the Corn Belt, but the very future of America depends on how we meet this problem. One thing we must never forget; there never was land so good that it couldn't be ruined."

CHAPTER XVI

Builders All

WE HAVE NOW traced the achievements of the corn breeders who labored at the seven principal centers in the corn belt where the revolutionary ideas and techniques worked out at the Connecticut Experiment Station were employed to develop the new hybrid corn. Other important work has been done at other points throughout the corn belt and elsewhere in the United States. While the work done at no one of these other points constituted a sweeping contribution such as was made in these seven principal centers, the collective contribution of all the other corn breeders has been of the greatest importance. Except for them hybrid corn could not have achieved so soon the signal success that it has attained.

For the most part, this work took place at the state agricultural experiment stations in corn-breeding programs undertaken co-operatively with the United States Department of Agriculture. This co-operative program produced such significant results that the men who shaped and executed it deserve special recognition.

The one man most responsible for this program was Frederick D. Richey. The idea had originated with Carlton C. Ball, senior agronomist in charge of the Office of Cereal Crops and Diseases under whose province the corn investigation work of the United States Department of Agriculture was done from 1919 until 1934. Richey, who became principal agronomist in charge of corn investigations in Ball's

domain in 1922, took the policy of co-operation with the
state experiment stations and fashioned it into the concrete
hybrid-corn breeding program that produced such important
results.

As we have already observed, the outstanding work done
at Iowa State College was a product of this co-operative
program, and the same program with one variation or
another functioned in other states such as Kansas, Ohio,
Missouri, Kentucky, Tennessee, Louisiana, Texas, Florida,
and Mississippi during the crucial years of hybrid-corn
development in the twenties. More recently, other states,
most of them in the South, have joined in the co-operative
effort.

Richey, as tall as he is outspoken, grew up in St. Louis
and on his grandfather's farm in LaSalle County, Illinois, a
hundred miles southwest of Chicago. Like so many good
Illinois farmers, his grandfather had selected his open-pollinated corn carefully for many years. In the fall of 1902,
when he was eighty and quite feeble, the older Richey charged
his grandson with responsibility of selecting out the ears to
be used for seed as the corn was being scooped from the
wagons into a crib. His orders were that the long slender
ears that were unusually solid and of good weight should
be put into the seed baskets.

The old gentleman died the following New Year's Day,
and young Richey stayed on the farm until spring to help
settle the estate and put things in order for a tenant farmer
to handle.

This was just about the time that the germination and
testing of seed corn were becoming recognized as one of the
measures of good seed, and although his grandfather had
never bothered to do it, young Richey made some cigar box
germinators and ran germination tests. He found that the
long, heavy, and somewhat smooth ears his grandfather had
instructed him to select as seed germinated well over ninety

per cent, while much of the show-corn seed available this particular spring in LaSalle County germinated very poorly. In all Richey had been able to save about fifty bushels of the kind of corn that met his grandfather's specifications, and after the fine germination test, he sold all but the four or five bushels needed to plant the acreage on the Richey farm, receiving $3.50 a bushel—then a good price for seed corn.

Later Richey went to the University of Missouri and took a general course in agriculture, thinking that he would return to LaSalle County and operate his grandfather's farm. Instead he took a job in 1911 with C. P. Hartley in the United States Department of Agriculture's Office of Corn Investigations. Always an apt student in mathematics and other subjects dealing with the sciences, Richey approached his open-pollinated corn selection on as nearly a graph and chart basis as possible. Almost immediately he saw the value of varietal crosses, and he was particularly interested in finding out what type of crosses would give the greatest increase in yield. Eventually he proved to his satisfaction that the highest yielding crosses were those bringing together the best of the southern prolific strains with the best of the northern single-eared varieties. This concept was largely responsible for his developing the variety of white corn, Delta Prolific, that is still used in Arkansas.

At the same time Richey began a systematic reading of everything ever written on maize studies and corn development. He did this largely because he had not specialized in plant breeding or corn improvement; his college work had been devoted to a general education in agriculture. This wide reading brought him into contact with the papers, bulletins, and articles written by such men as Shull, East, Hayes, and Jones.

While he began his inbreeding in 1916 before Jones reported the double cross, Richey says, "It was Jones' discovery of the double cross and his Mendelian explanation of hybrid vigor that cleared the air for me, and immediately I went ahead with a definite concept and with the fixed objective of establishing inbred lines and combining them into hybrids."

From the standpoint of developing inbred lines, this early work was not tremendously significant, but it did convince Richey that inbreeding, developing of pure lines, and crossing them into hybrid combinations was the most effective means of improving corn. This conviction was of great importance to the development of the new hybrid corn, for on Richey was to fall the major responsibility for shifting the emphasis of the Department of Agriculture's corn investigations from open-pollinated corn improvement over to the development of hybrid corn.

Richey continued to work with his corn inbreeding even though Hartley gave him no encouragement, and in 1920 he dared to come out openly and personally advocate hybrid-corn breeding. He did this in an address delivered December 31, 1920, at a meeting of the American Society of Agronomy held on the campus of the University of Chicago. Richey said, "The possibilities of progress under pure-line breeding methods is largely theoretical so far. . . Nevertheless, the entire evidence from all corn breeding investigations for the present points to pure-line methods as the only sound basis for real improvement of corn." These were bold words from a man whose own organization, the Department of Agriculture, was as yet completely committed to the further improvement of open-pollinated corn.

Less than sixty days after he replaced Hartley as principal agronomist in charge of corn investigations, Richey issued the "Magna Carta" under which the co-operative work in hybrid corn breeding was to be done. On March 31, 1922, Richey issued this manifesto, which began right where his address in Chicago left off, the first paragraph reading, "All experimental evidence indicated that the older methods of open-fertilized breeding of corn varieties are of little value. . . On the other hand, there is good evidence that methods involving selection within self-fertilized lines offer the greatest immediate practical possibilities in the production of higher yielding strains of corn. Futhermore, the fundamental problems of corn improvement can be solved only through investigations based upon self-fertilized lines. For these reasons, a program of corn-breeding investigations should concentrate principally on pure-line methods as a means of obtaining larger acre yields of corn, and the following program is concerned chiefly with such experiments."

There was no trace of compromise in his three-thousand-word pronouncement. The old order was ruthlessly rejected, and the stage was set to promote to the limit the corn inbreeding work that had already begun to spread from the Connecticut Experiment Station into important centers in the great corn belt.

On April 21, 1925, the directors of the North Central District of the corn belt experiment stations met in St. Louis and voted to make corn improvement a co-operative project, providing a sound basis for common objectives in corn improvement in the twelve states of Illinois, Iowa, Indiana, Ohio, Missouri, Kansas, Nebraska, South Dakota, North Dakota, Minnesota, Wisconsin, and Michigan. The same year the first Purnell conference was held at Michigan State College at East Lansing. These Purnell conferences, held once or twice each year during the late twenties and early thirties, made a great contribution because they provided an opportunity for hybrid-corn breeders to exchange ideas, past experiences, and even inbred material.

While the plan for co-operation between the state experiment station and the Federal Department of Agriculture was highly elastic, matters usually worked out with Richey's federal department providing personnel and the state experiment station supplying facilities for the conduct of the co-operative corn-breeding program. As a result the responsibility fell to Richey to secure the trained men capable of making contributions as hybrid-corn breeders. As we have seen, the first corn belt state to undertake the new co-operative program was Iowa, and to this state Richey assigned Merle T. Jenkins, who later justified his judgement by doing a remarkable job. Except for Jenkins, Richey depended to a considerable degree on graduate students of Dr. R. A. Emerson and Dr. E. M. East to staff these important posts.

In 1923 Richey established the same type of arrangement with Kansas State College in Manhattan, and he arranged for Dr. A. M. Brunson, who had just completed his graduate work at Cornell with Dr. Emerson, to direct the corn breeding there. Although Brunson did not achieve the dramatic results that Jenkins did in Iowa, his work was in some respects equally remarkable. He worked in Kansas during some of the toughest drouth years of record in that state, and despite all the hardships and disappointments imposed by this weather hazard, Brunson managed to develop some outstanding inbreds, including the great Ky line, that are now used in hybrids all over the south central and central part of the corn belt. Brunson stayed in Kansas until 1939, when he was transferred to the Agricultural Experiment Station at Lafayette, Indiana.

Dr. Brunson had also distinguished himself in the breeding of hybrid popcorn in Kansas. He managed, despite repeated disasters due to the drouths, to develop several good popcorn inbred lines. When he went to Indiana, he took his popcorn inbreds and began immediately putting them into hybrid combinations. Seed of Brunson's hybrid popcorn was produced in Indiana on field scale for the first time in 1940. Glenn Smith, the sweet-corn breeder who developed Golden Cross Bantam, joined Brunson on the Indiana popcorn breeding project, and together they have developed what are probably the best and most widely used popcorn hybrids. Their hybrids have yielded on an average about one-third more than adapted open-pollinated varieties of popcorn as well as being superior to the old corn in popping and field performance.

Dr. R. W. Jugenheimer, trained at Iowa State College, followed Brunson in Kansas. By making use of Brunson's inbred lines and other preparatory work and taking full advantage of the improved weather of these more recent years, he made remarkable progress in providing Kansas farmers with hybrids adapted to practically every section of the state. Jugenheimer left Kansas in 1944 and is now directing the hybrid-corn breeding at the University of Illinois.

Lloyd A. Tatum is now in charge of the Kansas Experiment Station's corn-breeding program. As a result of the work done at Kansas State College and by private hybrid seed corn organizations, Kansas farmers have shifted rapidly to the use of the new hybrid corn. In 1938 only three per cent of the Kansas corn acreage was planted with hybrid seed, but by 1947 hybrid corn was grown on seventy-five per cent of all land planted to corn in Kansas.

In Ohio, Richey established the co-operative program in 1923. The first inbreeding in Ohio was done by Marion T. Meyers, who began working on a small scale in 1920 while he was still a student at Ohio State University. Meyers studied the work done at the Connecticut Experiment Station, and grew Donald Jones' Burr-Leaming—the first hybrid corn grown in the Buckeye State. Meyers even produced a limited amount of the seed of the Burr-Leaming hybrid for Ohio farmers in the early twenties, becoming the first person in the corn belt to produce for sale seed of a double-cross hybrid. G. H. Stringfield, who did his first work with hybrid corn breeding in Nebraska with Dr. T. A. Kiesselbach, came to the Ohio Agricultural Experiment Station in 1924 and has remained there ever since. The work done by Meyers at Ohio State and by Stringfield at the state experiment station was combined into one project in 1929 with Stringfield taking charge. Meyers made a further contribution not only to hybrid corn advancement in Ohio, but throughout the corn belt, by becoming one of the first persons to go into large-scale production of experiment station foundation materials—inbreds and single crosses.

A number of inbred lines, especially Oh–07, Oh–26, Oh–51, and Oh–51A, have been developed by Stringfield and have been used in hybrids from Nebraska to the Atlantic seaboard. Particular attention has been paid to hybrids which are resistant to corn borer, since Ohio was the first major growing area in the corn belt to be invaded by this insect pest. Dr. L. L. Huber and C. R. Newswander took a prominent part in this phase of the work.

In popularizing the new hybrids in Ohio, R. D. Lewis, who was extension agronomist from 1930 until 1946, had an important part. He interested both farmers and hybrid-seed producers in the new opportunities presented by hybrid corn. Dr. Lewis and D. F. Beard served as secretaries of the Ohio Seed Improvement Association, an organization through which effective promotion was given hybrid corn in Ohio. In 1936 as little as two per cent of the Ohio corn acreage was planted to hybrid corn, but in 1947 almost one hundred per cent of the corn raised in the Buckeye state was hybrid corn.

While the co-operative program was carried on in corn belt states such as Iowa, Kansas, Ohio, and Missouri, other state experiment stations were breeding the new hybrid corn entirely with their own funds. Minnesota is an excellent example of this type of work. In 1915 H. K. Hayes went to Minnesota directly from his important work on the new hybrid corn done with Dr. E. M. East at Harvard and the Connecticut Experiment Station. Because his colleagues at the University of Minnesota were unable to appreciate the possibilities of corn hybridization, Hayes was unable to make a serious start on corn inbreeding until 1920. Thus Minnesota relinquished a golden opportunity to become the great hub from which the new concept of corn breeding might have been dispersed to the entire corn belt.

After Hayes got started, progress was made rapidly at the Minnesota Experiment Station, and today hybrids developed by Hayes and his co-workers through the years, P. J. Olson, F. R. Immer, H. E. Brewbaker, C. W. Doxtator, Dean C. Anderson, Iver J. Johnson, Royse P. Murphy, H. H. Kramer, Y. S. Tsiang, Emmett L. Pinnell, and Ernest H. Rinke, are grown on more than a third of the tremendous Minnesota corn acreage.

The University of Illinois and its Agricultural Experiment Station at Urbana have made contributions to the development of hybrid corn of an important and unusual nature. First, the agronomists of probably no other state university or experiment station have taken more interest in encouraging private seedsmen to do outstanding research on hybrid corn and seed production and processing than Dr. W. L. Burlison and his staff. This group, through the years, has been made up of such men as C. M. Woodworth, W. J. Munn, G. H. Dungan, A. L. Lang, E. E. De Turk, Ben Koehler, Oren Bolin, and R. W. Jugenheimer, as well as the University of Illinois entomologists, the late W. P. Flint, John Bigger, and George Decker. This encouragement is the end product of an attitude that has characterized the relationship between the Illinois Experiment Station and the University's College of Agriculture and the farmers of the state ever since Eugene Davenport became director and dean on the Urbana campus nearly fifty years ago.

This co-operation and encouragement have been an important factor in establishing Illinois as the center of the new hybrid seed corn industry. Illinois is foremost among all other states in two respects. For one thing, probably more of the seven million bushels of hybrid seed corn produced for planting in 1947 were raised in Illinois than in any other state. In addition, Illinois organizations each season sponsor the production of large acreages of hybrid seed in other states from inbreds and foundation seed stocks maintained and produced in Illinois. Three of the four leading hybrid-seed producing organizations of the country have headquarters in Illinois.

The University of Illinois and its Experiment Station also stimulated the development of hybrid corn through its Illinois Corn Performance Test, which has provided one of the most accurate hybrid-corn testing opportunities to be found in any state. The University of Illinois' testing plan was the first to provide for a performance score which was based, in addition to yield, upon all of the many phases of performance by which farmers judge their corn. Previously, the strains tested were usually ranked in the order of their yield without sufficient regard for other characteristics important in determining a good hybrid. In the Illinois corn test the highest yielding hybrids are sometimes found ranked well down on the list because of other shortcomings. Other states have since come generally to adopt one variation or another of the Illinois plan.

In Missouri hybrid corn breeding work was begun shortly after F. D. Richey began organizing the co-operative program among the state experiment stations. L. J. Stadler, well known geneticist who worked with Dr. R. A. Emerson at Cornell for a time, has been associated with the program in Missouri almost since it began. In recent years M. S. Zuber has worked with Dr. Stadler, directing the Missouri corn breeding programs.

Although corn is an important crop in only the southeastern and eastern parts of South Dakota, the Agricultural Experiment Station at Brookings has taken a major interest in corn development for more than half a century, the first publications about corn having been issued by Luther Foster as early as 1889. By 1910 corn had become a crop of sufficient importance that one of the Station's publications said with understandable pride, "South Dakota is now one of the corn producing states of the Union." Many of the fine corn investigations in the years since have been conducted and published by A. N. Hume. The hybrid corn breeding in South Dakato is now directed by D. B. Shank, and the Experiment Station has released a number of hybrids. Two-thirds of South Dakota's more than four million acres of corn are planted with hybrid corn.

The question has many times been raised as to why hybrid corn did not develop as rapidly in the southern states where the total corn acreage is comparable with the corn acreage even in the great corn belt. The general assumption has been that the job of breeding hybrid corn for the South is more difficult and consequently a task requiring more time. Actually, while the additional insect and disease hazards found in the South have been a retarding factor, the major reason adapted hybrids are not yet in extensive use in the South is that the southern experiment station seedsmen haven't taken the interest in corn hybridization that has been shown in the northern states. Merle Jenkins, in charge of the United States Department of Agriculture's corn investigations, explains, "Corn hybrids now available for planting in the South represent only a preliminary effort in the breeding of special types for this area. They are the product of only a fraction of the time, energy and funds that have been devoted to the development of corn hybrids for the corn belt. It is not surprising, therefore, that they answer the requirements of their region less precisely than do the hybrids now available for the corn belt. . . Considerable time will be required for the breeding . . . of the outstanding southern hybrids of the future."

The Federal Department of Agriculture offered the southern experiment stations the same opportunity to launch the co-operative corn-breeding programs as was offered to state experiment stations in the corn belt, but except for Louisiana and Tennessee and later three other states, no breeding work of a sustained nature has been conducted. Even in Tennessee and Louisiana, the support given the co-operative program has until very recently been indifferent. The major reason for the disinterest in the South has been that while corn acreage has been large, cotton has been the major crop. Now that the South is generally seeking to diversify its agriculture and is anxious to increase its production of livestock, the increased interest in corn hybridization within a few years will undoubtedly produce highly significant results. On February 24, 1939, the directors of the southern agricultural experiment stations met in New Orleans and voted to make hybrid-corn breeding a co-operative program, the same action which the corn belt experiment station directors took at St. Louis in the spring of 1925. Much credit for having brought this about is due Fred H. Hull, corn breeder at the Florida Agricultural Experiment Station.

Strangely, the same F. D. Richey, so largely responsible for originating the program of co-operation among experiment stations a quarter of a century ago, is directly in charge of the increased co-operative work now being done in the South, although in the meantime he served as associate chief of the Bureau of Plant Industry and was for a time engaged in the development of his own hybrids in Ohio. Richey now has his office at the Tennessee Agricultural Experiment Station at Knoxville, Tennessee, from which he co-ordinates the breeding programs undertaken jointly by the Federal Department of Agriculture and the several co-operating state experiment stations.

He and Mrs. Richey live in a small but attractive Cape Cod house among whose chief appointments is their remarkable collection of objects associated with corn gathered from all over the world. It is undoubtedly the finest collection of its kind.

The first corn inbreeding in the South was done by H. C. Kyle, in 1916, as a staff member of C. P. Hartley's Office of Corn Investigations. Kyle did work at a number of places including Tiffin, Georgia. While he early developed some promising inbreds from southern varieties, he found it extremely difficult to maintain his lines under Georgia growing conditions and nothing of consequence came of his program.

Dean of all the active hybrid-corn breeders of the South is Hugo Stoneberg, a federal plant breeder stationed at Baton Rouge, Louisiana, since 1924. At Pee Dee, South Carolina, in 1921 Stoneberg started a corn inbreeding program that was cancelled after one year of work through no fault of his. He then spent two years working under Richey's direction at the federal experiment station at Arlington Farm in Virginia before going to Louisiana. Since he worked most of these years in Louisiana with little if any opportunity to exchange inbred lines with neighboring experiment stations, progress has been understandably slow. However, by 1945 Stoneberg had released five hybrids for Louisiana farmers, three of which were white hybrids. Enough seed was produced so that 150,000 acres of these hybrids were grown by southern farmers in 1946, or a little more than one per cent of the 1,250,000 acres of corn raised in Louisiana.

In Tennessee a program has been in progress under the direction of L. S. Mayer during the same years that Stoneberg worked in Louisiana. Mayer worked almost entirely with the Neal Paymaster, the open-pollinated corn so outstanding in Tennessee that in the state capitol in Nashville there is exhibited a "Hall of Fame" bust of the originator, William Haskill Neal, with the inscription, "In 1898 W. H. Neal of Lebanon, Tennessee, began field selection of corn and by 1914 had developed a variety of corn that produced two ears known as Neal's Paymaster that has added two and one-third million bushels to Tennessee's annual yield." By 1935 Mayer had developed a number of white inbreds from Paymaster. After Dr. Jenkins became principal agronomist in charge of corn investigations, he spent a considerable amount of time with Mayer. Together they developed from the Paymaster inbreds two white hybrids known as Tennessee 10 and Tennessee 15 which have become the standard for white corn in the Middle South, just as Neal Paymaster was for a generation the standard among white open-pollinated strains.

In 1927 Paul Mangelsdorf, who learned about the new hybrid corn directly from East and Jones in New England, began inbreeding in Texas. Mangelsdorf was impressed with the difference in the weather hazards in Texas, greater even than in the corn-growing areas of his native state of Kansas. Especially was it difficult successfully to grow inbreds, naturally less vigorous than other corn. Mangelsdorf was joined by Dr. R. G. Reeves in 1928, and the work has continued unbroken, thanks to the collective efforts of Reeves, John S. Rogers, C. H. McDowell, and D. H. Bowman, and a number of hybrids have been released for Texas farmers by the state experiment station. While Texas is in the group of Southern States, its breeding program is more closely akin to that of Kansas. Many of the inbred lines brought in from other experiment stations have come from a program conducted by Brunson in Kansas. Texas farmers are now beginning to reap the benefit of all the years of work done on hybrid corn. In 1947 well over one-fifth of the state's corn acreage, which in an average year amounts to about five million acres, or about half the acreage in the state of Iowa, was planted to the new hybrid corn.

In Florida, which ranks thirtieth among the states in corn production, a hybrid-corn breeding program has been in progress for several years. Fred H. Hull of the Agricultural

Experiment Station at Gainesville has directed the work with his attention naturally focused on the northern half of the state where corn is the principal grain crop. Dr. Hull has developed several good inbred lines from Whatley Prolific, Cuban Yellow Flint, and other late varieties, these inbreds being among the latest maturing lines used in the United States. Hull's first hybrid, Florida W–1, is a white corn made up entirely of his inbred lines. W–1 early demonstrated its capacity to outyield Florida open-pollinated varieties by as much as forty per cent.

A most promising program is now being sponsored co-operatively in North Carolina by the Agricultural Experiment Station at Raleigh and the United States Department of Agriculture. P. H. Harvey has developed some unusual yellow inbreds and his station has already released four yellow hybrids, nearly 50,000 bushels of seed having been produced for use in 1947. Since North Carolina stands sixteenth among the states in corn production and each year plants about $2\frac{1}{3}$ million acres, the volume of seed of its Experimental Station hybrids as yet is not large. Harvey has also worked with white corn, and the North Carolina Station has already released a white hybrid.

In Arkansas the first work on hybrid-corn breeding was done as early as 1923 by L. W. Osborn. In 1926 C. K. McClelland took over the project. Unfortunately in 1930 the material was lost in a severe drouth, and although a new start was made immediately, the great drouth in 1934 destroyed all of the Arkansas inbred material. In 1935 Dr. L. M. Humphreys inaugurated a new program at the Cotton Branch Experiment Station at Marianna, Arkansas, in the belief that weather hazards would not be so great at this place. D. B. Shank took over the direction of Dr. Humphrey's program in 1941, and some promising material has been developed since. Ben D. McCollum now directs the work, and it is expected that the Arkansas Experiment Station will begin releasing hybrids this year or next. However, the private organizations engaged in developing hybrids for the Arkansas area have done a sufficiently good job that more than forty per cent of the state's approximately two million acres were planted with hybrid corn in 1947. Especially outstanding among the men associated with the private organizations developing hybrids adapted to Arkansas conditions is Bob Ayers of Little Rock, who has perhaps done more than any other one person to bring to the farmers of Arkansas the benefits of the new hybrid corn.

Investigations into the breeding of hybrid corn began in Kentucky as early as 1922. The plant pathologist, William Dorney Valleau, one of the first men to study with Dr. H. K. Hayes after Hayes went to the University of Minnesota from the Connecticut Experiment Station, began inbreeding corn early in the twenties. Dr. Valleau was interested primarily in breeding for disease resistance, but when E. J. Kinney took over the breeding in 1925, he placed major emphasis upon higher yield and generally improved field performance. By making use of inbreds developed at the stations in nearby states, L. M. Josephson, who took over the Kentucky corn program in 1943, is recommending for use on Kentucky farms yellow hybrids, Kentucky 102, Kentucky 103, and the famous U. S. 13. The Kentucky station has also two white hybrids, Kentucky 72B and Kentucky 203. Kentucky farmers have been quick to switch to the new hybrid corn. Although little use of hybrid corn was made before 1940, approximately seventy-five per cent of the state's corn acreage in 1947 was planted to hybrid corn.

The breeding of hybrids is now being done at experiment stations in well over forty states, evidence not only of the widespread interest in this type of work but also dramatic testimony to the general importance of corn itself in the United States. While a number of state experiment stations co-operate with the federal program, special mention should be made of the work done independently of that which Merle T. Jenkins of Washington, D. C., has charge. There are, in addition, an unknown number of privately sponsored corn-breeding programs.

In addition to the programs that we have already described, work is now being conducted by other experiment stations which deserve mention. T. H. Rogers has charge of hybrid corn at the Alabama Agricultural Experiment Station at Auburn, Alabama. Francis L. Smith is breeding corn at the California Agricultural Experiment Station at Davis, California. W. H. Leonard is directing corn breeding for the Colorado Agricultural Experiment Station at Fort Collins, Colorado. C. E. Phillips is breeding hybrids at the Delaware Agricultural Experiment Station at Newark, Delaware.

Work is being done at three places in Georgia with G. A. Lebedeff directing the work at the Georgia Agricultural Experiment Station at Experiment, Georgia, and W. H. Freeman handling the program being conducted at the Georgia Coastal Plain Experiment Station at Tifton. Work is also being done at the University of Georgia at Athens.

Warren K. Pope is working with hybrid corn at the Idaho Agricultural Experiment Station at Moscow, Idaho. In Maine the emphasis has been on sweet corn, and the work is in charge of Russell M. Bailey. R. G. Rothgeb directs the breeding for the Maryland Agricultural Experiment Station at College Park, Maryland. In Massachusetts, work is being done both on field and sweet corn, H. M. Yegian directing the breeding of field hybrids and W. H. Lackman having charge of the hybrid sweet corn.

E. E. Down is the corn breeder in charge of the work being done at the Michigan Agricultural Experiment Station at East Lansing, Michigan. The work in Montana is sponsored by the Montana Agricultural Experiment Station at Bozeman and the work is being conducted by H. K. Schultz. In

Mississippi, R. C. Eckhardt is directing the work on hybrids of the Mississippi Agricultural Experiment Station at State College, Mississippi. In New Jersey work on both field corn and sweet corn is being done at the New Jersey Agricultural Experiment Station at New Brunswick. J. C. Anderson has charge of the field-corn work, and Robert S. Snell of the sweet-corn program.

In New York the Cornell work is directed by R. G. Wiggans, the program being sponsored by the New York Agricultural Experiment Station at Ithaca. Sweet-corn breeding at the Experiment Station at Geneva is directed by Curtis Dearborn. William Wiidakas handles the breeding of the North Dakota Agricultural Experiment Station at State College, North Dakota. In addition to the work already described in Ohio, J. B. Park also is conducting a project at Ohio State University in Columbus.

James S. Brooks directs work at the Oklahoma Agricultural Experiment Station at Stillwater. The program of the Oregon Agricultural Experiment Station at Corvallis is in charge of R. E. Fore. Hybrid corn work in Pennsylvania is being done on both field and sweet corn. L. L. Huber directs the work on field corn, and M. T. Lewis has charge of the sweet corn. The South Carolina Pee Dee Experiment Station has just begun a breeding program with Alfred Manwiller as its director.

The hybrid-corn breeding of the Virginia Agricultural Experiment Station at Blacksburg is in charge of C. F. Genter. The West Virginia Agricultural Experiment Station has a program conducted by J. L. Cartledge.

The breeding of hybrid sweet corn has become such big business in the United States that it deserves additional mention. Whereas in Colonial times much of the corn raised in America was used directly for human consumption, now only sweet corn is eaten in large volume in an easily recognizable state, most of our vast corn crop now being converted into meat, milk, or other food products. Sweet corn is raised on field scale on tens of thousands of acres of our best corn land as well as in millions of gardens.

Exploiting to the full the opportunities which breeding methods afford to develop special purpose types, the sweet corn breeders have channelled their efforts into two general types—one of which is used as canning corn and the other of which is best adapted for roasting on the ear as quickly as possible after it is secured from the garden or market. The Golden Cross Bantam, whose story we have already told in Chapter 11, is the outstanding example of the new corn for canning. A number of other breeders, such as Ralph Singleton of the Connecticut Agricultural Experiment Station, have specialized in breeding the garden and market strains of sweet corn.

Singleton's project at Connecticut is an outstanding program for the development of the garden and market types of sweet corn, and was begun as a direct result of the early work in hybridization at the Connecticut Station done by East, Hayes, and Jones. In fact, Jones had begun work on hybrid sweet corn before Singleton joined the staff of the Connecticut Station in 1927.

By 1931 the Connecticut Station had developed one or two hybrids of sweet corn. During the sweet corn season of that year Singleton had an interesting and significant visit with Birdsey A. Farnham, who has a farm at the edge of New Haven and who prides himself on having good sweet corn for market by July 4. Farnham told Singleton in just about the minimum words required to tell it that none of the hybrids developed at the Connecticut Station were any good and that he would have nothing more to do with them.

"This made me mad," said Singleton, "but fortunately it also set me thinking, and what I thought was that this man Farnham will one day grow sweet corn hybrids developed by the Connecticut Station and like it. He has been doing this for the last four or five years," adds Singleton significantly.

Singleton introduced some new approaches to the breeding problem. One of the most important was that he began making careful inspections of his material in the green stage, whereas before the records had been based largely on observations made of the dried ears and upon the date of silking as an indication of earliness. The first year some of the best of the strains developed earlier were discarded when they were inspected at the "roasting ear" stage because they failed to measure up to desired standards. After a few years of hard work, the new garden and market sweet corn hybrids that have won wide recognition for the Connecticut Station and Singleton began to appear.

The Connecticut Station now has an almost complete line of sweet corn hybrids ranging from early to late maturities. Singleton, who could have been a fine historian had he not chosen to become a plant breeder, has a most interesting system of naming the Connecticut Station's hybrids. They are named for famous persons in American history with the earliest maturing strains being given names of early Americans, and the medium to late strains being assigned such names as Wilson. Singleton confidently believes that one of his new experimental hybrids will be the latest and among the best hybrids yet developed at the Connecticut Station, and if and when this comes true, there has already been reserved for it a very special name. If this new hybrid proves deserving, it will be named for the man whom the Gallup poll found was the most popular American in both 1946 and 1947—Dwight Eisenhower.

A number of private breeders have made outstanding contributions, especially to the canning hybrids. Lloyd Koritz of Rochelle, Illinois, is one. His sweet corns have been distributed as the well-known Del Monte brand of canned corn. Stuart Smith, also an important breeder of field corn hybrids, has developed sweet corn that is used extensively by the canners.

The state experiment stations in Iowa and Illinois have

conducted projects that have resulted in the development of outstanding strains. W. A. Huelsen began inbreeding sweet corn at the University of Illinois Experiment Station in 1922. Dr. Huelsen has worked largely with the Country Gentleman variety, and his hybrids are extensively used in Illinois and some other sections of the corn belt. E. S. Haber has also worked with Country Gentleman at the Iowa State College Experiment Station. His Ioana strain is an unusually popular white hybrid sweet corn, and he has developed a number of yellow sweet corns too. A more recent program, already producing results, is that sponsored by the University of Wisconsin with the noted field corn breeder, N. P. Neal, and R. H. Andrews in charge. Wisconsin in recent years has become one of the leading producers of sweet corn in the country, and reflecting this trend the Wisconsin program was begun in 1938.

One of the things which have enabled the breeders to make new hybrids so quickly available to the public was the discovery that southern Idaho provided a nearly ideal area for seed production. Credit for this discovery belongs to George Crookham, Jr., and Don Baldridge, two young men who got out of college about the time Glenn Smith completed the development of Golden Cross Bantam. These two men foresaw the tremendous demand for Golden Cross Bantam seed, and as a result went into the business of producing this and other hybrid sweet corn seed. They discovered that southern Idaho land, properly irrigated, brought together a number of conditions that made it remarkably well suited to the production of many types of seed. Since then practically all of the large growers of hybrid seed have transferred their production to southern Idaho until today most of the seed for the vast American sweet corn acreage is produced in this northwestern state.

CHAPTER XVII

New Temple on Old Foundations

YOU CAN'T plant a pedigree. Which is a way of saying that more than plant breeding has been needed to give American farmers the miracle of hybrid corn. The long years of work done carefully, brilliantly, and patiently by East, Hayes, Jones, and all the other hybrid-corn makers would have come to little or nothing had not the often discussed system of private enterprise stepped in and matched, in a sense, the genius of the corn breeders by raising up a new industry to convert the fruits of their research into something corn farmers could use. This new industry invested the resources and took the risks involved in a quick building of a new business, so that in a remarkably few years the benefits of the new kind of corn were spread to farmers scattered all the way from Canada to Texas and from Oregon to Georgia.

Over all, this new business in hybrid seed that passed from babyhood to manhood within a single decade has performed two vital services. First, it developed methods required to preserve in seed corn the precious characteristics developed in the new hybrid strains by the breeders, an assignment the exact like of which no group of seedsmen ever faced before. Secondly, the new industry demonstrated and convinced millions of farmers of the merit of hybrid corn in a period so short that even yet the possibilities of doing it appear only a little short of the fantastic.

This job of translating the new corn from the laboratory

stage into something of practical and nearly universal importance could have been done so effectively in America only by calling into play the tremendous forces at the command of our free enterprise system. Although the basic breeding concepts upon which hybrid corn rests today were almost all the product of work done in state and federal supported experiment stations, not a single crop of hybrid seed corn has ever been offered to American farmers by a government-owned or government-controlled institution.

From the moment Donald Jones of the Connecticut Experiment Station decided that seed of the first double cross hybrid should be produced on George Carter's farm by the ocean, the trend toward placing in the hands of private enterprise the task of producing hybrid seed corn for our farmers has never been reversed or even substantially altered. This is true even though an important percentage of the hybrid corn used on American farms is produced from foundation seed stocks—the inbreds and single crosses—supplied by the state experiment stations.

Although a significant volume of hybrid seed corn is produced by individuals and organizations with no previous experience in producing farm seed, by far the largest part of the new industry is built upon the solid foundation of regular seed businesses. Providing farm seeds in this country has to a rather remarkable degree been associated with certain families in somewhat the same way that banking and finance have been linked with the Rothschilds and the Morgans. To these organizations long associated with family names, such as the Funks in Illinois, Mangelsdorfs in Kansas, the Robinsons and Coys in Nebraska, the Peppards in Missouri, the Fields in Iowa and the Hoffmans in Pennsylvania, has fallen a big share of the responsibility for supplying seed of the new hybrid corn to American farmers.

Add to these organizations the others not so long established that were in the business of producing open-pollinated seed corn such as the De Kalb Agricultural Association of Illinois, Lester Pfister of Illinois, Northup King of Minnesota, and scores of others—and well over eighty per cent of all the hybrid seed corn industry is included. The bright exception is the Pioneer Hi-Bred Corn Company that was organized from scratch by Henry Wallace and his friends for the expressed purpose of producing hybrid seed corn. The whole matter adds up to this: by and large, the new hybrid seed corn industry was raised against the background of the old and established American farm seed business.

Within five years after the new hybrid corn was being distributed in more than experimental amounts, the methods of producing and processing seed corn had been completely revolutionized, converted from a job that almost any careful farmer could do with little special machinery, into a high-precision business which required both knowledge and equipment beyond the means of the farmer who selected seed corn.

As soon as corn farmers accepted the fact they could neither select seed from their own fields nor profitably maintain the breeding plots necessary to producing their own hybrid seed corn, the way had been opened to building the new hybrid seed corn industry. Within a few years this industry acquired a trained personnel and specialized machinery and equipment that quickly outmoded all previous methods and made available seed of a quality never before known.

Let us take three examples of these revolutionary changes introduced into each of the three most important phases of securing seed corn—the growing of the seed, harvesting it, and handling and storing it. Consider first the matter of growing the seed in the field, to which the average farmer, before the coming of hybrid corn gave no special attention since he expected to select his seed from the regular crop each fall. Now, fields for the production of seed corn are selected with great care both in respect to soil fertility and for a location that gives maximum protection from weather hazards.

One of the most exacting jobs in growing hybrid seed corn is the removal of tassels from the ear parent rows so that all pollen must necessarily be supplied by the pollinator foundation strain. Depending upon the rate of planting in the field, it is necessary to pull from 5,000 to 8,000 tassels from each acre of land devoted to hybrid seed corn, and the tassels must be removed quickly after they appear, else they will commence to shed unwanted pollen. This detasseling job was at first done, and still is in a significant part of the total production, by crews of trained detassellers moving up and down the rows on foot.

Lester Pfister, the most mechanically inclined of the hybrid-corn makers, developed a "detasseling machine" which enables the detasseling crews to ride through the field at about the height of the tassels. Except in very wet weather which makes ground muddy and the machines difficult to pull through the corn fields, the machines have the advantage of preventing the detasseler from tiring so quickly and of enabling the crew's foreman, who usually is the driver, to give better supervision.

Corn detasseling has become an American institution during the last fifteen years, and a full story of it would constitute a significant commentary upon life in this country during that period. The first large scale detasseling was done during the thirties when the general employment level was not high, and the detasseling crews were made up largely of men and older boys accustomed to farm work. However, as less farm labor became available in the years just before America entered the war, younger farm boys appeared in the detasseling crews, and it was not uncommon for groups of boys from urban areas to be recruited and transported to the area to handle the detasseling job. Then during the acute

In this well-isolated, seed-producing field six successive
rows of seed parent foundation strain were alternated with
two rows of the male foundation line. Before pollen shedding began, crews of detasselers removed the tassels from
the seed parent rows, forcing a cross of the two foundation
strains

Demonstrating how the tassels are removed. During the crucial labor shortages of the war years, women carried out a large part of this tedious job

labor shortage of the war years, detasseling was done almost entirely by girls, women, and young boys. In a very real sense it was these thousands of women, girls, and boys who made it possible for us to have ample supplies of hybrid seed during the crucial war years when food production would have been sharply curtailed if farmers had been unable to raise hybrid corn. American women deserve much more recognition than they ever received for volunteering to do this job that at the best is strenuous and at the worst can be one of the most disagreeable kinds of work.

Certainly the detasseling of hybrid corn has thrust upon our public in general and corn farmers in particular a new appreciation of the function and importance of the corn tassel, if not the science of plant breeding as a whole. The Indians never discovered the significance of the corn's tassel.

The second important step in securing seed corn, the harvest, has also been completely changed by the coming of hybrid corn. With open-pollinated corn there were almost as many ways of harvesting next year's seed as there were farmers. Some went into the field as soon as the corn was well glazed and marked certain choice ears which they would go back and gather as soon as they were sufficiently dry but in advance of the regular corn harvest. Others made a practice of carrying a little box in the wagon at corn picking time and placing in it any unusually large, sound, and heavy ears from standing stocks. Some farmers, and some of the most successful too, picked out their seed as they fed corn to the hogs out of the crib. Now the producers of hybrid seed watch their fields anxiously as the corn approaches maturity so that they may begin the harvest as quickly as possible after the corn is ripe. No longer do we wait until corn dries down in the fields to safe storage level. Instead, tests are made at frequent intervals, and just as soon as the kernel moisture is down to thirty per cent and sometimes when it is even higher, the harvesting is begun and the seed corn is rushed to plants where it is dried down to safe storage levels by artificial means.

What happens in the drying of a kernel of seed corn is a dramatic story, and explains why the new seed industry could never exist as it does now until some effective means was found to dry seed corn. The tiny germ in a kernel of good seed is a living, breathing thing. In favorable surroundings, this germ will remain in good health for considerable periods of time—several years. The little germ develops shortly after pollination and fertilization have taken place. Even in the soft milk stage, when the new kernel is only a few days old, it will germinate or sprout, but so long as the moisture in the kernel remains high, the germ is subject to a great many hazards that can snuff out its life in a short time.

Only when the seed is mature or reasonably so and its moisture is reduced by natural or artificial means down to about thirteen per cent or less is the germ safe from these hazards. Drying does many things for the kernel, not all of them explainable. Perhaps most important, drying has the effect of putting the germ in its resting stage, inducing it to "sleep," and in its "sleep" much less of its precious energies are exhausted. In this kind of sleep, somewhat akin to the hibernation or "little death" of bears and other animals, the corn germ is not hurt either by subzero or fairly high temperatures, and the chances of its becoming diseased are very slight. Until the kernel is dry, the germ is sensitive to extremes of temperature, especially cold, and to many diseases. This is why the producers work at a feverish pace every fall to get their crop out of the field and dried at the first possible moment and before severe weather begins.

The man chiefly responsible for development of the first seed drier capable of drying a large volume quickly, safely, and inexpensively was Andrew H. Wright of the University of Wisconsin. Andy Wright and F. W. Duffee, university engineer, developed the bin-type drier for use in processing open-pollinated seed corn in Wisconsin, but the drier was perfected near the end of the open-pollinated era and has found its greatest usefulness in drying hybrid seed.

Before Wright worked out the bin-type drier, there had been scores of other plans developed for the drying of seed. Probably nowhere in the United States had there been more work done on this problem than on Funk Farms in Illinois where shortly after 1900 special drying plants were built in which the seed ears were placed in boxes like orange-crates over which air was forced by huge fans. The boxes were even turned at intervals so that air could strike all sides of them. Even in Nebraska where normally the fall is dry, J. C. Robinson and his seedsmen in the Elkhorn Valley were using special seed driers as early as 1908. Plans developed elsewhere provided for laying the corn out on drying floors, and in some instances air was forced over them. Others used racks, and one method provided for placing each ear on a hanger-like ice pick so that air could circulate freely around all its surface. The trouble with all of these plans was that they required too much space and handling and simply weren't practical when there was a large volume of seed to be dried.

Andy Wright was reared on a farm in Oklahoma where as a boy he saw corn subjected to natural heat from 105° to 115° which, when it came late in the season, was a great help in drying the crop quickly to safe levels for storage. After attending college at Oklahoma A & M, where he was an agricultural student and star athlete, at one time holding the half-mile record of the Southwest Conference, Wright took additional courses at Kansas State College and then came to Wisconsin to do graduate work. His work attracted such favorable attention that he was given a position on the College of Agriculture staff. Then he ran into the problem of drying seed corn, which under the short Wisconsin growing season is a much more critical problem than in Oklahoma.

Wright faced the problem for several years, and in 1924

he decided to do something about it. He couldn't forget those hot fall winds in Oklahoma that would blow first from one direction and then another, drying down the corn quickly and safely. Why not, he reasoned, duplicate those conditions in a small compartment, perhaps using a special bin specially constructed so that hot air could be forced through the corn first from one direction and then from the opposite side. He took the matter up with his good friend, Engineer Floyd W. Duffee, and together they built a test model. Using a large discarded wooden packing box for the bin, they cut holes in it so that hot air could be forced through, first from the bottom and then from the top. An old blacksmith's fan was pressed into service to supply the forced hot air. That was in 1926.

Then they filled the old wooden box with soggy corn, turned on the blacksmith's fan, and waited. The answer was not long in coming, and, says Andy Wright, "It worked right from the start. It was one of those dreams that clicked the first time, and we just didn't have any trouble at all. A number of persons have tried to make changes and improvements on it since. We've tried to make some ourselves, but they didn't work as well as our original plan."

Today Andy Wright's bin seed drier is the very foundation of hybrid-corn processing, being used generally throughout the United States and Canada. It is even being used in the dry southwest from whence Wright got his impressions which led to the development of the Wisconsin drier. Not only are all of these driers built on the same general plan as the first model built by Wright and Duffee, but they are operated in a similar way. All of them use forced air, heated to about 110° F.—just about like the hot Oklahoma winds that blew across those corn fields when Wright was a boy there. With the new drier it is possible to reduce a thousand bushels of seed corn from thirty per cent moisture down to thirteen per cent in about seventy-two hours under average working conditions, something that was utterly impracticable before Andy Wright went to work on the problem.

Undoubtedly the first Wisconsin-type drier to be built and used exclusively for the drying of hybrid corn was the one erected by Pioneer Hi-bred Corn Company at Johnston, Ohio. The story of this drier was told in Chapter X. Later the Campbell Furnace Company of Des Moines learned about the problem of forcing heat through Wallace's drier, and after doing a considerable amount of research, developed the Campbell combination oil burner and fan unit that is now widely used throughout the hybrid seed industry.

Finally let us consider the third and last important phase in the preserving of seed corn, that of the handling and storage until planting time in the spring. Farmers used to meet this problem in a wide variety of ways too, but most of them put their seed ears in the driest, most rodent-proof place they could find, and then toward spring they shelled the seed so that it would be ready on planting day. A few made germination tests, but they were the exception rather than the rule.

Now the producer of hybrid seed takes the seed ears from the drier and after one or several inspections, shells them, but the job of processing is just beginning. The shelled corn goes into various machines which separate kernels of various sizes and shapes so that 800 to 1000 kernels on an ear are divided into perhaps a half dozen uniform types, such as large-sized flat kernels, medium-sized flat kernels, small-sized flat kernels, and similar grades of round kernels. This grading enables the farmer to use practically any size of seed kernel with the same ease and does away with the need for the old practice of discarding all but the flat kernels in the center portion of the ear. The seed is stored in dry, rodent-proof warehouses until it is delivered to the individual farmer in the spring, and continuous germination tests are made during this storage period; but the new industry goes even further and performs an additional operation of which neither the Indians nor our own farmers before the coming of hybrid corn ever dreamed. Drawing upon the wonders of the new world of science, most of our seed corn is now chemically treated to destroy not only disease organisms that may be living within the seed kernel but also to retard the development of soil-borne diseases which might attack after the seed is planted in the spring.

As early as 1916, Jim Holbert began experiments with chemical seed treatment, using the inorganic mercury compounds which did give some fine results on the germinator but which were disappointing in the field tests. The problem was similar to that confronting a physician treating a disease within the human body: some chemical had to be found that could destroy the disease organisms and at the same time not injure good seed. Holbert had tested literally scores of different chemicals and had largely dismissed the matter from mind until C. S. Reddy, a graduate student of Dr. A. G. Johnson at the University of Wisconsin, became interested in the matter during the summer of 1921 while he was working with Holbert at the Federal Field Station at Bloomington, Illinois.

Reddy was doing his graduate work on bacterial diseases of corn with a special interest in Black Bundle Disease. He began to probe the possibilities of controlling this disease by seed treatment, and he demonstrated that some of the German organic mercury compounds, released to this country after the German defeat in the first World War, could wipe out these seed-borne disease organisms and even retard the damage done by soil-borne diseases in corn and still not impair the value of the seed. These chemicals, developed by the Germans to combat venereal diseases, were promising for their high degree of effectiveness and low degree of toxicity. It was suggested that they might be useful in fighting plant diseases as well. Some of them, especially the organic mer-

cury compound known as Uspulun, did prove to be effective
when used as a water solution treatment on seed corn.

Reddy made a big contribution when his early work first
demonstrated that there were real possibilities of controlling
at least seed-borne diseases in corn by chemical treatment.
He has continued to maintain his interest in this problem,
and today as a member of the Iowa State College staff, Reddy
is one of the country's foremost authorities on seed treatments.

The water solution treatment probably could never have
come into wide usefulness, as it requires that seed corn be
soaked in a chemical solution for considerable periods of
time. Shortly thereafter, Holbert discovered that the more
or less insoluble organic mercury compounds, applied to seed
corn as dry dust, were as good as Uspulun in water solution
or better in controlling seed-borne diseases and to some extent soil-borne diseases. Holbert's discovery opened the way
to the development of rapid mechanical processes for applying the chemical treatment to seed corn.

Although the German chemicals were useful in demonstration work, they were not the final answer to the problem because a number of factors discouraged their widespread use.
The Du Pont organization became interested in the matter,
and a full-blown research project was organized with Du
Pont chemists—one of them the same man, Dr. Max Engel-
man, who was associated with the development of Uspulun
in German laboratories—working tirelessly to produce new
and better chemicals. Holbert, aided by Ben Koehler of the
University of Illinois, did the work of testing and evaluation
in the field.

Although several years of work were required, from this
project came the first of the potent new chemical dust treatments for seed which could discourage seed-borne diseases
as well as retard many that are soil-borne. Holbert and
Koehler found that it was not uncommon to add as much as

ten bushels an acre to production on corn belt farms as a result of treating the seed with the new dusts when periods of extremely adverse weather followed corn planting.

More recently the control of seed decay as well as seed infections is being recognized as an important factor in securing satisfactory field stands of corn. Newer organic compounds, non-mercuric in composition, have shown real merit in improving field stands and increasing yields under adverse conditions where seed infections are not involved. Of this class of seed treatment, Arasan is generally recognized as superior. P. E. Hoppe, of the United States Department of Agriculture, who is stationed at the University of Wisconsin, has developed effective techniques for more quickly evaluating new preparations as they appear.

The scope of seed treatments is likely to be broadened beyond any now in use. Much research work is already being done looking toward the introduction of DDT into a treatment which would protect the seed from insect damage. The time seems close at hand when we shall have treatments which will be fully effective in controlling seed infection, seed decay, damage from insects while the seed is in storage, and, at the same time, be nonpoisonous and nonirritating to those who treat and handle the seed.

Some limited treatment was given to open-pollinated seed corn, but it was not until the new industry began to develop that the practice of treating seed chemically became general. Today most of the millions of bushels of hybrid seed distributed to farmers each spring have been given chemical treatment. This treatment, along with the improvement in hybrid corn itself, accounts for the tremendous improvement in field stands and the resulting higher yields traceable to heavier and more even distribution of plants in the field.

Working out the processes by which hybrid corn could be made practical and available to millions of corn farmers on

this continent was, however, only one of the important accomplishments of the seed industry. No less imposing is the
job that has been done in demonstrating the value of hybrid
corn to American and Canadian farmers.

"Great things seldom come with convincing labels on
them," says R. R. St. John, a maker of hybrid corn, and the
new corn was no exception. Farmers are by nature careful
judges of new propositions, and they might have been expected to take a generation or perhaps more to convince
themselves of the merits of the new corn. That farmers in the
great corn belt were convinced in less that one decade is
dramatic evidence of the kind of job the seed industry has
done in popularizing hybrid corn.

There is no greater myth connected with the story of
hybrid corn than the popular notion that it sold itself to
American and Canadian farmers. The fact is that no more
effective and intensive job of selling a new development was
ever done in all the long history of American agriculture
than the fledgling industry did on hybrid corn. One of the
things that made the promotion so effective was that the
seedsmen chose to popularize their new product by almost
totally new methods.

For the first time on such a scale farmers were enlisted to
become chief promoters of a new product, and in the corn
belt and in many other corn growing areas, it was a case of
farmers convincing their own friends and neighbors of the
value of the new corn. In the short space of a decade some
50,000 farmers associated themselves with this task.

The principle of being a good neighbor figured heavily in
the rapid spread of hybrid corn. Almost everyone enjoys
being the bearer of good news and introducing his friends to
some advantage not previously enjoyed. These farmer-salesmen were perhaps motivated as much by their desire to enable their neighbors to get a better corn crop as by the

incentive of profit. They were so confident of the miracles which their new corn could perform that some interesting schemes were used to secure its immediate acceptance.

By 1930 Bob Garst had convinced himself that well-adapted strains of hybrid corn could outyield the old open-pollinated corn by an average of at least twelve bushels an acre. In the early spring of 1931, he suggested to his friend, Clyde B. Charlton, an attorney in Des Moines, that he plant hybrid corn on his farm in Pocahontas County, Iowa, explaining that Charlton should pay half the cost of the seed and that Hoskins, his tenant, should pay the remainder, since they would benefit equally from the increased yield. Charlton said that his tenant would have to be guaranteed that the corn would outyield his open-pollinated crop enough to justify the extra cost of the seed.

Garst immediately proposed to furnish the seed free on the condition that he be given one-half of any increased yield his hybrid might produce above the yield of the open-pollinated corn. Both Charlton and Hoskins thought this a fine arrangement, and accordingly their land was planted with the two kinds of corn—forty rows of hybrid to twenty rows of open-pollinated. Garst furnished six bushels of seed, which planted about forty-five acres.

That fall the yield of the hybrid corn was 80 bushels an acre compared to 58 bushels an acre for open-pollinated corn. Garst's share of the increased yield was about 500 bushels, worth at that time about 50 cents a bushel. Under the terms of the agreement Garst received $250—something more than $40 a bushel for seed which he had offered to Charlton in the spring for $10 a bushel.

Garst and his farmer salesmen made hundreds of arrangements like this, and the practice spread rapidly through several states during the first years that hybrid corn was being introduced. As farmers realized its power to increase yields, they were no longer interested in such arrangements to share the increased yield. But one such example in a county focused the attention of farmers on the value of hybrid corn and won rapid and general acceptance for it.

Garst employed another practice in popularizing hybrid corn which is still in use. In 1932 he began selling 95 per cent of his available supply of seed and then sacking the remaining 5 per cent in eight-pound bags, which held enough corn to plant an acre, and giving them to farmers who had not yet planted any of the new hybrid. Its performance was so outstanding that in the great majority of cases the farmers would plant an important part of their acreage to hybrid corn the following year. This meant that by dividing a bushel into eight-pound samples, Garst was likely to have seven more customers the following year, whereas if he had sold the entire bushel to one farmer, he would have secured only one convert.

The proving ground was another powerful aid in the tremendous campaign to acquaint hundreds of thousands of farmers with the advantages of the new crosses. Russell Rasmusen, of the De Kalb organization, which early established itself as a leader in the relentless campaign to uproot the old open-pollinated corn, introduced it as a major aid to sales. His first step during the late thirties was to locate proving grounds on farms in strategic places, where he put all of the hybrids which De Kalb breeders thought might have any usefulness for the area in question. The farmer on whose land the corn was planted or some of his neighbors were quick to spot the outstanding hybrids. They recognized that a revolution in corn growing had suddenly occurred and immediately carried the good news to the limit of their opportunities.

The importance of these converts is hard to overestimate. Rasmusen can recall the names of a dozen men still with his organization who took up the crusade in 1937 and were more or less responsible for introducing hybrid corn within a year or two into important sections of the corn belt. Among them were Charles Allen at Storm Lake, Iowa; George Gardner, Monmouth, Illinois; Neal Kennedy, Blue Earth, Minnesota; Kenneth Scott, Spencer, Iowa; Fred Fraser, Rennsselaer, Indiana; R. A. McWhorter, North Bend, Nebraska; John Bonner, Jewell, Iowa; Felix Witt, Jasper, Michigan; Floyd Ambrose, Maryville, Missouri; Bert and H. E. Nolin at Bondurant, Iowa; Albert Morehouse, Humboldt, Iowa; and his brother, S. E. Rasmusen, of De Kalb, Illinois, who had worked for farm bureaus before enlisting in the cause.

The next year there were more proving grounds and more converts, and the year following still more. Within a remarkably few seasons De Kalb hybrids were a household name in the corn country. The method was not only a merchandising achievement; it was also an accurate barometer of the amazing rapidity with which the educational campaign popularized the new corn.

The several thousand of farmers who became the foot soldiers in the campaign to sell the new corn were directed not by high-powered sales executives imported into the industry but by men specially trained in modern agricultural practices, men who had the confidence and respect of farmers in their own right. Most of those charged with these responsibilities of distribution were county agents, farm advisers, or vocational agriculture teachers.

Three Illinois agriculturists, Rusty Laible, Steve Turner, and Russ Rasmusen, are typical of the men called to direct the tremendous job of acquainting farmers with the great advantages of hybrid corn. They were all graduates of the University of Illinois' College of Agriculture. They all became farm advisers, or county agricultural agents as they are called in many states, in Illinois, and all moved into the hybrid seed industry as sales managers at about the same time.

Laible joined forces with the Funk organization, and the

title under which he handled his sales work still is "agricultural adviser," giving an idea of the service approach by
which the seed was sold to corn growers. Turner took charge
of sales for Lester Pfister's organization, and Rasmusen
was put in charge of De Kalb's distribution. These three
men have directed the distribution of more hybrid seed corn
than any other ten men. Their methods have been remarkably
similar in that they have all relied to an important degree
upon the method of schooling farmers to become seed salesmen and putting upon these farmers the major responsibility
for getting the story of hybrid corn across to their friends
and neighbors.

In the job of acquainting a million farmers in the heart of
the United States with the advantages of the new corn, these
farmer salesmen collectively made a momentous contribution.
Without them, all the fine efforts of the experiment station
extension workers, the farm bureaus, the vocational agriculture and 4-H club demonstrations, and work done by other
agricultural educational agencies might have taken a generation or more getting the complete acceptance that has
been achieved for hybrid corn.

How did this small army of farmer-salesmen become interested, able, and willing to accomplish their difficult task?
The experience of Dan Hayes, an east central Nebraska
farmer, is more or less typical. Hayes had a little farm and a
big mortgage near the small town of Silver Creek, a hundred
miles due west of Omaha in a country where people still living can remember having seen the last herds of buffalo roam-
ing in the 1880's.

In the spring of 1934 a man came to Dan Hayes' farm one
evening about milking time and told him he should plant
some hybrid corn. Hayes' acquaintance with hybrid corn
was limited to having seen it mentioned several times in the
Nebraska Farmer, but his visitor told him that the new corn
would yield twenty to twenty-five per cent more than his

open-pollinated corn and would stand the drouth much better. The result was that although Hayes didn't have enough
ready cash to his name at the moment to pay the ten dollars
for a bushel of the seed, he took it. Considering the state of
the Hayes family finances, he didn't tell his wife about it,
and Mrs. Hayes didn't know about the transaction until she
found the bushel of seed resting on the back porch. Then
Dan explained the deal, and his wife went to the sack to
have a look at seed corn that could cost ten dollars a bushel
when the best open-pollinated seed could be had for a trifle
more than the market price of corn. She opened the sack
and looked inside.

"You don't call that stuff seed corn," she exclaimed as
she beheld the small kernels her husband had bought. The
price on small kernels was less than on regular flat kernels
generally used.

Dan Hayes, a little embarrassed about it all and fearing
that perhaps he had been swindled, planted this hybrid corn
back from the road where it wouldn't be in common view of
the neighbors. About the same time he learned that his
neighbor, Henry Galus, had bought a bushel of another
hybrid. The two Silver Creek farmers visited back and forth
about their new hybrid corn frequently as the season advanced. Dan Hayes thought his hybrid corn looked a little
better than his open-pollinated, but Mrs. Hayes was by no
means sure that it looked enough better to justify having
spent ten dollars a bushel for the seed. Henry Galus was
better pleased with his, or at least he said so.

Then on the Sunday afternoon before Labor Day, Dan
suggested to his wife that they go over and visit the Galus
family. Dan's general idea was to be neighborly, but his
specific objective was to have a chance to go out to Henry
Galus' cornfield and see if his new hybrid was actually as
much better as he said it was.

"When I got to the corn field, I didn't have to be told where Henry had planted his new hybrid corn," recalls Dan Hayes. "You could see it a half-mile away. There it stood green and in good shape while the open-pollinated corn right next to it was going to make only half a crop on account of the drouth. That sold me on hybrid corn. My own hybrid corn did a lot better than I thought it would. It repaid me for the extra cost of the seed and then some.

"That fall as soon as the heavy work was over, I told my wife that I could sell that new hybrid corn and earn some badly-needed money during the winter. I inquired of Henry Galus where his hybrid seed had been produced. He told me that it came from the Robinson Seed Company at Waterloo, Nebraska. So about a week later I went to Waterloo, met Ted Robinson and Bob Herrington, and told them I wanted a chance to sell their new hybrid seed corn in the Silver Creek community. Bob Herrington was a little reluctant to let me do it until he found out that I had actually observed the performance of one of their hybrids on Henry Galus' farm, because he said that he didn't want anyone selling their seed unless he had had personal experience with hybrid corn and was convinced of its superiority.

"I went home and began working. I would get up before five o'clock in the morning, do the chores, eat breakfast, and be on the road to sell hybrid seed corn by daylight. Naturally it was slow work because most of my neighbors hadn't any more than heard of hybrid corn and some of them hadn't heard of it at all. I worked from dawn to dark every day I could spare that winter and spring until planting time, and I sold 434 bushels of the new hybrid seed corn—most of it in 1- and 2-bushel orders to farmers who were—like me the year before—just trying it.

"I got along all right, but it wasn't as easy as it sounds," recalls Hayes. "This was especially true as I got farther away from home and wasn't so well acquainted. I sometimes asked a farmer whom I knew and who was better acquainted in his particular neighborhood than I to ride with me.

"On the particular day I have in mind, my good friend Harold Lundeen had been riding with me all day, and we hadn't sold a bushel of corn. Toward evening and chore time, Harold pointed out the home of a prominent farmer. I told him, 'We'll stop and see him and make just this one more call, and if I can't sell him some hybrid seed corn, we'll give him some corn.' After talking a few minutes to the man, I saw that we could not sell him, so I said to him, 'Mister, I've got two seed samples of this new hybrid corn in my car. I'm going to give you these and I want you to plant them and let us know how they come out.'

" 'No thanks,' the man replied, 'I don't think I want to take a chance on anything like that.'

"I'm sure he never would have taken them either, but his Missus had heard us talking, and she came to the door and said to her husband, 'Why, I think you're foolish. These man are spending their time trying to sell you something that sounds like it might be a good thing, and you won't take it on, so they're offering to give it to you. I think we should try it.' With that the man took the samples, and from that day to this he has been a devoted hybrid-corn customer of mine."

One of the circumstances which made this sampling approach so effective during the mid-thirties was the outstanding performance of the new hybrid corn during the severe drouths that swept across practically all of the corn belt in 1934 and 1936 and on a more regional scale during other years. Farmers who had either bought or had been given the little four- or eight-pound samples of seed voluntarily wrote thousands of testimonial letters to the producers, letters that read like this: "My hybrid corn didn't make much corn this year, only fifteen or twenty bushels to the acre, but it was a big improvement over my open-pollinated corn which wasn't worth picking. I'm not going to plant anything but hybrid corn next season."

The next year Hayes was able to sell more than 750 bushels. At the same time he was planting the new corn on his own farm and beginning to reap the benefits of tremendously increased yields and other rewards that came to the farmers who switched from their own open-pollinated corn to a well-adapted hybrid.

Up to this point Dan Hayes' experience was typical of thousands upon thousands of these farmer-salesmen. A few of them such as Hayes were called on to take even more responsibility. Bob Herrington, who has in the years since become one of the foremost sales executives of the new industry in the great Missouri River Valley, was so impressed with Hayes' work that he asked him to take over the responsibility for schooling other farmers in the distribution of hybrid seed. Gradually Hayes took over supervisory responsibility for Herrington in the historic Platte Valley section of Southern Nebraska.

"I'll tell you this opportunity to help with the selling of hybrid corn has been a great thing for me and lots of other farmers," says Dan Hayes. "The extra income this work has brought to us has helped meet many a mortgage installment, pay many a doctor's bill, and buy many a new stove, refrigerator, or other piece of badly needed equipment in the home or on the farm. I could point out lots of such examples among the farmer salesmen I know, and the same thing has been true to one degree or another all over the corn belt."

However, there is another and more important benefit. As Dan Hayes says, "I feel that the eight years I've spent selling hybrid seed corn has been the equivalent to a college education for me. I've had to learn many new things, not only about corn but about better farming, both from the men in our organization and from the farmers I've met in my regular farm calls. I think the methods used by the producers of hybrid seed corn in distributing their products has been very beneficial to agriculture because it has been a great education for thousands of fellows like myself."

Experience with hybrid corn has been educational, not only for the several thousands of farmers who have distributed it, but for farmers in general. County agents, university extension workers, and seedsmen have repeatedly pointed out in recent years that hybrid corn has done more than anything else to convince the average good farmer that the research work done by scientists in their laboratories is one of the important keys to better equipment and better living on the farm. Hybrid corn has helped develop in farmers a receptive frame of mind. When his county agent, the state experiment station, a seed company, or any other organization in which he has confidence brings out a new product such as a new strain of hybrid oats, a new selection of wheat, or even a new hybrid chicken or hybrid hog, this farmer is immediately receptive, ready and willing to give such new products a thorough testing. Thus hybrid corn has done much to banish among farmers the outmoded adage, "It was good enough for my grandfather, it was good enough for my father, and it's good enough for me."

To these farmer salesmen is due the credit for the rapid and dramatic success of hybrid corn. Leading agronomists of the open-pollinated corn era openly insisted that the new hybrids could never materially influence the average per acre yield of an important corn-growing area because farmers would never make wide enough use of it, and if they did the extra drain on the soil would soon offset any advantages the new corn might have. Government reports on corn yields in the state of Iowa stand as powerful refutation and a great tribute to the work of the hybrid seed corn industry in providing a fine product and to its farmer salesmen who secured for the new corn such wide and immediate acceptance. Never during the days of open-pollinated corn did the state of Iowa have an average yield per acre of more than 46 bushels, but in 1946 when practically all of the corn in the state was hybrid, Iowa's average yield per acre was 62½ bushels.

Today the hybrid-seed industry is solidly established, in a position to maintain and increase its service to American and Canadian farmers. Undoubtedly the new industry's resourcefulness will continue to improve seed production and processing techniques and machines so that our farmers can expect a better product at the same or even less cost. In the matter of hybrid corn research, the future is especially bright. The state experiment stations are continuing and in some instances increasing their interest in corn breeding, and at the same time privately conducted corn breeding has reached major proportions. Leaders in the new industry with their research directed by such men as Gunn, Baker, Holbert or St. John have already demonstrated ability to take over full responsibility for their breeding programs.

Together these resources of breeding, producing and distributing hybrids possessed by the industry are a promise and a reasonable guarantee to American and Canadian farmers not only to maintain a high standard of quality in hybrids but to go on constantly developing better strains — hybrids of the future that will continue to make farming in great areas of this continent more profitable than it has ever been before.

CHAPTER XVIII

Distinguished Service

MAIZE HAS ALWAYS been the crop that enabled people of the Americas to be well-fed, happy, and strong, and the coming of hybrid corn has in many a respect increased our dependence upon this great crop rather than diminished it.

Because corn is so important in so many areas of our country, hybrid corn has now become an invigorating influence throughout a large part of our agricultural economy with its ramifications branching in an octopus-like manner into many other phases of our national life. The effect of hybrid corn has already been felt in America's social, industrial, and even political institutions, and the new maize has even had a hand in shaping this country's relations with the rest of the world.

The opportunities which hybrid corn has brought directly to our corn farmers, especially those living in the great Upper Mississippi, Ohio, and Missouri River Valleys, are the most easily seen. The new maize, increasing our corn yields from twenty to thirty per cent, cuts down the work needed to produce a bushel of corn and opens vast new possibilities for the management and operation of our farms.

Beginning with the season of 1936 down to the present, hybrid corn has so increased corn yields that farmers have harvested the equal of two extra corn crops of the size needed to feed and sustain us in years of peace. Or described another way, if we had planted the same number of acres of corn from 1936 to 1946 inclusive, and raised on them the old open-pollinated corn, we would have harvested about five billion bushels less corn, and five billion bushels of maize measured in terms of the health, happiness, and security of a nation is of such great value that there exists no adequate scale for its evaluation. Undoubtedly the most futile attempt to measure such a value is in dollars, since all the dollars in the world cannot provide an extra bushel of corn in the hour of a people's need if that bushel has not been grown by some corn farmer somewhere in the year or years before.

One of the men who saw this drama of expanding corn yields unfold during this first golden decade of hybrid corn was the kindly and philosophical A. J. Surratt of Springfield, Illinois, a real veteran among America's government crop statisticians upon whom many people and enterprises have come to depend in recent years. The job of Surratt and his staff is to report the prospects for the corn crops and to estimate the probable size of the new crop on the first of each month from July 1 until the harvest is complete. Over the years, Surratt and his associates in the Division of Agricultural Statistics have reduced the job to a fine art by which they can be sure of anticipating weeks in advance almost the actual size of the coming crop. A normal for corn crops had been carefully established during the open-pollinated era of the twenties and early thirties, and a normal crop was considered the average of the best corn crops ever raised, a basis that made it extremely rare for a reporting farmer to give an estimate for any new crop that exceeded 100 per cent.

Imagine Mr. Surratt's surprise when his reporters, who had begun using the new hybrid corn, began estimating their prospects at 110, 115, or 120 per cent of normal. Eventually, the new corn made it necessary for Mr. Surratt and his staff to work out an entirely new formula for reporting the condition of Illinois corn crops or estimating the probable yield at the end of the harvest. Similar steps had to be taken by agricultural statisticians in all the other corn growing states where hybrid corn had become widely used.

"The tremendous expansion in the use of hybrid corn in Illinois from 10 per cent of the total corn acreage in 1936 to 98 per cent in 1946 increased corn production in our state by the enormous total of 477 million bushels," says Surratt. "Sixty-six to 75 million bushels were added to our annual production during each of the war years, and this increase in the nation's food supply stands as a mighty contribution to the winning of the war by our farmers, hybrid corn seedsmen, and our state and federal hybrid corn research organizations."

W. F. Callander, assistant chief of the federal Bureau of Agricultural Economics, who has been in a unique position to observe the influence of hybrids in all of the important American corn-growing areas, says, "In 1946 about 67.5 per cent, or 2 out of every 3 acres of corn grown in the United States, was planted with hybrid seed. In 1933 only about 1 acre in 1,000 was planted to hybrids. In the corn belt about 91 per cent of all corn acreage was planted with hybrids in 1946 and probably 80 per cent of the entire United States 1946 corn production grew from hybrid seed. Yields from hybrid seed in 1946 averaged about 21 per cent above yields from open-pollinated varieties in states where the use of hybrid corn has become general."

Hybrid corn did much more than increase corn yields. In the corn belt it is in the process of revolutionizing our agriculture as completely as the steam engine revolutionized the industrial world. It is changing not only methods of farm management and farm operation, but also the social pattern of the farm family and the rural community.

Ever since the American industrial advancement that accompanied our participation in the First World War, there has existed a strong movement toward mechanized farming in our most concentrated and highly productive farming areas. Tractors were introduced along with a host of machines that were more efficient than the old horse-drawn implements.

One job, however, could not successfully be done by machine, and that was the harvesting of corn. Our farmers had to keep their horses for harvesting corn in the fall, and since they could not afford to let the horses remain idle the rest of the year, they were forced to cling to much of their old horse-pulled equipment. Inventors had tried in vain, especially after the great success of the McCormick reaper that banished the need of harvesting small grains by hand, to develop a practical corn picker, but their best efforts produced nothing of much more than novelty value until the coming of hybrid corn.

The new corn provided the two things that had prevented mechanical pickers from being successful. It would stand in the field until long after the regular harvest time if necessary, and the ears of hybrid corn were so uniform in size and position on the stalk that it became simpler to develop successful mechanical corn pickers.

With the coming of the successful mechanical corn picker, many a corn belt farmer sold his last pair of horses and swung over to a completely mechanized type of farming. This put his farming operations on a basis of greater efficiency and resulted in his producing the greatest number of pounds of food per man in all the long history of agriculture. He soon discovered that he could handle a larger acreage, and this accelerated the trend toward fewer and larger farms.

The mechanical corn picker, its effectiveness and wide use made possible by hybrid corn, was quickly adopted by corn belt farmers. In 1935 only fifteen per cent of the corn in Iowa was harvested by machine, but in 1945 approximately seventy per cent of the Iowa corn crop and more than fifty-five per cent of all the corn in our corn belt was mechanically harvested. Only a severe shortage of mechanical corn pickers during the war years kept Iowa farmers harvesting as much as thirty per cent of their corn crop by hand.

During this same ten-year period the number of farmers in the United States declined by thirteen per cent, the average size of the farming unit increased by twenty-six per cent, and the number of tenant farmers declined from approximately three to two million.

As the size of the farm unit increased, fewer workers were needed and a large number of tenants retired from farming to work in our towns and cities, a trend that was encouraged during the war by the need for men in military service and for workmen in war factories. As a result our farm population has declined one-fifth while the nation's population was increasing. These trends have been most in evidence in the great corn-growing areas, and they have been, to an important degree, the by-products of higher yields and complete farm mechanization which have followed the wide use of the new hybrid corn.

Sidney Cates, noted agricultural writer, summarized the development this way: "No other nation produces food—even in normal times—with the effort of less than half its workers. And the nations with lower economic standards take more than 80 per cent of their labor force to do the task. Hybrid corn has done more to put us further out in front, releasing our strength for other tasks than food getting, than has any other factor in modern times. Corn is the strength of the nation. And the hybrid gives heretofore undreamed-of strength to corn."

The advent of the mechanical corn picker and the complete mechanization of farming which followed wrought important social changes in the rural community. The mechanical corn husker could harvest from 7 to 15 acres of corn a day and as much as 30,000 bushels in a season. No longer was it necessary to furnish board and room to hired men during the fall and early winter while the corn was being picked. This ushered in a whole series of subtle but, in a collective sense, important changes.

The farm wife's responsibilities were reduced materially. Most sociologists regard the farm wife and mother as by all odds the hardest working woman in the land, so this is no mean consideration. Mechanization of the corn harvest reduced one of the most gruelling jobs on the farm to a task that is not distasteful or of long duration, creating greater leisure for the men in the farm family too.

Absence of young hired men in the farm community, with corresponding decrease of opportunity for young couples to take up farming as was such a common practice a generation ago, is but another of the ever widening effects of fully mechanized farming that followed the widespread use of hybrid corn.

Farming practices have inevitably been changed by this great industrial revolution in the corn belt. Many fears were expressed that the higher yields of hybrid corn would drain our soil of fertility more rapidly than it could be replaced, eventually leaving the great American breadbasket a vast carpet of impoverished and gullied fields similar to the old tobacco and cotton lands of the South. While the higher yields of hybrid corn do require greater amounts of soil fertility, these same higher yields create opportunities for better soil management which point the way to improvement of the general level of soil fertility in our most intensive corn-growing areas.

Greater corn yields mean that a farm's corn requirements can be produced on fewer acres, providing a chance to retire from intensive cultivation the land least suited to corn or other row crops. These acres retired from intensive cultivation can be put into forage crops, affording a chance not only to build up the level of fertility but to reduce greatly the hazards of erosion. The extra forage crops encourage a greater use of livestock that under modern farming methods can promote still further soil-building practices.

Even on the land best suited to intensive cultivation, hybrid corn offers incentives for building up soil fertility that never before existed. Although agronomists constantly urged soil conservation to maintain the highest possible levels of fertility during the era of open-pollinated corn, farmers took only casual interest, because in the final test it did not increase corn yields. In other words there was not a sufficient reward for following careful crop rotation and soil-building programs. This was true because open-pollinated corn did not have the capacity to use the extra plant food found in soil of high fertility and convert it into extra bushels of corn. The fact was that open-pollinated corn yields actually tended to drop in many instances on unusually fertile soil because of the old corn's tendency to produce a greater number of barren stalks and a greater number of diseased plants on unusually rich soil.

Hybrid corn has brought a complete about-face into this situation. Corn farmers now have a great incentive to use careful systems of cropping and to raise their land to the highest possible levels of fertility. By using these practices they can add five, ten, or perhaps fifteen bushels an acre to their yields, for hybrid corn has the capacity to utilize this additional food and convert it into bigger crops.

Many of the most respected soil experts in the corn belt now regard the new hybrids and their skyrocketing yields as the backbone of a movement which, over the years, will increase the general fertility in our most intensive corn-growing areas. One of these men is A. L. Lang, an authority on soils improvement at the University of Illinois.

"The coming of hybrid corn has been the greatest stimulus ever given our soil-conservation and soil-building programs in the corn belt," says Mr. Lang. "Over a period of say twenty-five years, I don't think there is any question that the use of hybrid corn and other higher yielding crops will result in a general improvement of our soil.

"Our farmers at last have a real incentive to improve their soil fertility to its highest possible level. This is already clearly shown in the farm management records at the University. In the years since hybrid corn came into general use in Illinois, our farmers have doubled and redoubled their use of limestone in order to lay the foundation for sweet clover acreage and other soil-building projects. Our work among farmers, the government soil conservation programs before the war, and other factors have encouraged this development, but the coming of hybrid corn, more than anything else, made it profitable and in the final analysis practical."

The great crisis in which America was forced to fight for survival revealed fully the power of the new kind of maize. An important part of German and Japanese war strategy was aimed directly at the American farmer. The Axis war lords figured that with America depending upon the Far East for billions of pounds of fats, oils, and fibers and practically all of its raw rubber each year, closing the western Pacific to our cargo ships would be a staggering blow to American agriculture. The enemy strategists planned not only to shut off the Pacific, but with German submarines virtually to isolate the United States from raw material sources in South America and Africa as well. This would, they hoped, leave the American farmers with the job of feeding the armed personnel, the civilian population and hard-pressed allies—and the momentous task of replacing the oil and fiber imports lost in the blockade without which American industry could not hope to respond to the call for the food and weapons needed for victory.

Although Japan's fleet and air force broke our routes to the western Pacific like a finger ripping away the supports of a spider's web, and though German submarines sank our

ships off the Jersey coast and near the mouth of the Mississippi River, America was not fully isolated from basic supplies. The tide of war rolled against us on front after front,
but there was one on which we ran up a convincing victory
during those dark months of 1942. This victory was won on
the American farm front.

Food, fiber, and oil-bearing crops moved off American
farms in a volume that surpassed anything the world had
ever seen. Never had so much been produced by so few.
Practically every farmer in the land had a hand in this first
great victory on the home front, but the farmers of the corn
belt helped immeasurably to set the stage for the smashing
defeat of the Axis' strategy of strangulation.

Using hybrid corn on most of the corn ground in the
corn belt, our farmers produced the greatest volume of corn
ever raised in the United States, a record of 3.2 billion-bushel
crop, and did it with one-fifth less corn ground than was
planted in 1917 to raise our greatest corn crop of the first
World War. This "surplus" land, amounting to nearly
twenty million acres, was planted to soy beans and other
special war crops.

A dramatic example of what had taken place was to be
found on the Paul Peabody farm in Christian County, Illinois, a few miles south of the capital city of Springfield.
Peabody, a pleasant, hard working corn and meat expert
of English descent, planted 94 acres with hybrids developed by Dr. Jim Holbert and harvested an almost unbe-
lievable yield of more than 11,000 bushels—an average of
117 bushels an acre. One 10-acre field of gently-rolling
prairie on the Peabody farm entered in the contest sponsored
by the University of Illinois and the Illinois Crop Improvement Association yielded an average of 191.64 bushels of
corn per acre—hailed by farm magazines and newspapers as
a world's record for 10 acres.

"I never saw corn fall into a wagon so fast," observed

Peabody. "I began using hybrid corn six or seven years ago. Before that, say back during the last war, the average corn yield for this whole farm wasn't more than fifty or sixty bushels an acre."

But the 1942 production of food, oil, and fiber was only the beginning. American farmers maintained this terrific pace through all the war years and have continued through the early reconstruction period too. Only three times in all the history of open-pollinated corn did we harvest 3-billion-bushel crops, but using every-increasing amounts of the new hybrid corn our farmers averaged such crops from 1942 until 1946—five consecutive years during which nearly 16 billion bushels of maize was harvested, more than 3 billion bushels yearly.

From this vast stockpile of corn was drawn the bulk of the foods that supplied our citizens in armed service, our allies around the world, and our civilian population that manned the war factories from which rolled the guns, tanks, planes, and countless other weapons that made America the arsenal of democracy. The high-energy foods such as pork, milk, butter, cheese, and eggs were processed from corn in such amounts that, except for battle emergencies, American armies were never without an adequate supply of food. Much of our lend-lease food exports were made up of canned or dried pork products, dried milk, cheese, and dried eggs. Still there was enough corn left to make available these same foods in record amounts to American civilians who were fed well at a time when hunger was sapping the efficiency of practically every other nation involved in the great war.

Through a careful husbanding of our maize resources and because the three-billion bushel crops kept coming regularly each season, there was still enough corn to provide a countless list of raw materials to our wartime industry. Important amounts of corn, along with wheat, were converted into alcohol used in the new synthetic rubber which staved off an especially critical situation by replacing the natural rubber lost when Japan plunged the Pacific area into war. Even the corn cobs were processed into a number of useful wartime products, such as an abrasive used in removing carbon from airplane engines, cutting to a fraction the time necessary to perform this common operation of engine overhauling.

Hybrid corn helped supply the energy that powered not only America but, in an important degree, our allies as well, and contributed to bringing about an actual reduction in the number of farmers necessary to provide these record amounts of food and industrial fiber products. The men and women thus released went into the armed services and into our war factories and made great contributions to achievements on these fronts.

Merle T. Jenkins, in charge of the federal work on corn, draws an interesting contrast between American corn production during World War I and World War II.

"In the three years of World War I, we produced 8 billion bushels of corn on a total of 311 million acres. During the three years of World War II, we produced 9⅓ billion bushels on only 281 million acres. During the three years of World War II, therefore, we produced 1,366,201,000 more bushels of corn on 30,522,000 fewer acres.

"This is equivalent to 15 billion pounds more meat, or 5 billion pounds more meat per year, which is the equivalent of 38 pounds more per person each year. When you look back to the fact that there were times when our meat rationing got down as low as 115 pounds per person per year, the importance of this extra production can be more easily appreciated."

Viewed from another important consideration, hybrid corn enabled our farmers to produce on only four acres what it had taken five acres to produce with the old open-pollinated corn. Without the new kind of corn, we should have had to allocate enough man labor, farm machinery, and tractor fuel to raise one-fifth more acres of corn to meet our food production goals. These resources would have had to be subtracted from production of other war crops of food or fiber, from the man power in our war factories, or from the personnel of the armed services. These alternatives pose serious problems when a nation is struggling for its existence.

Our maize stockpile was fortunately not exhausted at the end of the war when most of the productive power of our enemies as well as our major allies lay on one degree or another of prostration. During the grave food crisis that enveloped the world early in 1946, the United States rushed vast quantities of its food to civilians of both former allies and enemies. Wallace Duel, writing for a chain of America's foremost newspapers in an article that received commendation from government spokesmen, said that America's food shipments during the first months after the war had averted utter collapse in no less than nineteen nations and eased starvation in a score of others.

These are the people with whom we and our children will have to deal in an effort to stabilize mankind's relations in a world torn apart by the two greatest wars of all time which came within a single generation. The help we were able to give them—help delivered largely in the form of the products of corn and wheat—will contribute to the possibilities of improved relations between peoples for a long time to come. Thus the influence of the new hybrid corn has been felt not only in Des Moines and Chicago, Portland and Philadelphia, but all along

> "the road that goes down through a
> Philippine town,
> And it hits Highway Seven, north of Rome;
> It's the same road they had coming out of
> Stalingrad,
> It's that old Lincoln Highway back home!

Through Chungking and Paris and up along
the Rhine,
And out across the Java sea;
Through the snow and the sand, across every
land,
Wherever men fight to be free."

Processing plant for hybrid seed corn where millions of bushels are dried, scalped to remove light or broken kernels, graded into uniform kernel size, and treated to kill seed-borne diseases

Prophet of Plenty

CHAPTER XIX

Just the Beginning

WHAT of the future? What kind of corn will farmers be growing in 1960 or the year 2000? What ultimately comes of this new kind of work begun on a strip of prairie at the edge of Urbana in Illinois and carried on in Connecticut's Land of the Sleeping Giant.

The achievements of hybrid corn have been so great and so concrete that we generally think of its goals having largely been attained, of its development having reached a relative state of maturity. The fact is that the work of the hybrid-corn makers is just begun.

The misunderstanding that hybrid corn is a completed development is nowhere any greater than among those who have been benefitted most directly—our American corn belt farmers. The memory of man is not long, and already evident is an inability to retain a full appreciation of what the new kind of maize has meant. This is due mainly to two things. First, a good ear of almost any kind of corn has the same general appearance, and there is not, therefore, an opportunity to see that the hybrid-corn makers are constantly introducing new hybrids that are as much improved and as completely different as a succession of new models in an automobile. Second, because the environmental conditions under which each successive crop of corn is grown are constantly changing, it is extremely difficult to make continuous long-range comparisons of the performance of the new corn. On farms where soil fertility has not been maintained at a constant level, and this unfortunately includes a majority of our acres at this time, the problem confronting the hybrid corn breeders is especially difficult. On these farms each new hybrid actually has less chance to perform well than the obsolete hybrids used in the years before. This is such a situation as might exist if we were constantly to let our highways fall into greater disrepair so that each new model of our automobiles would be forced to operate over roads which each year placed new and greater hazards before them.

Undiscouraged, the hybrid corn makers are going right on with their research programs which will result in the introduction of constantly better and better hybrids. Not only will these new hybrids be capable of increased yields on constant levels of fertility, but they will gradually give our farmers even greater protection against irregularities of weather and the hazards of insects and disease.

The future, however, holds even more important tasks for the hybrid-corn makers. Farming practices change, and not infrequently new hazards from disease and insects appear. Sometimes these are introduced from other countries; sometimes they merely move from parts of our own country into previously-untouched corn-growing areas. Contrary to the popular opinion, strains of hybrid corn do not have blanket resistance to insects or disease. The characteristics in a hybrid that discourage and repel one insect may actually make the hybrid more susceptible to another enemy. The hybrid-corn breeder therefore often has to do a vast amount of work to develop resistance to a new insect or disease.

Future breeders may also adapt the maize plant to many new uses. D. Howard Doane, who has earned the respect of two generations of farmers in the great Mississippi basin for his work in farm management, has dared to predict that the hybrid-corn makers will someday produce new kinds of maize to replace other staple crops at present widely cultivated here and throughout the world.

"As a lay breeder of plants and animals," says Mr. Doane, "I like to contemplate the work of the real plant breeders of the future and think particularly of the opportunities of the hybrid-corn breeders. A great illustration of what they can do is what has been done with waxy maize.

"Here the breeder has, for all practical purposes, hooked a fleshy root crop from the tropics on a stalk of corn growing in Iowa or Illinois. Waxy maize grows and looks like ordinary corn, but waxy maize is as new a crop as soybeans were a few years ago. It's a new crop in an old dress. The old garment permits the corn grower to use all his old methods and tools, but he harvests an entirely new noncompetitive end crop.

"When the full significance of the meaning of this new approach to plant breeding is understood and applied," says Mr. Doane, "we may expect changes *within* the corn plant as great as changes which result from going from one plant species to another. Such developments may in the future make this outstanding cereal plant, discovered and nurtured by the American Indians, the great mother of numerous special-purpose crops that collectively would have the effect of raising maize from merely a worthy colleague of wheat and rice to being the master of all mankind's plant servants."

The real importance of what the hybrid-corn makers have done can only be fully appreciated when we realize what powerful influence their achievements, the natural laws they have exposed, and the practices they have developed have exerted upon not only the improvement of other plants of economic value but upon the breeding of animals as well. Even before hybrid corn registered its first great success in the heart of the corn belt, some of the hybrid-corn makers and other scientists saw that what was being done with corn could also be done with many other plants and animals. Then as hybrid corn came into its own, plant and animal breeders began to reappraise their work in light of the new development, and within a few years hybridizing assumed the proportions of a movement that promises within the foreseeable future to populate our farms and gardens with an entirely new galaxy of plant and animal servants.

In the Spragg Memorial Address delivered at Michigan State College in 1938, Henry A. Wallace said:

"The corn breeding experience of the past twenty years is certain to have a most significant effect upon genetic thinking. . . In the long run, this effect is likely to be felt even more in the field of livestock breeding than in plant breeding."

Writing in the July 7, 1947, issue of *The New Republic* and referring to his Spragg Memorial address, Wallace observed, "Ten years ago I predicted that the principle of controlled heterosis would spread from corn to chickens, from chickens to swine and finally to cattle. On a recent trip, I came across a group of ex-county agents in northern Iowa who are applying a modified form of this program to hogs. What they are preparing to do is to furnish farmers of Iowa this fall with one thousand boars at $150.00 each. They will not have the specific and direct control over heredity which we have in hybrid corn and hybrid chickens, but rather an intermediate approach through bringing in two or more inbred lines on the sire side. . . . At six months the pigs (offspring of the hybrid boars) weigh 20 to 30 pounds more than the average, and if crossbred sows are saved for breeding, one or two more pigs per litter will survive."

Wallace took the lead in endeavoring to employ the inbreeding and hybridizing technique in the improvement of livestock. Even before his program for breeding hybrid corn had yielded anything of general significance, Wallace was experimenting with the inbreeding of hogs and poultry and encouraging others to take up the work.

Especially in the breeding of hybrid chickens, Wallace's interest has produced dramatic results. Wallace's work with inbreeding poultry began much as did his work with inbreeding corn. In the same garden in Des Moines where he made his first selfs on corn, he established a chicken pen in the mid-twenties. One new element in this situation was to prove of the greatest importance. Wallace's oldest son, Henry B. Wallace, although only a lad beginning his teens, showed an interest in the handling of poultry.

During all the time that Henry B. Wallace was in high school, he continued to develop his small chicken flock. This project grounded him in the fundamentals of poultry improvement in much the same way that his father had first learned about corn from his three-acre ear-to-row planting of P. G. Holden's show corn in 1904 and 1905. Although Henry B. Wallace's work hardly achieved the status of inbreeding before he sold off his prized birds and went to college, he did become so interested in the possibilities that he specialized in poultry at Iowa State College.

While young Wallace was away at school in 1934, Raymond Baker decided independently that there was an opportunity to use his knowledge of hybridization in the development of a new kind of chicken. Enough inbreeding of poultry had been done at Iowa State College so that some promising inbred lines were beginning to emerge. Baker reasoned that by developing additional poultry inbreds and crossing them with the ones developed at Ames, a private breeder might offer farmers and commercial poultrymen the first hybrid chicken developed by the same techniques that had made possible the new hybrid corn.

The job of carrying on his regular corn breeding and poultry breeding as a personal project soon proved to be too great, and he invited one of his friends, Hugh Morrison, to join him. After they had been working for two years, Henry A. Wallace learned of the project and was immediately impressed with its possibilities. As a result, he bought a third-interest in the venture, but after another year all three men turned the entire project over to the Pioneer Hi-Bred Corn Company. Baker continued to direct the poultry-breeding program alone until young Henry B. Wallace joined him after his college work was completed. Young Wallace soon demonstrated such interest and ability that he assumed entire direction of the poultry-inbreeding program.

The first of the Wallace's new chickens became commercially available in limited numbers for the first time in 1942, and farmers began pitting them against their standard-bred chickens just as they had tested the new hybrid corn against their old open-pollinated corn a few years before. The verdict on the first of the new chickens bred like hybrid corn was immediately favorable. Increases in egg production ranging up to forty and fifty per cent—strangely similar to the advantage the new hybrid corn demonstrated in many of its tests—were soon being reported on Iowa farms where flocks of both the new hybrid chickens and the standard breeds were tested under comparable conditions. The new chickens molded by Wallace on the hybrid corn pattern were entered in the 1945 Illinois Egg Laying Contest, sponsored by Illinois' State Department of Agriculture. The new chickens outlaid the best standard-bred hens by a wide margin.

The success of this project in breeding hybrid poultry has been so pronounced that in 1944 another of the leading organizations in the hybrid-seed corn industry, De Kalb Agricultural Association, began a long-range project for breeding poultry from which it is expected the first hybrid chickens will be available for farm use in 1948 or 1949. A number of state experiment stations and members of the private poultry industry, some of whom had experimented with inbreeding in years past, are now beginning inbreeding projects to follow in the steps of Baker and Wallace, and the prospect is for a revolution in the general improvement of poultry that will eventually approximate that brought about in our great maize crop by the coming of hybrid corn.

Another instance in which the inbreeding and crossing technique contributed directly to improvement of livestock is to be found at Blakeford Farms on Maryland's famous Eastern Shore area. George M. Moffet, for many years head of America's largest wet-milling organization for the processing of corn and long a friend of Jim Holbert, watched Holbert's achievements with hybrid corn. He was so impressed that he determined to exploit the knowledge of the hybrid-corn makers in giving new objectives and direction to the line breeding and inbreeding of Guernsey cattle that was already under way.

In addition to producing and processing seed of the hybrids developed by Jim Holbert and his staff for Maryland and Virginia corn farmers, Blakeford Farms has launched under Guy Harmon's direction important programs to hybridize swine and dairy cattle. Mr. Moffet has set up his Blakeford Farms as a foundation so that this type of work, on which progress is necessarily much slower than with corn or poultry, can go on without interruption for a long time. The Blakeford Farms program for inbreeding dairy cows is being conducted with Guernsey stock. Begun in 1936, already some significant results have been secured, giving indication of developments which may bring about an increase in the productivity of dairy cattle.

One of the earliest plant inbreeding programs using principles demonstrated in corn hybridization was with alfalfa. This work was inaugurated at the University of Nebraska, where one of the early corn-inbreeding programs was conducted. Alfalfa inbreds have been established, and within a few years there is the prospect of the new hybrid alfalfa offering forage crop farmers an opportunity to increase their yields of this great legume hay by fifteen to forty per cent. In addition, the first farm tests of the new alfalfa, bred in the fashion of hybrid corn, show that the first adapted strains are highly resistant to the dread wilt diseases that have taken heavy toll in many areas.

Another example of employing the methods of breeding developed by the hybrid-corn makers on another plant of economic importance is Raymond Baker's work with watermelons. At about the same time that he was intensely interested in developing hybrid chickens, Baker began as a personal hobby a garden-sized breeding program to develop hybrid watermelons. The watermelon is a cross-pollinated plant like corn, and within a few years Baker succeeded in developing watermelon inbreds and crossing them into some excellent strains of hybrids. When Henry A. Wallace was vice-president, and hence presiding over the Senate, he made a practice each year of presenting to his colleagues a remembrance. On one of these occasions he presented them with a small package of seed from one of Raymond Baker's best strains of hybrid watermelons.

In recent years a large number of plant and animal improvement projects have been launched with a view to taking full advantage of the new understanding first worked out by the hybrid-corn makers. The state and federal experiment stations are devoting an increasing amount of their resources to exploiting these new opportunities. Much of this work is being done by the federal Department of Agriculture at Beltsville, Maryland, research center for the development of new plants and animals, and the projects range all the way from garden crops to beef cattle.

Nor is this revolution in plant and animal improvement confined to the United States. Probably in most instances the knowledge of the hybrid-corn makers will be first used in other lands, just as it was in the United States, to produce new and better kinds of corn. This is logical, since corn is the most widely used cereal, being an important source of food in more countries of the world than any other crop.

Hybrid corn has spread rapidly into Canada, where breeding is now being done at three government-supported experimental farms. Work at the Dominion Experimental Station at Harrow, in southern Ontario, has advanced to the point where the first double-cross hybrids made up entirely of inbred lines developed in Canada by G. F. H. Buckley were released for general farm use in 1946, attracting favorable attention not only in southern Canada but in the states of Wisconsin and New York as well.

A great incentive to adoption of hybrid corn by southern Canadian farmers has been the fact that the European corn borer damaged open-pollinated corn so severely during the late thirties that many farmers had been forced to give up growing corn for grain. Many of the hybrids developed for use in the United States were found to be useful in the heaviest corn-growing areas of Canada. In the counties of Essex and Kent, just across the border from Detroit and eastern Michigan, practically the total corn acreage is planted with hybrids developed in the United States.

American hybrids have been of little use, however, in the potentially large but short-seasoned areas of northern and eastern Ontario along Lake Erie and Lake Ontario. Hybrids for this and similar areas concern the Canadian breeders working at the Central Experiment Farm at Ottawa, Ontario, and the Dominion Experimental Station at Morden, Manitoba. In charge of the program at Ottawa is Professor F. Dimmock, who began inbreeding a number of years ago at the Harrow Station.

Agronomists of Macdonald College of McGill University in Quebec have also been breeding hybrid corn for a number of years. Professor L. C. Raymond is in charge of this project, the objective of which is to develop better strains of silage corn, much of Quebec being too far north to make it appear practical to the McGill scientists to attempt the development of corn for grain.

Programs have been inaugurated at a number of other places in North and South America. Probably the most comprehensive program going on outside the United States is that sponsored by the Rockefeller Foundation in Mexico. In the Fall of 1941, when Henry Wallace went to Mexico to represent the United States at the inauguration of the new Mexican president Avilo Comacho, he was profoundly impressed not only by the complete dependence of the people upon corn, but also by the primitive agricultural methods. Shortly after his return to the United States, Wallace had lunch with Raymond Fosdick, president of the Rockefeller Foundation, and Wallace pointed out the opportunity that existed for an organization such as the Rockefeller Foundation to render a great service by promoting the improvement of Mexican agriculture. Fosdick was immediately interested. The Foundation sent a special commission to Mexico composed of Dr. E. C. Stakman of the University of Minnesota, the noted authority on wheat culture, Dr. Richard Bradfield of Cornell University, an expert on soils problems, and Dr. Paul Mangelsdorf of Harvard, who as a result of his work with East and Jones and his work on corn in Texas was qualified to appreciate the possibilities for improving corn in Mexico.

As a result of the commission's study, the Rockefeller Foundation in 1943 began an agricultural research project which included corn breeding. Dr. J. G. Harrar, then plant pathologist of Washington State College, was chosen to head the four-man team of scientists who would do the work for the Foundation in Mexico. Harrar and Mangelsdorf, who continued as an adviser on corn breeding, were able to interest Dr. E. J. Wellhausen, who was at that time corn breeder for West Virginia University, in taking over the direction of the Mexican program. Wellhausen, who spent his early childhood on an Oklahoma dry-land farm and his later boyhood on an irrigated farm in Idaho, learned about corn breeding at Iowa State College. Wellhausen and Mangelsdorf mapped the program, and work began in 1943. Because of Wellhausen's capacity for hard work and the fact that he can raise two corn crops a year in Mexico, work has progressed more rapidly than perhaps any other corn program ever conducted.

Although Wellhausen considers it only a stop-gap measure, he began by developing new open-pollinated varieties which have demonstrated yield increases of twenty to twenty-five per cent over the native corn in general use. At the same time he is carrying on an inbreeding program so large that Dr. Louis Roberts, a graduate student of Mangelsdorf's at Texas, has been engaged to assist him. Wellhausen and Roberts began in 1947 to increase their inbred lines, looking forward to the release of double-cross hybrids. Some of the double-cross experimental combinations have indicated greater and more dependable yield increases than the new open-pollinated varieties that have already come from Wellhausen's work. One of the first steps to be taken under this program will be the building of the first plant in Mexico for processing the seed of hybrid corn. Senator Gabriel Ramos Millan, president of the Mexican senate, headed a commission that spent several weeks in the United States studying American methods. From Jim Holbert the commission secured plans for a plant capable of processing 20,000 bushels of seed in a period of two months. The progress of this breeding program has so impressed agricultural leaders in Mexico that in 1947 the government appropriated four million pesos (approximately $800,000) for increasing these new varieties and making them available.

Organized breeding of hybrid corn is being done at two other research centers in Central America. Eduardo Lomon is directing work in Mexico at the Campo Agricola experimental farm at Leon, Guanajuata, and recently Iowa State College corn breeders began an intensive program in Guatemala.

Iowa College chose Guatamala as the site of its Tropical Research Center because it is believed that many of our useful plants, including some varieties of corn, were first developed there and in Southern Mexico. Iowa State scientists think that this is probably the best place in the Western Hemisphere to study the direct connections between the wild flora and the differentiation of the resulting species. Logically, the first plant singled out for study and breeding was corn; many new and little-known varieties have already been found.

Dr. I. E. Melhuse, director of the Guatemala Tropical Research Center, describes its objective as follows: "The first step is to study the growth and development of these corns in their native climates and then to screen out such characters that may through hybridization enhance our own corns. The second step is to fix this promising exotic germ plasm in combination with our well-known inbreds and make it available to science in this country. While these studies are being made, it is planned to improve the corns of Guatemala and Central America and in this way contribute to the corn production programs in these neighboring countries."

Work done recently in Costa Rica by Walter Bangham, plant scientist for the Goodyear Rubber Company, gives an indication of the problems and opportunities for the corn breeder in the Caribbean. Bangham learned about hybrid corn directly from Dr. E. M. East, with whom he did graduate work at Harvard. He tackled the problem of corn improvement in Costa Rica as a means of increasing the food supply of natives who were employed by the Goodyear company. He subjected a number of Caribbean strains of corn to inbreeding and in addition received both open-pollinated and inbred material from the United States. Bangham left Costa Rica in 1947 after demonstrating two things to his satisfaction. He found that it was extremely difficult to develop hybrids with inbreds derived entirely from Caribbean varieties of corn; and he discovered that his experimental hybrids involving some germ plasm from United States varieties were so superior to native corn both in field performance and yield that an immediate demand for them was created.

Programs are also being conducted in Brazil, Argentina, and Venezuela. The work at La Plata University in Argentina is being directed by Dr. S. Horovitz. Dr. C. A. Krug, a German who received his training in the United States, is breeding hybrid corn at Instituto Agronomico at Sao Paulo in Brazil.

Probably the most advanced breeding program in Latin America is conducted at Instituto Experimental de Agriculture, El Valle, Caracas, Venezuela, by Dr. D. G. Langham, a former Iowa plant breeder who received his training at Iowa State College and Cornell University. Langham began breeding hybrid corn in Venezuela eight years ago and has already developed a number of inbred lines from native Venezuelan corn and crossed them into some promising hybrids that have demonstrated the capacity to outyield native corn twenty to fifty per cent. These new hybrids in Venezuela, as in all other Latin American countries, will develop only gradually, since many factors impede both the development and the distribution which were not present in the United States. But, if the difficulties which must be overcome are greater, so also are the ultimate benefits. This was brought out in a recent visit which Dr. Langham made to the United States.

"How much of your corn in Venezuela is fed to hogs?" asked a friend.

"When corn costs $3.50 a bushel, you don't feed it to

hogs," he replied. "You eat it yourself. We have a new government bulletin in Venezuela that gives 400 recipes and ways of preparing corn for table use."

We in the United States find it difficult to appreciate what hybrid corn combined with soil improvement work can mean to the people of Latin America, where, to many, a good corn crop means being well fed and happy and a poor corn crop means actual hunger and malnutrition. Here is a new and worthy opportunity to promote a good-neighbor policy in the Latin American countries, and here, too, is a dramatic example of how the work begun by two or three men at the foot of the Sleeping Giant in Connecticut can be projected into better living for peoples in the farthermost corners of the earth.

Evidences of the interest in hybrid corn throughout the rest of the world have poured into the United States from every continent since wartime censorship and other restrictions on communication have been eliminated. Research workers and seedsmen in other countries are turning to our corn breeders to see if the benefits that have come to American farmers may also be made available in their countries. Naturally their immediate hope is that some of the American varieties will prove to be well adapted to their needs so that they may regularly import seed from the United States.

In a period of only a few months covering the last weeks of 1946 and the early weeks of 1947, R. J. Laible, who answers inquiries received from other countries by Funk Brothers Seed Company of Bloomington, Illinois, received more letters from overseas than at any other time since the Funk organization began inbreeding corn more than a quarter of a century ago. Typical excerpts follow:

"Please be so kind as to write me by return air mail about the following subjects: I shall need several varieties and quantities of field MAIS Hybrids . . . for irrigated and others for dry land. I am interested, before all, in the earliest yellow and white varieties. . . For ensilage I shall also need 1 or 2 varieties. Looking forward to hearing from you, I am,

Sincerely yours,
[Signed] Francois de Mauthner

Av. 5 d'Outubro, 23–4°dt°,
Lisbon, Portugal."

"I would appreciate very much if you would send me some seeds at your earliest convenience, about 50 pounds will be preferred for experimental and variety tests. Send it C. O. D. because our planting season is almost over. Thanking you, I am,

Yours truly,
[Signed] Tamao Otani

Waiakoa, Maui, Hawaii."

"It is the interest of this Company to deal with Hybrid Seed Corn. Corn in Egypt is still of the open-pollinated type.

"There are recent trials, however, to produce local inbred lines from a high yielding Egyptian variety. These trials are being made by both Ministry of Agriculture and the College of Agriculture here in Egypt. We do not expect any results for few years to come.

"So we plan to try your hybrids under the Egyptian conditions, and we hope that one or more of the hybrids might outyield our best open-pollinated varieties. If we get such good hybrid, we would order large quantities of its seeds every year.

"Egypt grows over two million acres of corn annually. Most of it is white dent used as human food. Yellow corn is not yet appreciated by the Egyptian farmer, whose interest is to have a high yield of white grain.

"Corn is grown in Egypt under irrigation. The growing season varies from 100 to 130 days, from July 15 to about the end of November. Our weather is similar to that of Southern California, Arizona, or in general, like the Middle and Southwestern States. . .

Thanking you, we are,

Yours very truly,
[Signed] Hussein Mourad

The Nile Valley Seed Co.,
35, Emad El Din Street,
Cairo, Egypt."

"Being someone like your county investigation directors, for the French Yonne county, I would be glad if that is possible to know if you have in your corn varieties anyone would be able to grow in four months. The weather of our country is with last frosts on the 10th of May and on the 15th of September. So that our French varieties which grow in more than four months exceptionally come to maturity. That's to say once each three or four years when it freezes but in October. I hope you could give me a good answer.

Sincerely yours,
Y. Gagnet

Office Agricole Departmental,
4 Rue Marcelin-Berthlot,
Auxerre, Yonne, France."

"We obtained a ton of hybrid corn through the firm of Luthi of New Orleans, a few months ago. Since we wish to make new orders on the different classes of corn raised in your country, I would like for you to send me a list of the different classes which you might be able to export, whether it is the one that produces in 150 days, or the one that produces in 90 days in high land altitude . . .

Sincerely yours,
Alfonso Alehos

Negocios En General, Oficina: 6ª
Avenida Norte. N°1 B,
Guatemala, Central America."

These letters are typical of many hundreds received by American institutions well known for their interest in hybrid corn breeding. As a result American varieties are this year being tested in experimental quantities on every continent and in most countries of the world.

American hybrid corn has already been used to increase

food production in a number of European and other countries. Ever since Allied armies began turning back the Axis
legions in 1943 and 1944, many countries freed from their
bondage have received supplies of hybrid seed corn. More
than 650,000 bushels of hybrid seed were sent abroad for
planting in the spring of 1947, reaching a new high for shipments of corn. A few thousand bushels were sent to the
Orient, mostly to China, and the remainder went to European countries.

A number of countries made arrangements for the pur-
chase of large amounts of American hybrid seed corn to be
used for regular plantings in the spring of 1947. With food
so desperately needed, farmers in many areas were unable
to save even enough corn to be used as seed. Rumania, for
instance, sought 20,000 long tons or nearly 800,000 bushels
of seed, much of which was shipped from the port of New
Orleans late in March. Allowing for difficulties of procure-
ment and distribution and Rumania's prewar corn acreage,
this would be enough seed to plant hybrid corn on perhaps
one out of every three acres grown in 1947 in this Balkan
nation, which has for a generation been the foremost corn-
producing country in Europe. Belgium, France, and Hol-
land also planted sizable amounts of American hybrid seed
corn in 1947. Rather extensive experimental plantings representing wide ranges in hybrids and growing conditions
were made in the spring of 1947 at several other places in
the Danube River basin, Greece, northern Italy, and Egypt.
Should this seed prove adapted to the soil and climatic conditions of any of these nations, a sharp demand for hybrid
corn may develop before any progress has been made on
breeding it by the scientists of these countries.

When we project these prospective benefits of America's
hybrid corn to the other important corn-growing nations
and areas—Latin America, Africa, China, the Balkans, the
East Indies and elsewhere—it is then possible to appreciate

that the work of the hybrid-corn makers is only started. It is possible to see that the surface of the total possibilities has just been scratched, that this knowledge is to become one of the great gifts of our time to the rest of the world.

The principles and practices first discovered and developed by the hybrid-corn makers are destined through an ever-expanding application to generate a new kind of living for man on this earth. They are destined to banish hunger and want from places where enough food, clothing, and other minimum requirements for healthful, happy living have never been known before. A century from now, those hybrid-corn makers will more easily be recognized as the prophets of plenty—vanguard of a great world-wide army of scientists who will provide more abundant life for a constantly increasing number of people.

Thus this is not the end of the story of hybrid corn—only the beginning.

INDEX

Agricole Departmental, Office, 316
Agricultural Alumni Seed Improvement Association (Indiana), 184
Aikenhead, Daddy, 183
Alabama Agriculture Experimental Station, 260
Alehos, Alfonso, 316
Allee, George M., 66
Allen, Charles, 280
Ambrose, Floyd, 280
American Breeders' Association, annual meeting at Urbana, 30; Jenkins and East meet, 34; East hears Shull's paper, 45; Shull's first paper, 49–57; other Shull papers, 59–60; mentioned, 66–81
American Breeders' Magazine, 145
American Maize Products Company, markets waxy cornstarch, 197
American Naturalist, The, 44
American Seed Trade Association, 163
American Society of Agronomy, addressed by Wallace, 156–157
Anderson, Dean C., 252
Anderson, J. C., 261
Andrews, R. H., 264
Angle, Paul, viii, ix
Antioch College, 53
Arkansas Experimental Station, 258
Armour, P. D., 10
Ash, Thomas, 8
Associated Press, 135
Ayers, Bob, 259
Aztecs (Indians), 5

Bailey, Russell M., 260
Baker, Raymond, Early contacts with Wallace, 160–61; joins Pioneer, 162; begins poultry inbreeding, 305; hybridizes watermelons, 308; mentioned, 287, 307

Ball, Carlton C., father of federal-state cooperative program, 244
Bangham, Walter, conducts Costa Rica project, 312
Barnard, H. E., 195
Barry, L. A., 188
Bateson, William, recommended East, 68–69
Beard, D. F., 251
Beal, William James, first to cross varieties, 16; utilizes hybrid vigor, 41
Bell, Orton L., Gunn's assistant, 214; wanted to see hybrid corn in his time, 215; begins cornbreeding work, 216; mentioned, 226
Best, Richard, helps Holbert test hybrids, 125
Bigger, John, 127, 252
Bill, Frank, 127
Black Hawk, Chief, peace treaty of 1804, 9
Black Hawk War, fight for corn grounds, 9
Blakeford Farms, 307
Bloody Butcher corn, given to Wallace, 147; mentioned 114–15
Bloomington Pantagraph, 127, 235
Bolin, Oren, 252
Bonner, John, 280
Boone County White corn, entered in Holbert's plots, 114–15
Bowman, D. H., 257
Bracker, E. M. D., conducts first utility corn show in 1921, 119
Bradfield, Richard, goes to Mexico, 310
Brawner, Murray, joins Pioneer research department, 163
Breeders' Gazette, 96, 147
Brewbaker, H. E., 252
Brink, R. A., gets inbred material from Jenkins, 188; works with waxy

319

9 781258 154257